MISSISSIPPI NEWSPAPER OBITUARIES
1876 - 1885

By
Betty C. Wiltshire

Copyright 1998
Betty C. Wiltshire

3 4766 00283190 3

Some Other Books by Author:

Mississippi Newspaper Obituaries, 1862 - 1875
Register of Choctaw Emigrants to the West,
1831 & 1832
Choctaw and Chickasaw Early Census Records
Carroll County, Mississippi Estate Records, 1840 - 1869
Marshall County, Mississippi Will & Probate Records
Tallahatchie County, Mississippi Will & Probate Records
Yalobusha County, Mississippi Will & Estate Records
Mississippi Confederate Pension Applications,
A-G, H-O & P-Z
Abstracts of Choctaw County, Mississippi Records

Published By
Pioneer Publishing Co.
P. O. Box 408
Carrollton, Ms. 38917
(601) 237-6010

ISBN 1-885480-27-X

TABLE OF CONTENTS

Introduction	v
Tri-Weekly Examiner	1
Aberdeen Examiner, The	1
Tri-Weekly Examiner	3
Ashland Register, The	6
Batesville Blade	8
Pleader, The	9
Brookhaven Democrat	26
Brookhaven Leader, The	29
Brookhaven Ledger, The	33
American Citizen, The	38
Conservative, The	58
Carthaginian, The	62
Argus, The	64
Mississippi Baptist Record	64
Crystal Springs Monitor, The	80
Crystal Mirror	88
Meteor, The	89
Edwards Citizen, The	91
Forest Weekly Register, The	92
Friar's Point Gazette	92
Greenville Times, The	97
Weekly Copian, The	132
Copian Signal, The	133
Holly Springs Reporter, The	141
Comet, The	146
New Mississippian, The	164
Natchez Daily Democrat	167
Macon Beacon, The	181
Oxford Eagle	182
Ripley Advertiser, The	184
Summit Conservative Times	193
Vicksburg Daily Herald	208
Index	231

INTRODUCTION

Due to many requests for more newspaper obituaries, this book is a continuation of earlier books of newspaper obituary notices from throughout the State of Mississippi. This covers the years 1876 through 1885. These were copied from newspapers on microfilm available at the Mississippi State Dept. of Archives and History in Jackson, Mississippi.

These notices include accounts of accidents and murders as well as obituaries. Deaths of both blacks and whites are given. Most notices were copied exactly as found, but in some cases where the notice was very lengthy only the most important information was copied. These are so noted.

TRI-WEEKLY EXAMINER
Aberdeen, Ms.

May 30, 1883
Died at 2 1/2 o'clock, Sunday morning, April 15, 1883. after a long and painful illness of many months, Laura, youngest daughter of Thomas and Leatha Word, of Monroe County, Mississippi.

Died at one o'clock, Saturday, May 5th, 1883, from heart disease, after an illness of 15 months, Mrs. Leatha Lewis, wife of Thos. Word, of Monroe County, Mississippi. She was born in Virginia, 1811, married in Limestone County, Alabama, December 1830, moved to Monroe County with her husband in December 1840.

THE ABERDEEN EXAMINER
Aberdeen, Ms.

July 10, 1879
Died at the residence of his father, _____ Hollingsworth, Sr., in Mo___, on the 1st day of July, 1879, Thadeus E. Hollingsworth, in the 28th year of his age. (Editor's note - part of this article was missing)
Born in this county on the 11th days of April, 1851, married on the 17th day of December, 1871, to Miss Gillie McWhorter.

April 14, 1881
Died in this city, April 6th, Sallie Irene Dalton, wife of Robt. B. Burdine.

Died at her husband's residence in this city on Wednesday afternoon, of puerpal fever, Mrs. Sallie Dalton Burdine, wife of R. B. Burdine, Esq.

November 2, 1882
Katie May, daughter of Mr. H. E. Fitts, of this county, died on Saturday, October 21st, after a brief illness, aged 4 years, 10 months and 21 days.

March 8, 1883
Died February 27th, 1883, Allice, infant daughter of W. M. and Alice E. Ransom, aged one month.

March 29, 1883
Departed this life on the 26th of March, Mrs. Sarah E. Wamble, wife of T. J. Wamble and daughter of Wiley and Mary Harris. She was born at Quincy, in this county, on the 5th day of September, 1836, and was married to T. J. Wamble on the 22nd day of September, 1859. She joined the Methodist Church when she was 15 years of age.

April 26, 1883
Died at his home near Quincy, on the 19th of April, 1883, Licurgus S. Wood, youngest son of Joseph and Nancy Wood, in the 23rd year of his life.

May 24, 1883
Died at her residence in Aberdeen, Miss., May 16th, 1883, Mrs. C. C. Heisen, formerly Miss Celia T. Butler. She was born in Chicago, Illinois, October 29th, 1800. Her ancestors were among the founders and most prominent persons of that city. She was educated at the Chicago Young Ladies Seminary.

Died on the 14th of May, 1883, Phelan, only son of J. B. and Mattie J. Riggan, aged 15 years and 5 months.

October 4, 1883
Died at the residence of her husband, near DeSoto Front, Miss., September 24th, 1883, Mrs. Ira G. Holloway. Mrs. Holloway was the daughter of Capt. C. C. Love, and raised in this county, of which her husband, I. G. Holloway, was also a citizen.

February 7, 1884
Ira Baker, son of Leonard and Nancy Baker, was born in Union District, South Carolina, November 14th, 18_3. He grew to manhood in his native state. At the age of twenty-five years he moved to Tennessee where he remained six years. He was married on August 28th, 18_3 to Miss Sarah J. DePriest. He moved to Monroe County, Mississippi in the year 18__, where he remained until his death.

July 24, 1884
Lewis Gifford Knowles, only son of Hugh A. and Katherine K. Knowles, born February 6th, 1879 in New York City, died at Shuqualak, Miss., July 14th, 1884. He was buried at Odd Fellows Cemetery, Aberdeen, Miss.

June 11, 1885
David W. Jamison, after an illness of some months, died at the residence of his father, John T. Jamison, June 3rd, 1885. David was born in Monroe County, Mississippi March 17th, 1865, was only only nineteen years and a few months of age.

Died on June 1st, 1885, in the 23rd year of her age, Mrs. Emma Barton, after an illness of several weeks.

June 18, 1885

Died at the residence of her husband, A. S. Crump, son of the late and highly esteemed Joseph Crump, of this county, in the 35th year of her age, Mrs. E. S. Crump, daughter of Mr. and Mrs. Thompson Gregory.

TRI-WEEKLY EXAMINER
Aberdeen, Miss.

April 8, 1881

Jackson, Miss., April 5th noon - Last night a man named Brennan was found lying on the sidewalk with his throat cut. Suspicion pointed to a negro who had been seen near the murdered man just previous to the discovery of the murder. A search resulted in capturing a negro who was identified as the same.

April 11, 1881

During a rain and thunder storm at noon on Thursday, Mrs. Birch, residing on Mr. Joseph Adams' place, was struck by lightening and instantly killed. The discharge came through the roof of the house and struck the woman on the shoulder. Her bonnet and clothing were torn from her body and burned, her hair almost all burned, and the electricity passing to her feet tore off her shoes and shattered them into pieces.

May 6, 1881

Died in this city, April 25, 1881, Mrs. Mary Bashaw, wife of George W. Bashaw, Esq.

July 19, 1881

Lafayette Haughton was born near Huntsville, Ala., July 29, 1827; removed to Mississippi at the age of 18 years; commenced the practice of law in 1847; was married in 1857 to Miss Sallie Brownrigg of Columbus, Miss.; served during the Civil War as Staff Officer of Gen. Reuben Davis, Gen. Samuel J. Gholson and Gen. Charles Clarke respectively. He was appointed Chancellor of the First District of Mississippi in 1876 and reappointed in 1880. He died July 10, 1883.

July 27, 1883

Mrs. Emma A. Justice, wife of Mr. G. W. Justice, departed this life at Jackson, Hinds County, Miss. on the 10th day of April 1883, her death being caused by congestion of the brain. In the year 1875 she was unfortunate in losing her mind, hence she died as an inmate in the "State Lunatic Asylum". She was the daughter of H. T. Watrons, Esq., of Aberdeen, Monroe County, Mississippi and was united in marriage to Mr. G. W. Justice, of Aberdeen, Mississippi on the 12th day of September, 1866.

August 1, 1883

On last Friday evening, Mr. C. S. Jobes, while at the top of a telegraph pole on the C. A. & N. railroad, stretching wire, the wire slipped, striking Mr. Jobes in the breast, knocking him violently to the ground and it was thought at one time that he was fatally injured, but after he recovered the only injury he had sustained was a broken wrist. (Kosciusko Star)

August 3, 1883

Mr. J. M. Simmons, son of J. B. and N. P. Simmons, was born October 29th, 1869, and departed this life July 15th, 1883.

Miss Laura Reynolds, of the town of Winona, has shaken off the cares and troubles of this life on the 18th of June. She was born in Aberdeen, Monroe County, Miss., on February 14th, 1860. Her father died while she was quite young, leaving the care of raising a family of three little girls to the mother. In 1875 the mother, after a long lingering illness, found relief in death. After the death of her mother, Miss Laura lived with Mrs. Gregg, of Aberdeen, until 1880.

Mrs. Lilla Sykes Lewis, wife of Mr. Thomas A. Lewis and daughter of Mrs. Pollock Barbour, was born in Aberdeen, Miss., July 10th, 1862; was married in Louisville, Ky., July 20th, 1882; and died in that city July 15th, 1883.

August 17, 1883

Died at Buckatunna, Wayne County, Miss., July 28th, 1883, W. P. Gillespie, Sr. The deceased was born in South Carolina, April 15th, 1794; was 89 years, 3 months and 12 days old at his death. At the age of 18 he volunteered his services in the War of 1812, serving in the capacity of courier to Gen. Andrew Jackson. Serving out his term of enlistment, he returned to his native state; from thence he moved to Alabama; from that state he moved to Chickasaw County, Miss.

Needham J., son of Mrs. Lucy and the late Needham J. Whitfield, was born January 1861 and entered into the feet of Paradise July 17th, 1883.

September 5, 1883

Died suddenly, of heart disease, at his home in Aberdeen, Miss., July 18th, 1883, David Jamison, aged 65 years, 4 months and 2 days.

September 14, 1883
Died on September 8th, Charlie J. Peugh.

Mrs. Dorcas Hollingsworth was born June the 6th, 1806 and died August the 7th, 1883, aged 77 years, 2 months and one day. She was daughter of the Rev. Frederick Weaver and was married to Wm. Hollingsworth about the year 1845, and was the mother of the Rev. L. D. Hollingsworth. She has been a devoted member of the Methodist Church from childhood. She left one son and one daughter to mourn her loss.

September 19, 1883
Brother Joseph W. Hosea was stricken down in the morning of life by the dread messenger, the Angel of Death. Tributes of respect by: Wildey Lodge No. 21, I. O. O. F.; Aberdeen Lodge No. 32, A. F. & A. M.; and Apello Lodge No. 14, Knights of Pythis.

October 22, 1883
In Aberdeen, Miss., Oct. 10th, 1883, at the residence of the parents - Jesse J. and Julia S. Ellis, died little Wood Sadler Ellis. She was one year, two months and 22 days old.

The Supreme Ruler of the Universe, in His infinite wisdom has seen fit to bring to a close on the evening of the 16th, the life of General Samuel J. Gholson.

November 23, 1883
It has pleased an All-wise Providence to remove from our midst our esteemed brother, A. M. Kuffer, on November 17th, 1883. Aberdeen Lodge #32 A. F. & A. M.

December 7, 1883
On the 30th day of November, 1883, God saw fit to take from among us our friend and brother, C. Mauldin. Aberdeen Lodge #32.

December 19, 1883
Henry D. Spratt departed this life on the 13th December, 1883.

February 8, 1884
Ira Baker, son of Leonard and Nancy Baker, was born in Union District, South Carolina, November 14th, 1806. He grew to manhood in his native state. At the age of twenty-five years he moved to Tennessee, where he remained six years. He moved to Monroe County, Mississippi in the year 1834, where he remained until his death.

August 12, 1885
Little Bessie Davis, daughter of C. C. and Annie Boyd Williams, died July 26th, aged 16 months and 9 days.

THE ASHLAND REGISTER
Ashland, Mississippi

July 17, 1879
Died at Michigan City, Indiana, July 14th, Mrs. Clayton, wife of Hon. A. M. Clayton, of Benton Co. We learn his wife's health had been bad for some time and the Judge had started and got that far with her on his way to some watering place, whither he was going when she died.

August 14, 1879
Died at his residence one mile east of Ashland, on the 7th day of August, 1879, Daniel Rees, aged about 75 years.

Died at the residence of his father in Fayette County, Tenn., on the 6th of August, 1879, Armistead Thompson, infant son of J. W. and M. B. Mason, aged ten months and twenty days.

August 28, 1879
Green Houston, five miles south of Ashland, died of fever on the 26th inst.

September 4, 1879
Born August 28th, 1879, to Judge J. M. and Mrs. E. J. McDonald, a daughter, eleven and a half pounds.

Died on the 29th of August, at the residence of his son, Maj. W. G. Pegram. He had reached the extreme age of 93 years.

On the 29th of August, Mrs. Chas. Dawkins died at her home in Benton.

September 18, 1879
On the night of the 10th inst., about 7 o'clock P. M., Harrison Saxton, a clever colored boy who did not suppose he had an enemy on earth, was shot square through the body with an old army gun at or near the mill at Michigan City, in this county, and died about three hours later. Robert Fox, another colored man, is under arrest, charged with the killing. He had recently had some difficulty with a darkey named Deadner and is supposed to have mistook Saxton for Deadner.

October 9, 1879

Andrew Sumlim knocked Dickson H. Lewis on the head with a hand stick, at Cothran's saw mill, in the southern part of Benton, on the 25th September, from which blow he died in about four hours. From the best information we can obtain, they were brothers-in-law, and they, with several other relatives, are recent immigrants from Crenshaw County, Ala.   (Author's note - This was followed by a lengthy report)

Mrs. Alberson, wife of Wm. Alberson and sister of James W. Day, near Saulsbury, died last week.

Mrs. Mary Womack, wife of J. H. Womack, died at Michigan City, on the 4th inst.

October 16, 1879

The report that reached us of Mrs. Wommock's death last week, is now denied. She was very low, but is now hoped will recover.

November 6, 1879

Born to Mr. & Mrs. J. P. Byrd, of Ashland, on the first instant, a daughter. Mother and child are doing well.

It is with sadness we note the death of our friend Mr. C. F. Robinson's little daughter, Lillie, on the 1st inst.

It is with sorrow that we note the death of W. S., son of W. T. Ivie. At the time of his death last week he was 18 years and 6 days old.

J. R. Snodgrass, son of James and M. T. Snodgrass, died at Hickory Flat, Miss., Oct. 15, 1879, after several weeks with typhoid fever. He was born in Severe County, Ark., January 10th, 1863.

November 18, 1879

Last Friday morning, at 30 minutes after 11 o'clock, Robert Fox was seated in a buggy by the side of Mr. Doss Winborn, and started to the gallows. Rev. Smart Isom, a colored minister, sang and prayed with him. Sheriff Winborn read the death warrant, placed the rope around his neck, adjusted the black cap over head and face, then stepped down. The rope was cut 33 minutes after 12. 15 minutes lates the Drs. examined his pulse and he was cut down two minutes before 1 o'clock p.m. He met his fate without faltering. (Author's note - this is part of a lengthy report)

Bent. Oakley, son of Oscar and Alice Oakley, died on the 4th November, 1879, near Lamar, Miss., at their residence.

On the 5th Nov., 1879, the infant son of Walter and E. M. Hardaway, died at their residnece near Lamar, Miss.

November 20, 1879

Mrs. Elizabeth Reynolds, wife of Elijah Reynolds, died on the 17th inst., of consumption, in Benton County. Mrs. Reynolds was the daughter of Mr. T. J. Murray, who died on the night of the 12th.

BATESVILLE BLADE
Batesville, Mississippi

June 18, 1880

Died Saturday the 12th last, Arthur, infant son of Mr. & Mrs. H. E. Hall, of Courtland.

A fatal shooting affray occurred in this county last Saturday, west of Tallahatchie river, between Capt. W. W. Bailey and an old man named Spivey, in which the former lost his life and the latter badly wounded in both arms. Spivey gave the following account -- "My wife told me that Bailey had turned mules in crop and I wrote Bailey a note telling him to keep his mules out of crop or I would shoot them. Bailey became offended --- in a short time Bailey and Mayberry came to my house. Bailey told Mayberry to go and get his (Bailey's) gun and they would settle it. Mayberry brought the gun -- Bailey wanted me to come out and settle it. My son and I walked to another part of the room and I sat on the bed so as to be out of Bailey's sight. My wife and son told Bailey not to come in. Bailey said he would kill the whole d__d family or have revenge. My son fired -- I saw Bailey on the ground. I went back to get my gun and was myself shot." (Author's note - this is part of a lengthy account)

July 9, 1880

Died at his residence a few miles southwest of Batesville, of dysentery, June 25th, Wm. R. Martin, aged 68 years, 1 month, 18 days.

Died at his residence, June 7th, E. C. Blackwood, in the 46th year of his age.

August 27, 1880

Died in Wesley Chapel neighborhood, August 19th, Mrs. Lizzie Davidson, aged 40 years.

Died near Humanity, August 23rd, Mr. H. D. Bill, aged 73 years.

May 11, 1883
Died near Monat Olived, May 8th, of enlargement of the spleen, Mrs. S. A. Cox, aged 40 years. Mrs. Cox was born in Hardeman County, Tennessee and came to Mississippi in 1879.

December 5, 1884
Died, Mrs. Parish, at her home near Ptoccowa Springs, on the 2nd inst.

January 9, 1885
Tis with a heart steeped in anguish that we make mention of the death of Mrs. L. J. Pearson, after a brief illness, on the 4th iinst.

May 22, 1885
This community was startled yesterday by the announcement that a fatal and desperate duel with shotguns had been fought at Rolling Fork, between S. E. Sharkey, Chancery Clerk of Sharkey County, and Wm. K. McLauren, an attorney, both prominent citizens of Rolling Fork, resulting in the killing of the former instantly. The first intimation of the sad affair here was in a private telegram to S. M. Shelton, a cousin of the deceased. (Author's note - a lengthy report followed)

THE PLEADER
Booneville, Mississippi

November 4, 1880
In memory of Joseph B. O'Reilly, who died June 22nd, 1862. (Author's note - followed by a lengthy poem, signed R. E. O'R.)

    Just twenty-three years ago tonight
    My precious father took his spirit flight
    To worlds of love afar.
    There was no seemingly pain or fear of death,
    But gently yielding up God's given breath,
    Mounted the Golden Car.
        (continued)
    He rose in beauty to the upper air
    And stood a smiling planet there,
      in purest blazing light --
    From forth the window of my little room,
    Peering most brightly through the midnight gloom,
    I see him stil tonight.
        signed G. B. Ellington.

November 11, 1880

The killing of J. E. Ashcraft and J. T. Lockhart at Lexington: About 30 minutes before the polls closed, while a large crowd were around the polls waiting to vote, a dispute arose between J. T. Lockhart, then Chancery Clerk, and J. W. Ashcraft, father of J. E. Ashcraft, then Sheriff of Holmes Co. and a candidate for re-election, Lockhart struck J. W. Ashcraft over the head with his cane, and was about to repeat the blow when J. E. Ashcraft, seeing his father imperiled, drew his pistol and shot Lockhart in the abdoman. Lockhart instantly returned the fire, striking Ashcraft in the neck, under the chin. Ashcraft turned and Lockhart fired again shooting him in the back. Either wound was fatal and Ashcraft died instantly. Lockhart died at 7 o'clock the next evening.

February 10, 1881

Mrs. Sallie L. Wells, wife of Col. J. M. Wells, died on the 31st Jany., 1881, in the 73rd year of her age. She was born in Maury County, Tennessee, July 4th, 1808; was married Jany. 14th, 1830, and attached herself to the M. E. Episcopal Church in 1833.

July 7, 1881

Died at his daughter's residence, 6 miles northwest of Baldwin, in Prentiss County, Miss., after an illness of three months, June 21st, 1881, Mr. William B. Garrison, in the 75th year of his age. Mr. Garrison was born in Greenville Dist., S. C., February 12th, 1807; emigrated in 1842 to Tippah County, Miss. He was a devoted member of the Baptist Church over 45 years.

August 25, 1881

Col. Fleet T. Cooper, editor of the Comet, breathed his last on the 18th inst., after a protracted illness. Col. Cooper was one of the best newspapermen in the state.

October 6, 1881

The boiler of the steam mill of the Simpson Bros., 3 1/2 miles north of Ripley, exploded Monday morning, Sept. 26th, with fatal effects. Dr. Charley Rucker, who happened to be there on a visit, and Mr. Jessie Stubbs, were instantly killed, and Mr. A. B. Simpson so badly wounded that the died the same day. Sam Simpson, Charley Stubbs, Jr. and Dick May barely escaped with their lives.

October 13, 1881

With sorrow we chronicle the death of little Lillian Mathews, on the 30th day of September, 1881.

October 27, 1881

Col. D. L. Love, formerly a citizen of this state, was killed at Greenville, Miss., on the 21st inst., by J. T. Lanier, of Huntsville, Ala. Mr. Love, some years ago while editing a paper at West Point (Miss.)

killed Col. Louis A. Middleton, editor of a rival paper, for which he was tried and acquitted. (New Orleans Democrat)

D. L. Love, who recently made a publication reflecting on the virtue of a young lady that had just married Mr. Lanier at Huntsville, Ala., was killed here this morning. Mr. Lanier, on landing from the steamer *Grand Tower*, in company with the young lady's father, armed with a double barrelled shotgun, discovered Love in the rear of Compton's livery stable, and immediately opened fire with the shot gun, filling his head and face with buckshot. After emptying both barrells, Lanier then opened with two large calibre pistols and while Love was endeavoring to crawl off, shot him repeatedly, until his pistols were emptied and Love was dead. Lanier is in jail awaiting trial. (Greenville, Oct. 21.)

November 24, 1881

We regret to announce the death of Mr. John B. Donaldson. He died suddenly at his residence near town, of aneurism, Dec. 17, 1881. He was over 70 years old and leaves a wife, children and grandchildren.

December 8, 1881

A most horrible murder was committed near Aberdeen on the night of Nov. 26th. A small party of travelers, four in number, traveling west, camped near the Cummings place. They were found next day by some parties passing the road foully murdered in their beds. The result of inquiries by the Sheriff showed them to be the Walker brothers from Alabama. They were supposed to be murdered by a traveling companion. (Author's note - See the Brookhaven Ledger, Jan. 5, 1882)

Columbus, Miss., Nov. 30th -- John Abner, a negro from Oktibbeha County, was fatally shot about 3 o'clock this evening, by Mr. Hunter Sharpe, son of Gen. J. H. Sharpe, just beyond the county bridge over the Tombigbee (river). Two shots were fired by Sharpe, the second entering the right side, passing through the right lobe of the liver and passing out on the left side in the region of the left kidney. The negro died about 7 o'clock.

Bro. J. M. Brown departed this life at the residence of his brother-in-law, W. L. Neil, on the 2nd Nov., 1881.

January 5, 1882

Mr. J. B. Donaldson, son of Berkley Donaldson, was born in Williamson County, Tenn., Feb. 16, 1811; moved to Mississippi some 40 years ago where he has lived till the time of his death, which occurred Nov. 17, 1881.

January 19, 1882

We extend to Col. J. L. Power our sympathies in the lose of his son, Mr. Willie S. Power, which occurred on the 11th inst. by the discharge of a pistol in his own hand, producing immediate death. For a long time there has existed an attachment between himself and Miss May Ross. Her father objected to the possible union, and on Wednesday forbade the young man further attention to his daughter. About 5 o'clock he called on the young lady "to tell her goodbye." After the words of parting were uttered, and while her head was bowed, the sharp report of a pistol rang into her ears. She rushed to him to find him weltering in his very heart's blood.

February 23, 1882

Mrs. M. A. Barker, wife of Mr. S. N. Barker, died at the assylum in Jackson, on the 10th inst. She was taken sick last July and losing her mind from the severity of her illness her physicians advised her removal to the assylum. She was buried in the cemetery in Jackson, by the side of two of her brothers.

Mr. James Donahoe died in Humboldt, Tenn., February 17th, 1882, of paralysis. He had gone there to visit his married daughter the Sunday previous.

It is with deep sorrow we announce the death of Mr. Oscar Stevens. He died of consumption at his father's residence in Rienzi, Feb. 16, 1882.

March 23, 1882

The case of the State -vs- Prof. S. P. Brown, for the killing of Dr. Sadler, was commenced Monday and late Thursday evening was submitted to the jury. The jury brought in a verdict yesterday that Brown be sent to the penitentiary for life. (Ripley Adveretiser)

April 20, 1882

We stop the press to announce the death of Capt. M. Surratt, which occurred last night, the 19th, after a brief illness. Capt. Surrett was one of our most prominent citizens and identified with the history of North Mississippi for the last thirty years.

April 27, 1882

The loss of Mrs. Malissa Williams, daughter of Rev. Wm. G. Hawkins and wife of J. L. Williams, who died on the 16th inst., is felt by almost every one in our community. She attached herself to the Methodist Church in youth. She was the mother of seven children.

May 18, 1882

Mrs. Nancy Barnett, wife of Mr. J. T. Barnett and daughter of the late John R. Martin, died at her residence Saturday afternoon, May 14th, 1882.

May 25, 1882

B. W. Phillips was killed in Holmes County on the 15th, by Wm. Harrington. They fell out about some cattle claimed by both. Harrington emptied the contents of a double barrelled shot-gun into Phillips' body and had not been arrested at last accounts. The occurrance took place at the Christmas plantation in the swamp.

July 13, 1882

Tom Jones, a lad, was killed in Louisville, Miss., last week by one F. L. Jones, an artist. It seems Tom reported that F. L. Jones had used some disparaging remarks about a lady. Jones asked Tom about it, when Tom repeated that he did say so. Upon this F. L. Jones shot Tom five times, causing his death in two hours. Some bystander hit Jones on the head with a brick while he was shooting Tom, but as ill luck would have did not kill him. Another was about to shoot him, but was prevented. F. L. Jones was arrested.

July 27, 1882

Leonard Haynes killed W. C. Cummings, District Attorney at Loredo, Texas, on the 16th inst., for seducing his sister. He was son of Col. Jno. L. Haynes, collector of the port of Brownsville, Texas, and formerly a citizen of Lexington, Miss.

Col. Beverly Matthews, one of the ablest lawyers in the State, died at Columbus on the 19th inst. He commenced practice in 1844 or '45 and was competitor at the bar with W. S. Barry, Jas. T. Harrison, Richard Evans and others.

Among the victims from the disaster at Texarkana, Texas, on the 12th inst., caused by a two-story brick house being struck by lightening and torn to pieces, the walls falling upon a smaller building and killing thirty persons, we notice the name of Mr. W. B. Russell, formerly of Carrollton, Miss. He was the son of the late Daniel R. Russell, a well known Mississippian before the war, who distinquished himself greatly in the Mexican War at the storming of Monteray.

Mr. N. W. Posey died at the residence of Mr. W. H. Shackelford, on Mackey's Creek, Tishomingo County, Miss., on the 22nd, from the bite of a ground rattle-snake on the area just above the wrist. He was bitten the 18th. It seems he was destined to be snake bitten, having been bitten by a ground rattle-snake on the hand March 27th, 1880; again on the 8th of May, 1880 by a cotton mouth snake on the big toe through a hole in his boot; again about the last of May, 1881 he was bitten by a cotton mouth on the side of his foot through a hole in his shoe; again June 3rd, 1882 he was bitten by a cotton mouth on the hand while hauling rails and again on the 29th of the same month he was bitten on the leg by a copper head while plowing. In addition he was bitten twice by snakes in

Alabama, by a rattlesnake when about 10 years old and by a copper head last spring while on a visit to his relations.

Mr. Posey was only about 25 years of age. He came to this county from Coosa County, Alabama, Feb. 25th, 1880 and was employed by Capt. W. A. H. Shackelford to work on his farm. He was married to Miss S. A. Hagood, July 2nd, 1882.

August 10, 1882

We regret to announce that Mrs. Fallis, wife of Mr. N. L. Fallis, was struck and instantly killed by lightening during the storm Tuesday afternooon. She was at the time on a visit at the residence of her father, Mr. Peter M. Dubois, two miles northeast of town.

Miss Nancy Robertson died at the residence of Mr. J. V. Alexander, August 7th, 1882. She was the aunt of Mr. J. V. Alexander.

August 31, 1882

Dr. Isaac B. Clayton, who killed Freeman Lester last January, was assassinated near Goodman, Miss. on the 28th inst., ten buckshot in his body. The murderer has not been arrested.

September 14, 1882

We are pained to announce the death of Col. Mose McCarley, which occurred at his residence on Wednesday, September 13th, 1882. He had been ill only four or five days. He leaves a wife and four children. Col. McCarley was formerly a citizen of Tippah County, where soon after the war he was twice elected to the office of Sheriff. He moved to this place about the year 1873.

Mr. Thomas Palmer died one day last week, in this county.

Mrs. Caroline Doty, wife of Mr. P. L. Doty, died at her residence near town, Sept. 8th, 1882, in the 69th year of her age. She was an old member of the Methodist Church.

October 5, 1882

Mr. George Alcorn, son of Robt. J. Alcorn of Jackson, Miss., accidently shot himself on Saturday night, 23rd, at the railroad convict camp near Red Banks. He stood leaning on a double barrell shotgun, the muzzle being under his arm and the gun loaded with twelve buck shot, which passed through his shoulder and head, tearing off the top of his skull and killing him instantly. (Holly Springs South)

Died near Waterford, Miss., Sept. 25th, 1882, Miss Nettie Henderson, of Augusta, Ark. She had spent the summer in Miss., in Booneville and Marshall Co., visiting relatives.

October 12, 1882
A dispatch from Crystal Springs says: "The northbound freight train on the Jackson railroad this morning ran over a mule near here, causing a wreck of fourteen cars. Riley Hawkins was killed, being buried under the ruins."

October 19, 1882
Hon. W. M. Lowe, Greenback candidate for Congress in the 7th District of Alabama, died at Huntsville, October 12th, of bronchitis.

Died near Booneville, October 16th, 1882, Mrs. Sarah J. Young, wife of Mr. Geo. F. Young and daughter of Rev. P. R. and Mrs. Ellen E. Hoyle. She was born March 3, 1853 and was married to Mr. Geo. F. Young, Nov. 6, 1873. She attached herself to the M. E. Church. She was buried at the cemetery in Booneville.

October 26, 1882
Bishop Robert Paine, of the Methodist Church, died at his residence in Aberdeen on the 20th. He was 83 years old and entered the ministry at the early age of 19. Bishop Paine was born in Person County, N. C., Nov. 12, 1799. His father, James Paine, Esq., removed to Giles County, Tennessee when Robert was a youth. (Author's note - a lengthy report followed)

November 23, 1882
Died at his home in Rienzi, Miss., Nov. 10th, Rev. Wm. E. Ellis, aged sixty-three years. He had been for thirty-nine years in the ministry of the Gospel.

November 30, 1882
The Gillium brothers who were charged with the killing of Matt Sugg, in Attala County near Goodman, was refused bail by the Justice that tried them.

We have the intelligence from West Station, that on the 9th inst., Wm. Kyle, brother of the late Thos. J. Kyle, was found dead on the bank of the creek near his residence a few miles from the town. Mr. Kyle was about 76 years of age.

December 14, 1882
Col. William H. H. Tison, Speaker of the House of Representatives, lost his life by the hand of violence at his home in Baldwyn, Lee County, on the 4th. (Author's note - a lengthy report followed)

Died at his home six miles west of Baldwyn, Nov. 24th, J. H. Palmer, aged 47 years and 6 months.

Leon Stewart, of Scooba, Miss., committed suicide at the Markham House in Atlanta, November 26, by taking morphine. He had a wife and one child.

December 21, 1882
Mr. Wm. M. Caver died of malarial fever, near Mineral Springs, Ark., Nov. 11th, 1882, in the 21st year of his age. He was the son of Mr. W. L. Caver, of this county.

J. E. Sanders was brought to Baldwyn Friday of last week for the purpose of having his preliminary trial for killing Col. Tison.

January 4, 1883
In 1878, Wm. Avery killed in Madison County, Sam Brister, and fled to Yazoo County. He was arrested by John Briston, Sr., and other parties. The parties started with him to Canton, but never reached Canton, but killed the prisoner in the woods. Jno. T. Brister and Wm. Beall have been recently arrested and put in jail at Yazoo City, charged with murder.

Mr. Robert Donaldson died at his residence Dec. 23, 1882, after a brief illness, at a ripe old age. He left a number of children.

Mr. Henry Spain died January 1, 1883, at the age of 76 years. His disease was apoplexy and his illness was brief.

John Holland, a well known colored man, died near town, Dec. 23, 1883.

January 18, 1883
Died Dec. 9th, 1882, Mary Crow, wife of Fielding Crow and daughter of E. C. Mitchell, after an illness of several weeks, at the age of 23 years.

March 8, 1883
Miss Dora Smith died in Booneville, on the morning of March 1, 1883. Her disease was typhoid fever, complicated with pneumonia.

March 22, 1883
Brother T. M. Baldwyn died at his mother's residence two miles north of Marietta, March 9th, 1883. He joined the Baptist Church at Casey's Creek, August 31st, 1878.

April 12, 1883
The painful duty devolves upon us to record the death of Tabitha Richardson, the wife of Mathias Richardson. Sister Richardson was born in Moore County, N. C., Feb. 23rd, 1793, joined the Baptist Church in 1828 and died near Marietta, Prentiss Co., Miss.

March 15th, 1883, aged 90 years and 23 days. She was widowed for nearly 13 years.

April 26, 1883

John Moriarty, who killed J. W. Ricks at Deasonville a short time since, had a preliminary trial at Yazoo City.

Little Lucille, infant daughter of Mr. & Mrs. B. A. P. Selman, died April 21, 1883, age one year and four months.

May 10, 1883

All the papers of the State have announced the death of Eliza Pinkston, the famous colored woman used as a witness by the Louisiana Returning Board to count that State for Hayes. She died in Canton jail on a charge of larceny.

Mr. S. M. Thompson, editor of the Oxford Eagle, was shot and instantly killed Tuesday, at Oxford, by the Marshall of the town, while he was resisting arrest.

May 17, 1883

Died at his residence 3 miles north of Hazel Deil, Miss., on the 7th day of May, 1883, B. M. Stennett, of chronic bronchitis. He leaves a wife and seven children.

Mrs. Narcissa Jane Smith, wife of Thomas B. Smith, died of typhoid pneumonia. Born in Fayette County, Ala., April 10, 1830, aged 53 years and 20 days, she was a member of the M. E. Church South.

Died at his father's residence near Booneville, Miss., David Milton, son of T. J. & M. H. Wheatly. He was born Sept. 16th, 1859 and departed this life April 7th, 1883, age 23 years, 5 months and 9 days.

James Thomas Cook, infant son of J. P. and Ellen Cook, was born June 26, 1882 and departed this life February 10, 1883, age 7 months and 14 days.

May 24, 1883

The Ripley Advertiser of the 19th announces the death of Mrs. Lavenia Kendrick, which occurred at the residence of Mr. G. M. Bostwick, in that place, May 15, 1883. She was in the 90th year of her age and had been a citizen of Tippah County 45 years, and a member of the Presbytarian Church 68 years. She was the mother of Mr. J. W. Kendrick.

June 7, 1883

Miss Sue D. Ferris, daughter of William and Catharine Ferris, died May 9, 1883 in the 18th year of her age, after a long illness of rheumatism and miningitis. She joined the Methodist Church four years ago.

July 5, 1883

Vernon White, who was charged with the assassination of Macon Leigh last September at Charleston, has been tried at Grenada and acquitted.

July 19, 1883

The jury of inquest in the case of Capt. M. L. Cole, assassinated near Vicksburg July 2, have concluded their investigation and brought in a verdict that the deceased was killed by a gun shot wound fired by Dr. P. H. Cook, and his son Hewett was an accessory before the fact.

The body was discovered by Miss Lilly Cook, daughter of Dr. Cook. In her testimony she said that the murderer, when she saw him, was dragging Capt. Cole by the back of the neck, and when he cried for mercy the murderer would push his fact in the sand. She exhonorated her brother Hewett, but would not say that her father was not the murderer. She had separate property from her father and they did not agree. She was living separately from him. (Author's note - this was part of a much longer report)

July 26, 1883

G. B. Walker was born in Marion Co., Ala. on the 6th day of August, 1831, and departed this life in Itawamba County, Miss., on the 29th day of March, 1883. He joined the Methodist Episcopal Church South in which he lived a member until his death.

Gen. E. O. C. Ord died of yellow fever at Havanna, on the 23rd. He commanded here during reconstruction times.

We chronicle the death of Miss Callie Barnett. She breathed her last Friday morning, in the presence of her father, brothers and sisters.

August 9, 1883

Capt. H. P. Johnson, editor and proprietor of the Kosciusko Star, died August 1, near San Marcos, Texas, whither he went a few weeks ago for the benefit of his health. His remains were brought to Kosciusko for interrment. He entered into the practice of law in Lexington soon after the war and married a daughter of H. H. Fultz, Esq. He leaves a wife and four children.

The infant child of Dr. and Mrs. D. T. Price died 3rd August.

Mr. & Mrs. B. A. P. Selmon lost their little infant Aug. 4th. It was only a few days old.

Judge and Mrs. B. B. Boone were so unfortunate to lose their infant child after a protracted illnes, August 4th.

August 16, 1883

W. M. McNulty, Sheriff of Pike County, at Summit, Aug. 3, was struck by a passenger train and badly wounded. He was taken home in an unconscious state and has since died.

August 30, 1883

Jackson, Miss., Aug. 23: Fayette Knight, a bad negro who has served at least one term in prison, has been arrested in Rankin County, charged with the assassination of Jno. W. Pearson, who was murdered some weeks ago.

Mr. Anthony Keirn, son of Dr. W. L. Keirn, died at Lexington on the 21st August. He was 24 years old, a graduate of the University of Virginia.

The Ripley Advertiser of the 25th contains an account of the death of Mr. Charlie D. Carter, formerly of Ripley and known to many of our citizens. The following excerpt is credited to the Dardenelle (Ark.) Independent Arkansian.

Aug. 8th, 1883, Judge Carter had returned bringing with him the remains of his brother, Charles Dudley Carter, who was wounded in the fight which took place July 29th between the Sheriff's posse of this county, and two desperadoes known as Bud and Jack Daniels. The funeral procession started from the residence of Judge H. S. Carter and the services were conducted by Rev. J. W. Heagan.

Walter Suggs and George Morgan were killed by lightening on the 14th near Greenwood. They had taken refuge under a tree out of the rain.

September 27, 1883

Smith Shaw and Dick Shaw, charged with the murder of Gen. Tucker, prayed for a change of venue. Their trial has been moved to Pontotoc County and will come off next February.

October 4, 1883

On the 26th September, 1883, the Angel of Death visited W. L. Boren, who was a member of the Methodist Church. He was 32 years old at the time of his death and left a wife and one child.

October 11, 1883

Col. A. M. Nelson died at his home in Carrollton, Oct. 1st. He was a soldier in the late war and was private secretary of Ex-Gov. Stone.

Dr. J. M. Byrd has been indicted in Jasper County for the murder of H. M. Brame, late Sheriff of said county, and Henry Calhoun has been indicted for complicity in the same.

November 15, 1883

Last Saturday night Mr. John M. West was found dead in the road leading from the Square to this home. He had been at his store all day up to about half past nine at night. Mr. West was a native of Lexington and a member of the drug firm of Watson & West. He had been in bad health for some time, and his death was attributed to an over dose of chloral. He was about 35 years old and a member of the Baptist Church. He leaves a wife and daughter.

Benj. Jordan, mayor of Hazlehurst, was shot with buckshot on the night of the 9th, as he entered his gate. It is supposed he was mortally wounded. Assassin not known.

J. P. Matthews, ex-Sheriff of Copiah (Co.), was shot on the day of the election, by R. B. Wheeler, with a double-barrell shot gun, and instantly killed.

November 22, 1883

The news reached here last Wednesday, of the killing the night before, of young Dryfus, of Durant. It seems that his father went to supper, leaving his son in charge of the store, and when he returned he found him lying in the store with his skull crushed. The object of the murder is supposed to have been robbery.

November 29, 1883

We regret to announce the death of Mr. J. C. Hamilton, who died in Baldwyn on the night of November 22, 1883, of Bright's disease, in the 25th year of his age. His remains were brought to Booneville by train.

December 6, 1883

Mrs. Harriet N. Prewitt died at her residence in Yazoo City, Nov. 26th. She was the mother of Col. J. C. Prewitt of the Yazoo City bar.

George Harris, an escaped negro convict, was killed in Columbus last week, by Charles Townsend, a negro, for resisting arrest.

Died Nov. 22nd, Mr. J. C. Hamilton, formerly of Booneville. He was buried in Booneville on Friday.

Mr. John Wright, of Jackson, Tenn., died suddenly last week, of a congestive chill, and Mr. Sam Dupas, of Memphis, died the same day from typhoid fever.

December 20, 1883

Col. J. R. Powell, a wealthy citizen of Yazoo County, was killed at Modoe, in Washington County, Dec. 9th. Col. Powell had killed J. P. Robinson about two years ago, and was on his way to stand trial for that offense. He stopped at a house and met with Charles T. Robinson, said to be no relation of J. P. Robinson. A quarrel ensued, Powell raised a chair and Robinson shot him. He died in a few minutes.

Col. Powell came from Alabama and was a member of the Legislature of that state for several sessions. He was the founder of the town of Birmingham. His remains were carried to Alabama for interrment.

The death is announced at Jackson, Tenn., of Mrs. Jessie Kitredge McNeil, wife of Rev. E. B. McNeil. The deceased was born at Elm Hall, Assumption Parish, La., Jan. 5, 1845, and was married at Winchester Springs, Franklins Conty, Tenn., Oct. 13, 1867.

January 3, 1884

The negro Howard, who killed Pat Flinn, white, near Skipwith Landing, in the early part of December, with a billet of wood, was taken out of the hands of the officers and lynched by a mob of negroes.

Mrs. Carter, wife of Mr. J. C. Carter, died after a lingering illness of consumption, December 25th, 1883.

T. H. Weathersby, Sheriff of Madison County, bitten two months ago by a mad dog, has developed symptoms of hydropbia. It is feared he will not recover.

Mrs. Williams, wife of Dr. W. B. Williams, died on the 24th December, 1883, leaving a husband and a number of children.

January 17, 1884

Crystal Springs, Miss., Jan. 13th - Ed. Graves, son of Eli Graves, was assassinated last night on his way home from this place, by two negroes, supposed to be Luke and Richard Miller. The assassins have made their escape.

Hardy Skillman, the unfortunate boy mentioned last week as wounded with a toy pistol, died Saturday and was buried Sunday near old Farmington. He was perhaps 15 years of age. He was in the act of showing a younger brother how to load and fire the pistol, when it accidently fired. (Corinth Herald)

January 31, 1884
Last Wednesday morning, at the residence of R. H. Henry, in this city, the spirit of Harry Moss winged it's flight beyond the stars. He was the "Mark Twain" of Mississippi journalism.

February 14, 1884
J. C. Cameron, Sr., an old citizen of Madison County, was killed by a freight train at Madison Station, on the I. C. R. R. Feb. 2.

February 21, 1884
The *Aberdeen Examiner* announced the death of Hon. O. H. Whitfield, which occurred in his office in that city, on Wednesday of last week.

Hon. Ben King died at his residence near Beauregard, of pneumonia, aged 65 years. He was a prominent Whig before the war, and was a member of the State Legislature. He ran as an Independent candidate for Governor and was defeated. He died on the 14th of February.

Joe Alexander was killed by John McNeil some few miles from this place last Friday. It seems that McNeil had had his jug filled with whiskey at a neighboring grocery, and went by Alexander's, who was his brother-in-law. They imbibed from the jug, and a quarrel ensued. McNeil cut Alexander in the abdomen, from the effects of which he died. McNeil escaped and has not been arrested.

The Flatonia (Tex.) Argus of Feb. 14th comes in mourning for the death of Robert E. O'Reilly, it's late editor and proprietor. It will be remembered that Mr. O'Reilly was foreman in the office of the *Pleader* in the Fall of '80 and part of '81. His sickness was a protracted one. He died at the early age of 25.

March 6, 1884
Charles Cumming, Mayor of Brookhaven, died in that city on the 2_th of February, with consumption.

Jack McKenna, who killed Ed. Wilson in Vicksburg, has appealed to the Supreme Court.

Frank Long was mortally wounded in a street fight in New Orleans, during the Mardi Gras parade.

There was a fatal pistol and bowie knife duel in Vicksburg last week. Harry Stith, a colored policeman, arrested H. J. Johnson for committing a nuisance on the street. While taking him to jail Johnson slipped out his knife and cut Stith in the groin, severing the femoral artery. Stith stepped back a few feet and drawing his pistol, shot Johnson several times. Both soon died from the wounds received.

Capt. W. P. Towler, charged with the murder of Charles W. Wright on Jan. 31, 1883, was recently tried at Winona, and acquitted of the charge.

John McNeil, the slayer of Joe Alexander, was captured last Monday in Tishomingo County.

Died at his residence near Eddy, Texas, Mr. James M. Dorster, of pneumonia, Feb. 24th, 1884. He was a resident of Alcorn County previous to his removal to Texas last fall.

March 13, 1884
Died in Booneville, March 7th, 1884, Mrs. Eliza J. Walton, daughter of Robert and Cynthia Parsley, and the beloved wife of William H. Walton. Deceased was born in Raleigh, N. C., October 27, 1815, and was married at Wake Forest College, May 18th, 1841, removed to Tishomingo County, Miss. in 1851, where she has since resided with her family.

March 20, 1884
Mr. B. W. Grisham died at his residence near town, of pneumonia, March 18, 1884. He leaves a large family.

Died last Thursday morning, Mr. A. G. Williams. Mr. Williams has long been a resident of this place.

March 27, 1884
Bishop H. H. Kavanah, one of the oldest Bishops in the Methodist Church, died in Columbus on the 19th, in the 83rd year of his age.

April 10, 1884
George Lee, col., was lynched at McComb City, on April 4th, for rape committed on a white girl 14 years old. He was first taken to jail at Magnolia. A crowd of 100 men, more or less, went to Magnolia, took him from jail and back to McComb City, where he suffered death as the penalty of his crime.

Died near Baldwyn, Miss., on the 27th, Mrs. M. E. Yates, after a protracted illness of several months.

April 17, 1884
Mrs. Lina Wilson, wife of Dr. T. Wilson, died in Corinth, April 12th. She was a member of the M. E. Church, President of the Ladies Christian Aid Society, and also of the Ladies Temperance Union.

April 24, 1884

The funeral services of Mr. J. W. Kendrick was preached Sunday afternoon at the Presbyterian Church. Mr. Kendirck was one of our oldest and most esteemed citizens.

May 8, 1884

Col. Wm. French, of Vicksburg, a brave Confederate officer and bright Mason, died in Jackson, April 28th.

Samuel T. Wilson, a white man guarding convicts on Col. E. Richardson's plantation, near Skipwith's Landing, was hung by a mob of negroes, April 27th. It is charged that he had difficulty with a negro, took him in a boat and beat him severly and then made the convicts throw him overboard. He was tried by a negro Justice of the Peace and sent to jail without bail. He was taken from the hands of the Deputy Sheriff by the mob of negroes and hung before reaching the jail.

May 22, 1884

The Columbus Dispatch last Sunday contains an account of the killing of Robert B. Speirs by A. B. Meek, the son of Col. S. M. Meek. The two young men were friends and were playing, snapping what they conceived to be unloaded pistols at each other.

Col. J. F. H. Claiborne, the historian of Mississippi, died in Natchez last Saturday, aged 77.

Died on the morning of the 20th of May, 1884, near Pisgah Church, Mrs. Elizabeth Allen, wife of Jas. H. Allen, aged 60 years. She leaves a husband, children and grandchildren.

June 12, 1884

We learn that Mr. Rives, Editor of the *Optic,* killed a man by the name of Ford, at New Albany last Saturday, by shooting him with a pistol. No particulars.

June 19, 1884

Died last Thursday evening, little Joe, son of Mr. John Welch. He had been sick for several days but was not thought to be dangerously so.

July 10, 1884

Died of heart disease on Wednesday last, Dr. A. G. Smith, of Cross Roads. Although he had reached the advanced age of 78 years, he was hale and vigorous.

July 24, 1884

Two negroes were lynched near Starkville for poisoning two white boys two years ago. One Ned Mack, a "kunger," furnished the poison and the other, Newt Carpenter, administered it. A negro woman who knew the secret told on them and they confessed.

July 31, 1884
News reaches us through the *Times Democrat*, that Col. J. L. Murphy, of Mobile, was shot and killed by Reuben Tipp, colored, June 27th, at Tipp's home some seven miles from Mobile. Tipp claims that he acted in self defense. Mrs. Annie Murphy was his wife, and his children named Miss Lillie, James, Willie and Tommie Murphy.

Died on the 21st of July, 1884, Georgia Goodger, only child of Mr. & Mrs. D. A. Goodger. She would have completed her first year had she lived till the second of August.

September 4, 1884
We record the death of Viney Simmons which occurred near Marietta, Prentiss County, Miss., on the 28th day of May, 1884. Sister Simmons was born in Oglethorpe County, Georgia, June 20th, 1814. She was married to Bro. James Simmons at the age of 16. She joined the Baptist Church at an early age.

September 18, 1884
Little Marcus Boren, son of Mr. & Mrs. J. S. Boren, died Friday night the 12th, aged two years.

October 2, 1884
Died Thursday night, September 11th, infant son of Mr. & Mrs. A. T. Stocks, aged one year and five months.

Died September 12th, 1884, little Pe___ Elder, infant daughter of Mr. & Mrs. Thos. Elder.

Mrs. Provene died near this place on the 26th of September, aged 79 years and 10 months.

October 9, 1884
We announce the death of Mr. Joseph B. Alexander after a long illness from typhoid fever, on October 8th, 1884. He was a member of the Baptist Church.

October 30, 1884
We chronicle the death of Mr. Joe Alexander, which occurred at his father's home in Booneville, Miss., on the 8th. Mr. Alexander was W. U. night telegraph operator at this place. (Union City Anchor, Union City, Tenn.)

We regret to annouce the death of Mr. J. M. Savery, which occurred at his father's residence last Saturday night, after an illness of thirteen months.

November 13, 1884

Mr. W. C. Timbes died at his residence of typhoid fever, Nov. 6, 1884. He as an old citizen and one of our most successful merchants.

Mr. Billie Ross, of Tupelo, died on Monday night, of typhoid fever.

Died Oct. 28, 1884, Mrs. Josie Archer, at her home one mile from Marietta, Miss.

November 20, 1884

An old negro man named Calvin Johnson, living near Canton, committed suicide on the 13th, because he believed when Cleveland and Hendricks were inaugerated, he would be sold into slavery.

December 18, 1884

The *Lexington Bulletin* announces the death of Mr. J. N. McLean, Sr., at Shell Mound in Leflore County, at the age of 75. His remains were interred in the cemetery at Lexington. Mr. McLean was a prominent citizen of Holmes County in ante bellum days.

The *Water Valley Progress* of Dec. 6th, is in mourning for the death of Miss Minnie Brown, the daughter of Capt. S. B. Brown, editor of that paper.

John Moriarty, who killed James Ricketts in Yazoo County some years ago, has been tried, found guilty and sentenced to the penetentiary for life.

BROOKHAVEN DEMOCRAT
Brookhaven, Mississippi

September 1, 1883

Mr. Robert Claiborne is a brother to Mrs. T. P. Leathers, wife of the Captain of the *Natchez*. He is postmaster at Point Coupee (La.). Last Tuesday evening, while the steamboat *Blanks* was lying at the landing, Mr. Claiborne started down the levee toward where she was tied, followed a short distance behind by two negro men mounted on mules, carrying the mail bags. When nearly to the boat he was seen to fall to the ground suddenly beneath a white blaze of light that hovered around him for an instant, and the two negro men at the same time were hurled off their mules to the ground. Those on the boat who witnessed the phenomenon rushed ashore to where Mr. Claiborne had fallen. They found him a corpse, black as ink all over. The lightening traversed his body. The two negroes felt the force of the shock sufficiently to be thrown from the mules without being seriously injured. (Vicksburg Herald)

On August 25th, a negro boy by the name of Lymas Bridges, living on Pearl River near Monticello, while climbing a muscadine vine, lost his balance and fell to the ground, a distance of ten or fifteen feet, breaking his neck.

Dr. William Weathersby, the victim of assassination at the hands of one Dewitt Rollins, departed this life on August 25, 1883, after a prolonged period of suffering. During his confinement his son, Eugene Weathersby, once a promising youth, was sentenced to the penetentiary for theft.

Young Eugene Weathersby, lately sentenced to the penetentiary for theft, was killed, it is rumored, while attempting to escape. The particulars, as we heard them, are as follows: he became enraged at the guard while at work on the N. G. & C. R. R., threw a spade at him and then turned and fled, when the guard shot him dead. We do not vouch for the truth of this report.

Dr. R. H. Ryland, a prominent physician and planter at Bayou Sara, La., fell from his gin-house a few days ago and was killed.

Mary Thomas was found dead in Vicksburg, Miss., a few nights ago. When found she was dead with a wound ranging from the armpit up toward the neck. A knife was found in the bottom of the basket she carried, and although the Coroner's jury found a verdict of suicide, it has since been ascertained that the deed was committed by an enemy of Mary's, and an arrest is expected.

September 8, 1883
John Bowman, of this city, but at the time of the accident guarding convicts at Bogue Chitto, while coupleing lumber flats on the Wesson & Pearson branch, was caught between the cars and had his head badly crushed. He lingered some time in acute pain, when death finally came to his relief.

Died on August 31, 1883, of a painful illness, Fanny Decell, daughter of T. H. Decell and F. H. Decell, aged 18 years, a native of Brookhaven, Miss.

October 6, 1883
The news of the murder, without provocation, of Mr. Wm. M. Neely, and whose family, wife and daughter, now reside in McComb City, comes to us as having occurred on the Payne plantation, at Barbeck, La., where he was an engineer, on the 26th. Two men named Lane and Brown, who had secured work on the

place, became angry with Mr. Neely and Brown pulling out a pistol shot him three times in the back, producing wounds, either one of which would have proved fatal. These men made their escape and continued at large until the 29th of Sept., when Sheriff Dudson, of Eola, La., apprended the murderers on the Red River 42 miles from Eola, and demanded their surrender. They refused and opened fire upon the Sheriff and his posse, during which Lane was shot and killed and Brown taken prisoner.

Mr. Neely was about 55 years of age.

November 10, 1883

On Tuesday last our town was considerably excited over the news of the killing of J. P. Matthews, of Hazlehurst, Miss., by E. B. Wheeler, of the same place, by firing both barrels of a shotgun into Matthews' body. The news is so conflicting we forebear publishing anything in regard to the affair.

November 17, 1883

Wm. Deer, a nephew of Sam Magee, of this place, was found dead on the rail road track near Bogue Chitto, on Saturday morning. It is believed he was murdered and placed on the track to throw off suspicion. He was a citizen of Amite County, and lived near Summit, but had recently returned from Texas.

November 24, 1883

The Curtis brothers, who are charged with killing Jesse V. Piace near Winona, has turned up in Louisiana, where under the names of Lane and Brown they murdered a man; they resisted arrest and Lane was killed; Brown was captured and is now in jail in Winona.

December 1, 1883

Miss Alice M. Benton, one of the injured ones by the dreadful cyclone at Beauregard last April, died on the 10th inst., never having recovered from the injuries she sustained. Miss Alice was the sister of our esteemed citizen, W. H. Benton, and had spent the summer at his home near Rocky Springs. (Port Gibson Reveille)

December 22, 1883

Died in Lincoln County, at the residence of his son-in-law, Mr. F. E. Marsalis, about 18 miles west of Brookhaven, Mr. Ephram Marsalis, in the 78th years of his age. The deceased was the father of Mrs. C. E. Magee, wife of our fellow townsman, Mr. Sam Magee. The deceased was one of the first settlers of Amite County. He was a member of the Methodist Church.

January 19, 1884

Vicksburg, Jan. 17 - A murder was committed here last night. Jack McKenna, a notoriously bad character, killed Ed. Wilson in a faro saloon on Washington Street. Wilson was "dealer," and he prevented

McKenna from taking another man's chips. This brought on abuse from McKenna and a quarrel. Wilson attempted to make McKenna keep quiet, but the latter became more violent. When Wilson went to a colored servant and instructed him to bring him his pistol, and was in the act of getting it when McKenna fired on him, killing him almost instantly. McKenna fled, but gave himself up afterward.

March 1, 1884
The grim monster Death has once more knocked at the door of our friend Charles Cuming. Our young friend sleeps his last.

March 15, 1884
Last Monday evening our community was startled to hear that a man named Henry Rittman, a German, who was arrested in town on that morning, had ended his life by taking a tin cup and tearing it open to make an instrument for the purpose of committing suicide, cutting his throat from ear to ear.

March 29, 1884
J. R. Rawlston committed suicide in the Brookhaven jail a few days ago by severing the jugular vein with a knife made from a tin cup. He was arrested on suspicion of being the man who had beaten his wife and murdered an unborn babe near Yergersville, Granada County, some time ago. He was evidently insane.

Bishop H. H. Kavanaugh, of Anchorage, Ky., died on the 19th at Columbus, Miss. He was eighty-three years of age and had been a clergyman for over sixty years, of the Methodist Episcopal Church South.

THE BROOKHAVEN LEADER
Brookhaven, Mississippi

April 5, 1883
After a protracted illness, Frank A. Young died at his home in Jackson on March 30th.

April 12, 1883
Died on April 3rd, at her home in Lincoln County, Mrs. Sarah Margaret Johnson, aged 25 years.

May 17, 1883
The following particulars have been given of the killing of Col. S. M. Thompson, editor of the Oxford Eagle: The deceased was intoxicated and unarmed. Butler, without warrant, arrested him for offensive language and started with him to the Mayor's office, when

Thompson suddenly stopped and refused to go farther. A scuffle ensued during which the deceased clung to Butler's coat lapels with one hand. When the latter commanded him to let loose or he would kill him, Thompson said "Well shoot!" Butler fired, the ball passing through Thompson's head. Butler was indicted for murder.

The *Brandon Republic* of last Thursday gives the following account: Our population was thrown into a state of excitement by the intelligence that Mrs. J. M. Benson had committed suicide by taking rat poison. She gave birth to a child about five weeks ago and had been in feeble health ever since. She leaves a doting husband and three small children. (Author's note - this was part of a lengthy report)

July 5, 1883

Mrs. Holland, an old lady of 72 or 73 years, who had for a long time been the housekeeper of Mr. Jesse Warren, our Circuit Clerk, committed suicide on Thursday last by taking strychnine. For several weeks she had been in a demented condition.

July 26, 1883

Died at the residence of Mrs. V. C. Harris, Beauregard, Copiah County, Miss., April 22, 1883, Miss Mary Mikel, one of the victims of the fearful cyclone which devastated the town that day. Miss Mikel was born in Lawrence County, Miss., August 1849.

Mrs. Sarah Emily White was born in Lawrence County, Jan. 25, 1820, and was married to Capt. J. F. White, Oct. 19, 1853. They moved to Beauregard (Copiah Co., Miss.) October 4, 1871, where they both joined the Baptist Church. From that time until the day of her death she proved to be a "bright and shining light" in the Church.

George Adolphus White, a promising boy aged 15 years, 7 months and 10 days, was slain and borne from the ruins of their once happy home a mangled corpse. Likewise, the loving sister, Miss Mary, was brought bleeding and dying, calling upon "Emily" who though hearing her last, could not come to her calling.

August 2, 1883

Brakeman Ed. Porady tripped and was caught between the bumpers while coupling cars at Hoskins Mill switch on the H. & H. railroad last Tuesday afternoon, and was killed. He was a young man of about 24 and had a mother living in Memphis.

August 9, 1883

Died near Caseyville, Miss., on the 5th of August, 1883, of flux, Jones Neil, son of T. J. and D. S. McInis, aged 4 years, 4 months and 24 days.

August 16, 1883
Capt. Wm. M. McNulty, Sheriff of Pike County, died at his home in Magnolia last Saturday, and was buried with Masonic honors.

September 6, 1883
A. W. Barnett, Esq., a young lawyer of Hazlehurst, was shot Tuesday night, by a young man named Chas. Hart, a printer of the *Signal* office. We have not heard full particulars but understand that Barnett's wounds are mortal.

Died the 31st of August, at Maxwell's Mill in Lawrence County, Mrs. Lizzie Maxwell, wife of A. M. Maxwell, aged 33 years.

September 20, 1883
Died August 31st, 1883, on Fair River, Lincoln County, Miss., Mazilla Nations, wife of Wm. Nations, aged 40 years, 3 months and 26 days. She had been a member of the Baptist Church over 19 years. She left a husband and 7 children.

September 27, 1883
Died near Pleasant Hill Church, Copiah County, the 19th, of diptheria, Clifton, son of Jasper and Bedia Davis, and grandson of Dr. E. R. Applewhite, aged about three years.

Mrs. Dillon "Aunt D," an aged Christian lady of Monticello, died yesterday.

October 11, 1883
Miss Lillie Miller, a young lady of scarce sixteen summers and daughter of Mr. & Mrs. Geo. W. Miller of Copiah County, died last week.

November 22, 1883
Died of apoplexy on the 13th, at his residence in this county, Mr. T. J. R. Keenan, in the 63rd year of his age.

December 6, 1883
Capt. Robert Joselyn, formerly a well-known citizen of North Mississippi, died in Austin, Texas, on the 4th. Capt. Joselyn at one time edited a paper in Holly Springs and once filled a state office at Jackson. At the beginning of the war he was for several months private secretary of President Davis.

January 3, 1884
Hon. W. B. Stuart, president of the outgoing Board of Supervisors of Jefferson County, died on Dec. 24th, of a chronic disease.

Died at his residence near Monticello, Lawrence County, Dec. 26th, 1883, William Cameron, a native of Wilmington, N. J.

January 31, 1884

Mr. Shall Yerger, fifth son of the late Judge William Yerger, died in Bolivar County last week.

Dr. John W. Crisler, of Hinds County, died recently at his home near Byram, of pneumonia.

February 21, 1884

Hon. Benj. King departed this life at his home in Beauregard, on Feb. 13th, 1884, aged about 61 years. He had been in feeble health for a number of years and being attacked with pneumonia some two weeks ago caused his death.

Emanuel Myers, born in Raleigh, Smith County, Mississippi, Dec. 21st, 1867, died in New Orleans, Oct. 19, 1883.

Capt. James M. Buckley was born in Lawrence County, Miss., Nov. 19, 1830. On April 1, 1856 he was married, in Pike County, to Miss Bethany Craf. In 1862 he was elected Chancery Clerk of Lawrence County, which position he held until 1869, when he removed to Brookhaven. In 1872 he was elected Chancery Clerk of Lincoln County, and held that office until 1879, when he was made Deputy Auditor of State. Henceforth, his residence was Jackson, Miss. He died away from home, unexpectedly.

March 13, 1884

Died on the 3rd, after an illness of five days, Mary E., daughter of J. M. and M. L. Taylor, of Boguechitto, Miss., aged nine years, seven months and five days.

A sad and fatal accident occurred on Mr. Isaac Smith's place about 7 miles northwest of Brookhaven on last Monday. Albert Parr, a youth of 13 years, and a negro were riding in a dump cart loaded with corn and drawn by a mule, when the mule took fright and ran away. The negro jumped out, but Parr remained trying to check the mule. The cart finally struck an obstruction in the road, upset and struck him on the head, killing him almost instantly. The victim was a grandson of the Rev. Mr. Cooper who discovered the famous Cooper's Well. He leaves a mother and several brothers and sisters.

May 14, 1885

The usually quiet town of Magnolia is in ferment on account of a most foul and brutal murder by an unknown party last Tuesday night, upon L. L. Traube, a lawyer of our town. The particulars are: About 10 o'clock Tuesday night three pistol shots were heard in rapid succession and the cry of "murder" emanated from a point between the residence of Traube and the house occupied by James Ballard. Persons who went immediately to the spot discovered the dead body of Traube with two pistol shot wounds in his left side.

Mr. Philip P. Werloin(?), senior partner of Werleins(?) music store, of New Orleans, died last Saturday night, aged 73 years. He was in early life at the head of the Female Seminary at Clinton, Miss., and afterward resided in Vicksburg. He was born in Germany.

THE BROOKHAVEN LEDGER
Brookhaven, Mississippi

October 20, 1881

Died in New Orleans on Oct. 9th, Julia Simmons, only daughter of Dr. G. Farrar Patton and Clara M. Simmons, aged 23 days.

Died at the residence of his brother, near Summit, on the 16th, Rufus R. Ratcliff, aged twenty-five years, first son of Walter S. Ratcliff and Sarah J. Evans.

October 27, 1881

Mr. S. H. Whitworth, of Rising Sun, formerly of Brookhaven, who was recently compelled to kill John Murdock in Leflore County, has given us an account of that sad event. He says he and Murdock had had a difficulty about some sheep; Murdock went before a Justice of the Peace and had Whitworth put under a peace bond. While returning home, accompanied by S. S. Parker, he overtook John and Wm. Murdock. William hailed him and said he could not come any nearer immediately covering him with a double barrel shot-gun, snapping one cap. Whitworth then dismounted and drew his pistol; Murdock wheeled and fled. Jno. Murdock then remarked he would do the fighting, shot at Whitworth once with a pistol. Whitworth then fired four shots successively at John, killing him.

November 10, 1881

Two negroes, Isaac & Richard Hill, murdered a white man named D. A. Cameron, in Warren County, on the 6th. Cameron became engaged in a difficulty with the two negroes at a fair on the Oakland place, during which the negroes drew revolvers and fired upon him. Cameron fled but the darkeys followed in pursuit, both firing upon their victim. Cameron was shot twice near the spine, but continued to run until he reached his mother's, and on arriving was put to bed. He died in less than thirty minutes.

November 17, 1881

Died at her home on Fair River, Nov. 11th, Mrs. E. J. Carlisle, wife of J. J. Carlisle and daughter of W. B. Brewer. She leaves a husband, son and four daughters. She was buried at the Wilson graveyard near Monticello.

Mr. Jno. W. Bessonett, of Terry, died here Sunday, the 6th, of consumption. He leaves a wife and one child.

December 22, 1881

Mrs. Mayers, wife of Capt. P. K. Mayers, of Handsboro, died on the 14th, of consumption. She was a member of the Methodist Church. To her husband and son we extend our deepest sympathies.

On last Saturday, near Rockport in Copiah County, we learn that there was a boiler explosion at the steam mill of Dr. J. B. Catchings, resulting in the instant death of two persons- Mr. Frank Brooks and Dick Sartain, the latter colored. Their bodies were found horribly mangled, several yards from the engine.

January 5, 1882

The Aberdeen murderers, Jones, the white man recently arrested, and William Miller, the negro, both pled guilty and were remanded to jail. Our readers will remember the circumstances - three brothers named Walker were traveling from Alabama to Arkansas and were near Aberdeen, this state, when they were murdered by Jones and Miller. The youngest brother was only fourteen years of age.

January 19, 1882

On the night of the 16th, at Meridian, Mr. W. A. Pettus, of Newton, a drummer, was shot and probably fatally wounded by unknown parties in a house east of the Mobile & Ohio railraod track. The shooting was done through a window.

A four year old son of Mr. Vannoy Blanks, of this city, was accidently shot on Friday, by his little brother, about two years older, with one of the so called toy pistols. The weapon was loaded with turkey shot. (Meridian Homestead)

February 16, 1882

A shooting affray occurred in Jackson, on the 13th, between D. Harrington and Geo. Harrel. Harrington was dangerously wounded and is reported very low.

March 2, 1882

Died at her residence near Brookhaven, February 24th, 1882, Mrs. Jane Coltharp, wife of Mr. A. J. Coltharp.

March 23, 1882

Rev. Dr. W. E. M. Linfield died at his residence in Hazlehurst, on the 16th. For the past two years he had, on account of bad health, almost total blindness.

A man giving his name as J. R. Davis, was arrested in Corpus Christi, Texas, on the 20th, believed to be J. D. Gillewater, who murdered S. T. Eaton, in Smith County, Miss., last August.

Roderick Bowles, for the killing of Otis Reynolds, was tried at Batesville last week.

A negro man by the name of Ned Walker, a lunatic, was found dead in the woods in Clarke County. His death was caused by exposure, deprivation and want.

April 20, 1882

A few days ago, in Kemper County, a negro named George Hughes murdered the lady for whom he was working, Mrs. Alex. Hensod, and threw her body in a well.

James Bailey and John Robinson, of Charleston, Miss., were drowned while making a journey in a dug out last week. They had both been drinking hard.

May 11, 1882

Died in Monticello, May 5th, 1882, Marx Cohn, a victim of the late storm, in the 24th year of his age.

Dr. Preston E. Buckner, of Greenville, Miss., on Thursday night, entered a room where a man named Wentworth was sleeping, and as it was very dark and not being able to discern who it was, the latter called upon him to halt. Dr. Buckner paying no attention to the command, Wentworth fired, killing him almost instantly.

June 1, 1882

A man residing in Fayette County, Alabama, named Andrew Allen, visited his wife, from whom he had been separated several months, and shot her, killing her instantly. Her brother arrived soon after, and finding his sister dead fired both barrels of a shot gun into Allen, and he fell dead by his wife's side.

June 29, 1882

Died at McComb City, Miss., June 22nd, 1882, Eugene Stanley, youngest son of W. J. & Sallie Vanzant, aged 1 year, 3 months and 27 days.

Died in Brookhaven, June 24th, 1882, Annie Laura, daughter of R. H. and Mrs. Ida Henry, aged eleven months and four days.

July 13, 1882

Annie Laura Henry, daughter of R. H. & Ida J. Henry, aged 11 months and 4 days, was born July 20, 1881 and died June 24, 1882. She died of inflammation caused by inability to assimilate nourishment.

The body of a German named Hawke was found in a cistern in Yazoo County on the 10th. He is supposed to have been murdered by his partner, Chas. Parsons, who is missing.

August 3, 1882

Louis Rosenburg left Vicksburg very suddenly a few days ago. He had been tried and acquitted of the charge of killing Dr. Wm. Michoricsburg. Notwithstanding the decision, a number of people believe him guilty. Accordingly, a committee of citizens called on Rosenburg and told him he would find distant lands more healthy. He took the hint and left.

A few miles southwest of Lexington, the 13th, R. E. Cader, commonly known as Dick Cader, a man about fifty years of age, was engaged at repairing a well. He was standing on a platform that was suspended in the well, and fell off, going down to the bottom. When he was taken out life was extinct.

On July 22nd, a negro boy, Willis Bell, about sixteen years of age killed himself on the plantation of Dr. W. G. Ford, about three miles west of Wesson. The particulars, as related, are as follows: Some of the negroes on the place had traded a violin for a pistol and placed the same loaded in a trunk. Willis was lying on the bed alone in the room, and the trunk was at the edge of the bed. Leaning over, he took out the pistol, and in putting it back the hammer struck the lid of the trunk, exploding the weapon, the ball penetrating the lung. He died in ten minutes.

August 10, 1882

J. M. Niolin, Jr., the twelve year old son of Mr. & Mrs. Niolin, of Meridian, accidently killed himself at Portersville, on the sea coast, last week. He had cocked his gun to shoot at some cranes, and failing to get a shot, forgot that his gun was cocked, and in this condition punched at a lobster in shallow water with the butt of his gun, discharging it, the contents entering his head and killing him instantly.

Thos. Sullivan, who killed P. H. Higgins at Meridian, was tried last week and found guilty of manslaughter. Judge Terrel sentenced him to fifteen years imprisonment.

August 17, 1882

On Thursday of last week, the boiler of the steam saw mill belonging to J. C. Carter, 12 miles southeast of Booneville, exploded with terrific effect. Mr. John Odom and a negro named Bob were killed outright. Mr. Lindsey was badly, and it is feared fatally, injured. Mr. Jim Hodges had just stepped off to get a drink of water and in that was escaped with slight injury.

September 7, 1882

Died in Brookhaven, September 3rd, 1882, of laryingitis, Walter Trawick, youngest son of Wm. L. And Arcola Mitchell, aged four years, ten months and fifteen days.

Dr. I. B. Clayton, of Goodman, was found last Monday about a mile from that town, life being quite extinct and his body showing the lodgement of ten buckshot. At last account the proprietor of this deed had not been discovered. Dr. Clayton killed Freeman Lester last January, and was acquitted at the following term of Court.

September 21, 1882

Jessie Sessions passed from our presence to dwell with her Father in Heaven, Sept. 11th, 1882.

Mr. N. D. Link, an old and respected citizen of Yazoo County, died near Yazoo City last week.

October 12, 1882

Died at her residence in Franklin County, Sept. 23rd, 1882, Eliza M. Adams, aged seventy-seven years. She was the second of four children consisting of Hon. D. U. Hollis, of Moscow, Ala.; Mary Stodder, of Mobile, and Martha Hodges, of Booneville, who passed away a few years ago.

October 26, 1882

Died at her residence in Franklin County, the 20th of October, 1882, Mrs. C. A. Lee, with chronic bronchitis.

December 21, 1882

Died at his residence in the eastern part of Jefferson County, on Nov. 24th, James McDonald, in the eighty-third year of his age.

Died on the evening of the 12th, at her home in Lincoln County, Mrs. Elizabeth Smith, in the 79th year of her age. She was stricken with apoplexy, and in a few hours died. Sister Smith has a husband (Lott Smith) and six children who have trod the path of death before her, and leaves ten children.

THE AMERICAN CITIZEN
Canton, Miss.

April 13, 1878
Died on April 6th, 1878, in Phillips County, Arkansas, at the residence of her son-in-law, H. C. Bosworth, Mrs. Emily T. Walker, relict of the late Wm. F. Walker, for many years a resident of Madisonville, in this county. The deceased was a native of Greene County, Ga., and her maiden name was B__che. She was about seventy years of age.

April 27, 1878
A colored man named M. F. Daniels and two mules were instantly killed by lightening on Mr. J. N. Batley's place, in the southern part of this county, near Tougaloo, during a thunderstrom, on the 18th.

May 11, 1878
The death of Miss Ella, eldest daughter of the Rev. H. H. Montgomery, which occurred in Hazlehurst, Miss., on the 7th, we record with sorrow.

Died in this city on the 8th, at the residence of her mother, Miss Florence, youngest daughter of Mrs. Lucy and the late Harvey Latham. She died of heart disease.

May 25, 1878
It is our painful duty to record the death of Mrs. Emily Lee, wife of Dr. T. A. Phillips, which occurred on the 17th. She was a native of East Feliciana Parish, La. She completed her 41st year on the 12th of February last. She was married on the 9th of June, 1853, and removed to Vernon, Miss. She joined the M. E. Church the same year. In December, 1869, Mrs. Phillips removed to Canton.

Miss Kate Morris, aged 19 years, and daughter of Judge J. S. Morris, of Jackson, Miss., who was so badly burned in attempting to fill a lamp with coal oil on the night of the 10th, died on the 18th. She was a devout catholic.

June 1, 1878
Died at his residence in this place, on the 28th, of May 1878, Mr. Herman Peterson, in the 56th year of his age. Mr. Peterson was a native of Hanover, Germany. He had resided in Canton 19 years. He died of cholera morbus.

Yesterday morning James Bilbrew, colored, living on Mr. James Smith's place, was arraigned on a charge of murdering his wife. We give the affair as he confessed it:

Some four weeks ago there was a disagreement between the parties and the wife left the husband. Yesterday morning when both were in the field hoeing the wife stated to Jim that she had learned he had threatened to kill her, and if true he had better do it at once and with these words extended the hoe with which she was working and cursed him, adding that if he did not kill her she would kill him. He thereupon struck her a blow on the head. She repeated her threat. He again struck her a severe blow on the head with the hoe with which she fell to the ground. Bilbrew immediately came to town and gave himself up.

June 8, 1878

Died in Sharon, on Wednesday night the 5th, Miss Ella Wiggins.

July 6, 1878

We learn that Mrs. Foreman, relict of the late Dr. Foreman (pastor of the Presbyterian Church in this place), died at the breakfast table on the 30th. She died of disease of the heart.

A fatal affray occurred at Terry, Miss., on the 27th, which resulted in the death of Mr. J. H. Bracey, in a difficulty in which several parties were involved.

August 31, 1878

Died in this city, on the 24th of August, at the residence of Dr. A. H. Cage, Mrs. S. D. Garrett, aged 67 years.

November 16, 1878

Died on the 12th, of yellow fever, at the residence of her son-in-law, Mr. J. V. Fitchett, Mrs. Wilson, aged about _9 years.

November 23, 1878

Died Nov. 22, Johonie Jones Summerfield, son of William W. and May Summerfield..

Died on the Hardee plantation, Isaquena County, Miss., October 15th, of yellow fever, John Doyle, aged 27 years.

November 30, 1878

Died the 26th November, at her residence in this place, Mrs. Fannie W. Leitch, aged 56 years.

Lewis Kenoyer, many years a citizen of Canton, died on the 20th, of paralysis, after a lingering illness of four months.

Mr. James Lennard, while performing his duties as brakeman on the north bound freight train on Wednesday night, near Grenada, slipped and fell to the ground, the car wheels passing over both legs, causing amputation, from the effects of which he is not expected to live.

December 21, 1878
Died in New Port, Miss., on the 7th day of Dec., at the residence of T. D. Brown, after a lingering illness, Narcissa Elvira, only child of T. D. and Josephine Brown, aged 1 year and 4 months.

February 1, 1879
Died the 27th of January, of pneumonia, Maggie, aged four years, daughter of Mr. & Mrs. Jas. Monahan, of this place.

February 13, 1879
The killing of a mulatto girl, Kansas Foster, born in Canton and known here as Kansas Singleton, was given in the Jackson Clarion of the 15th.

A brutal murder was committed in West Jackson last evening. James Hicks, colored, shot and killed Kansas Foster, colored. They had a dispute about a handkerchief and a pair of sleeve buttons. He claimed he did not know the gun was loaded, but witnesses say that he did.

April 19, 1879
Died at her residence in this county, on the 14th, Mrs. Jane P. Divine, relict of the late Samuel Divine.

May 31, 1879
A serious affray occurred six miles from Canton on the 26th. D. McAllister shot and mortally wounded his son. An old family feud was the cause.

With deep sorrow we chronicle the death of Maj. B. J. Semmes, who breathed his last on the 28th, in his old home in this place, surrounded by grief-stricken relatives. His attack was sudden and violent.

June 7, 1879
James Bilbro, the negro who murdered his wife last summer, on the farm of James Smith, in this county, was hanged on Monday last. (Author's note - a lengthy report followed)

June 21, 1879
On Thursday night, as the north bound passenger train left Canton, a negro man named Richard Taylor got on for the purpose of riding to his home, about a mile from town. On nearing his house, Taylor attempted to jump off, but in some way fell beneath

the wheels and was shockingly mangled. He lived only a few moments.

July 26, 1879
Died on the 17th, Mary Clave, second daughter of Mr. Carroll Smith, in the 8th year of her age.

August 9, 1879
Died in Canton, August 2, 1879, Maggie, second daughter of Mr. R. B. and Mrs. Lucy Campbell, aged six months and twenty three days.

Died in Canton, August 5, 1879, of pneumonia, Josephine Barksdale, youngest child of Rev. R. D. and Mrs. Jennie Norsworthy, aged two years.

August 16, 1879
Ben Taylor shot and mortally wounded Joe Bates, at Goodman, late Tuesday, for the alleged seduction of his daughter. Bates has since died.

November 8, 1879
On November 2nd, the mortal remains of James McFarland, for many years a merchant and citizen of this place, was followed to the cemetery. His death occurred on the 1st of November, after an illness of nearly four weeks. He was a native of Strahan, Ireland, and came to this country when about 22 years of age. He had been thrice married and leaves a wife and three daughters. He was a member of the Presbyterian Church.

Louis George, second son of Mr. & Mrs. G. R. Kemp, of this city, on the 24th, was crushed to death by the fall of a heavy pile of lumber. He was three years and three months old.

Adaline Augusta Latimer, nine years of age and daughter of the late Robert and Mrs. Angie Latimer, departed this life on the 3rd day of November, after a few days extreme illness from croup.

November 29, 1879
Died on the 26th, of diptheria, John Robert, aged fifteen months, only child of Mr. Charles and Mrs. Gertrude Mayson.

Last week Mr. Jas. B. Otto had the remains of his beloved mother and brother, Mrs. S. A. Otto and Mr. Wiley L. Otto, who died in the country during the yellow fever epedemic of '78, removed and reinterred in the family lot in the city cemetery.

Some weeks ago, Mr. Emmett Drane (generally known as Buster), third son of the late Judge Wesley Drane, formerly a citizen of Canton, had accidentlly shot and killed himself in New Mexico.

January 17, 1880
Died on the 10th, after a brief illness, Mrs. Sara, wife of Mr. Samuel Aaron. Her remains were transferred to New Orleans, her former home, for burial in the Jewish cemetery.

February 7, 1880
Dr. C. M. Vaiden died at his home on the 6th.

March 20, 1880
Died at the residence of Rev. George C. Harris in Tennessee, Mrs. M. L. Johnstone. Mrs. Johnstone was only a few years ago a resident of this county.

March 27, 1880
Died in Canton on the 21st, of cancerous affection, Col. Willie Lyons, aged 79 years and 6 months. Col. Lyons had been a citizen of this city and county for more than a generation.

July 3, 1880
Paul Bass, a colored youth who formerly lived at Canton, was struck by lightening while fishing on the Pear river, last Sunday, and instantly killed.

July 10, 1880
Died at Madison Station, July 3rd, at the residence of her mother, Mrs. C. L. Lewis, Jennie Magruder, wife of D. P. Montgomery, of consupmtion.

July 17, 1880
Mr. Joseph Blake Jones, of this county, died in Oxford on the 3rd.

August 7, 1880
Mr. W. T. Williams, a merchant at Mechanicsburg, Yazoo County, was waylaid and killed near that village on the 24th. Tobe Hill, a negro, was arrested and confessed to being guilty of the crime, but claimed to have been paid to murder Dr. Williams by L. Rosenberg, Jr., another merchant of Mechanicsburg. Rosenberg was arrested.

We learn from the Macon, Ga. Herald that Dr. J. T. Holmes, a citizen of Canton, died at the home of his brother in Macon, on Saturday last.

August 28, 1880
Died at Benton, Miss., Aug. 15th, Mrs. Sue, wife of J. H. Avery.

October 2, 1880
Died at the residence of her mother, at Carthage, Leake County, on Monday last, Mrs. Clinton Hanson Luckett, wife of O. A. Luckett, Jr., Esq., and youngest daughter of the late Col. Hanson, of said county, in her 20th year. She was a member of the Methodist Episcopal Church.

October 30, 1880
Mr. Asa Coleman died at his residence in Sharon, on the 27th.

November 13, 1880
Died in Isaquena County, on the 29th, of swamp fever, Mr. James Dinkins, aged 21 years. He was the second son of Mr. James and Mrs. Margaret Dinkins, of this county.

Died at her residence near Madison Station, on the 7th, Mrs. Lizzie Stevens, oldest daughter of the Rev. John R. Lambuth, deceased. She was a victim of consumption. Her brother, Rev. Wm. R. Lambuth, our missionary to China, reached her bedside a few days before her spirit left.

December 4, 1880
Departed this life at his home near Livingston, in this county, after a short illness, surrounded by his family and friends, Gen. S. A. D. Greaves. He was born in Marion District, South Carolina, on the 7th day of January, 1819, and was in the sixty-second year of his age. In the year 1835 he moved to this state and settled at Raymond, Hinds County. He served in the Raymond Fencibles in the Mexican War, and saw service at Beuna Vista, Mexico.

About two o'clock last Thursday, an affray took place in the courthouse in Carthage, between Gassamore Hughes and S. D. McGaughey, in which the former received a pistol shot wound from which he died a few moments later. It is said that the difficulty grew out of business matters in connection with a third party -- a negro named Bill Cheshire. (Author's note - a lengthy report followed.)

Died on November 30th, 1880, at the residence of Mrs. Anna E. Ross, Mrs. Florence, wife of Col. Pritchard.

December 18, 1880
Died at his home in Concordia, Bolivar Co., Miss., on the 4th, of pneumonia, Mr. Robert C. Mayson, aged 58 years. He leaves a wife. He was the only brother of Mr. Jno. R. Mayson, of this place.

January 29, 1881
Died on the 28th, in Amite City, La., Mrs. Minerva J. Alsworth, wife of J. N. Alsworth, formerly of Madison County.

Mrs. Cartha, wife of Mr. Dan Hamblen, of Camden, Miss., died at her residence on the 23rd of January, 1881. She was born in Columbia County, Ga. on the 8th of July, 1815. She came to this State with her parents in 1858 and was educated at Salem, N. C. On the 6th of December, 1866, she was married to Mr. Hamblen. Eight children blessed their union, seven of whom survive. She joined the Methodist Church in 1876.

March 5, 1881
At Jackson, Saturday, Mr. Will H. Bailey, Chancery Clerk at Madison County, accompanied by Mr. T. J. Wharton, Jr., entered the restaurant of Henry Muller. During the meal the latter held a large raw oyster upon his fork and detailed the circumstances of the death of Hon. Walter Brooke, at Vicksburg, some years ago -- caused from an oyster lodging in his windpipe. The two without further talk proceeded to eat. Presently Mr. W. heard a gurgling sound and glancing to the face of his friend, discovered him with one hand around his throat and trying with the other to get something out of his mounth. A doctor was called for and reached the scene just in time to see the unfortunate man fall dead, with a piece of steak lodged in his windpipe.

Died on the 26th February, in Jackson, Miss., very suddenly, Mr. William U. Bailey, in the 39th year of his age. He was born and raised in Canton.

March 12, 1881
Died on the 6th, infant son of Mr. W. L. and Lena Mayson Craig.

March 19, 1881
Joe Maples, a young man, was shot and killed by a Mrs. Spaulding, a milliner, in Edwards, Miss., on the night of the 11th. About the only words Maples spoke after being shot was, "I do not know why that woman shot me." He died in about three hours. (Yazoo City Sentinel)

April 9, 1881
Died on the 4th at the residence of his mother, after an illness of two weeks -- Johnnie Luckett. He was nearly nineteen years of age and the oldest son of the late O. A. Luckett, Jr. His disease was typhoid pneumonia.

April 23, 1881

Mr. James L. Averitt died at his residence in this county on April 18th, from pneumonia. He was 46 years of age and leaves a wife, a son and little daughter. He was a native of Florida, educated at Chapel Hill, N. C., and removed with his father to this State and settled in Madison County.

The death of Mrs. Florence E., wife of Mrs. A. N. Parker, occurred on the 19th, at her residence in this place.

May 7, 1881

Grenada, Miss., May 2 -- Our community was shocked this morning by the explosion of a soda fountain generator at the drug store of W. P. Towler, which resulted in the death of Dr. H. J. Ray, a prominent physician, and the fatal injury of W. P. Towler.

May 21, 1881

Mrs. Reeves died at the residence of her daughter, Mrs. Augusta S. Bosworth, in Canton, Miss., May 16th, 1881, aged 81 years. Her maiden name was Walker. She was a native of Georgia but moved to Mississippi in 1844 and was a resident of Madison County for 37 years. She was twice married. Her first husband, Mr. John G. Towns, was the eldest brother of Governor Towns of Georgia. Four children were the fruit of this marriage, two of whom are yet living in Texas. By her second marriage she had three children, only one of whom survive her, viz: Mrs. Bosworth.

June 18, 1881

The trial of T. J. Bolton, for the killing of the Clark brothers, in Vicksburg, in February 1880, resulted in his acquital last week.

Mr. Jno. R. Hargon, an old citizen of this place, died the 12th, after a long and painful illness. He was sixty-five years of age. He leaves a wife and six children.

July 2, 1881

Died on June 27th, 1881, in Gonzales, Texas, at the residence of her son, Mr. Ned Anderson -- Mrs. Nettie Howard, after an illness of four weeks.

Died on the 5th of July, after a lingering illness, Mrs. Bettie G., wife of Chas. P. Moore.

Thos. N. Jones, Sr., departed this life at his home at Madison Station, July 3rd, 1881. He was born in Madison County, Al. in the year 1827, being 54 years of age at his death. He moved with his father to this county.

July 16, 1881

Died July 10th at her residence in this place, Mrs. Mary, wife of Samuel Ewing, at a ripe old age. She was a member of the Methodist Church.

July 23, 1881

We record the death of Mrs. Katie Winter, aged 22 years, wife of Mr. Stewart Cobb and daughter of D. A. T. and Mrs. Bena Semmes, which occurred on the 11th of July, 1881, at her residence in Brown's Valley, Minn., leaving an infant a few hours old.

B. F. Garey died suddenly from apoplexy, at the residence of his son, J. A. Garey, in this county, on the 13th day of June, 1881. He was born in Newberry District, S. C. in 1800 and was in the seventy second year of his age. He emigrated to this county in 1841.

August 20, 1881

Died at the residence of his son-in-law, Mr. Moore, on the 5th of August, 1881, Mr. James Simpson. He was born in York District, South Carolina, January 1st, 1802. In 1829 he came to this State. He lost three sons in the Confederate service and one since then, leaving him without a son. Of three daughters, only two survive him -- Mrs. Word and Mrs. Moore.

Died at the residence of her mother, near Central Academy, on the 11th, Mrs. Nora, wife of Mr. Chas. James, and third daughter of Mrs. Gus Coleman, aged about 20 years.

Died on the 17th at her residence in Yazoo City, Mrs. Nettie, wife of Dr. W. T. Martin, formerly of this county.

August 27, 1881

Died the 22nd of August, 1881, Katie Semmes, infant daughter of Stuart Cobb, of Brown's Valley, Minn.

Died near Canton, August 20th, Mrs. Sallie Fitzhugh Welbourn.

Col. Fleet T. Cooper, journalist who died at Jackson on the 20th, was a native Mississippian. Born in Lawrence County in 1835, he was barely 21 years of age when he entered the field of journalism. (Author's note - a lengthy report followed)

September 17, 1881

Died on the morning of the 16th, after a long illness, Miss Fannie, youngest daughter of Mr. R. Y. Seater.

September 24, 1881
Died at the residence of Dr. J. B. Catchings, Copiah County, Miss., August 28, 1881, Miss Millie Evelyn Harris, of malarial fever.

October 1, 1881
Died on the morning of the 29th, in this city, Mrs. Agnes M. Brown, in the sixty-eighth year of her age. She took to her bed one week previous to her death. She was a member of the Baptist Church. She was a devoted mother.

October 8, 1881
Died near Skipworth Landing, Miss., on the 14th of September last, B. Chase Alsworth, in the twentieth year of his age. He was a member of the Presbyterian Church.

October 22, 1881
Died on the 12th, Warren Tankersley, a colored man who had lived in this place for the past twenty years. His disease was flux. He was sick about two weeks. He had lived with and served Mr. J. V. Fitchett as undertaker, for the the last fifteen years.

October 29, 1881
Died at Centreville, La., on the 20th Oct., 1881, Miss Eliza B., second daughter of Mr. J. G. Fellowes. She was born in Nashville, Tenn., Feb. 5th, 1850 and was reared and educated in Canton, Miss.

November 5, 1881
Died on the 22nd of October, 1881, after a long and painful illness, Maud Mayes, third daughter of Mr. Mike and Mrs. Nannie Russell, aged about two years.

November 19, 1881
Died at his residence in this place, after an illness of several weeks, Mr. John D. Howell, aged 51 years. He was a native of Philadelphia, but removed to Huntsville, Ala. when he was about fourteen years old. Afterward he lived in Jackson, Miss., and came to Canton in 1855, where he has lived ever since, except during the time he served in the Confederate army. In the election last April he was elected city alderman. He leaves a wife and an infant son.

On Saturday last, Mr. J. Gray Thigpen breathed his last breath at the house of his friends, Mr. & Mrs. Will Walker.

December 3, 1881
Died 28th Nov., aged three years and five months, youngest son of Samuel Aaron.

December 10, 1881
Died on the 2nd day of December, 1881, in Texas, George Harvey, aged 12 years, only son of Mrs. Annie Harvey.

Died in Canton, after a lingering illness, the 12th(?) day of December, Mrs. S. U. H. Russell, aged about 50 years.

March 4, 1882
On the morning of the 27th of February, all that was mortal of Mrs. Effie, wife of Mr. T. N. Avery, of this city, was borne to the Baptist Church to receive the last tribute. She was a victim of consumption. Mrs. Avery's maiden name was Effie Wynne. She was reared in Yazoo County. He age was 33 years.

February 4, 1882
Died on the 28th, in this city, Miss Jennie Hinchie, aged about 50 years.

Died on the 28th of January, of pneumonia, Mrs. Mollie, wife of Thomas Sevier/Sevirt, leaving a son and two little daughters.

March 11, 1882
Died on the 22nd, after a few hours suffering from being burnt, Peter, aged 5 years, son of Mr. & Mrs. Henry Gwinner.

May 13, 1882
Vicksburg -- After the annual parade of firemen, while a small steamer was being pulled by hand, several of the members tripped and fell, one of the wheels passing over the head of Lee Hanly, killing him instantly, also severly injuring a young son of Major L. W. Magruder.

Died in New Orleans, La., April 18th, James Kelly. He was born August 12th, 1831 in Statesborough, S. C. and was a resident of this county for 22 years. He served throughout the late war in the 18th Mississippi.

Died on the 6th day of May, 1882, at his residence near Canton, Monroe B. Glick, aged 43 years. He was a native of Ohio, but had lived in Madison County for the last 12 years. He had been an invalid for several years.

June 17, 1882
We record the death of Mrs. Eliza Yandell, wife of Hon. O. R. Singleton, which occurred at his residence on the 16th, after a protracted illness. She was a member of the Methodist Episcopal Church.

July 1, 1882
Died in this city, June 26th, 1882, Samuel, infant son of Mr. & Mrs. Horace Handy.

August 5, 1882
Died on 30th, of congestion of the brain, at Deasonville, Yazoo County, Annie Moore Avery, eldest daughter of Mr. Thos. N. Avery, of this place.

Died at the home of her mother on July 29th, 1882, of paralysis of the heart, Eva, daughter of Mrs. M. A. Coleman, of this county.

September 16, 1882
Died in this city on the night of September 14th, Mrs. Mary M. Breck.

September 23, 1882
Died on the 17th of hermaturis, John Gabriel Davis, son of Geo. W. and Laura B. Davis, aged 12 years and six days.

September 30, 1882
Died in this city on September 26th, 1882, Adolphus Brown. Deceased was for the last 26 years Professor of Music in the Canton Female Institute. He was interred at the Jewish cemetery.

October 7, 1882
Died October 1st, 1882, Mrs. Mollie E. Richards, only daughter of Mr. W. J. Kendall and relict of the late Capt. Thos. Richards. She was 89 years of age on the 30th of September. She was a member of the Methodist Church.

November 3, 1882
Our community was greatly shocked by an accident that occurred at Gwinnet's store last Wednesday. It seems that Mr. Otho Billingslea had bought a pistol at the store some time previously and had called to exchange it for one of heavier caliber. He handed the revolver, a self-cocking one, to Mr. Will. Baldwin, a clerk in the store, and just as he passed it, the pistol was fired, the ball taking effect just below the left eye and penetrating the brain of Mr. Billingslea, who dropped dead instantly.

November 11, 1882
A telegram received by Mr. Harry Priestley on Saturday night last, from Breckenridge, Colorado, conveyed the intelligence that Capt. Turk has died on the 4th after two hours illness. A sad blow to his beloved sister Mrs. Harry Priestley.

December 16, 1882
Died on the 15th of December, 1882, Dr. Wm. Reid. He was an old citizen of Madison County.

January 6, 1883
Dr. William M. Reid was born in Union District, S. C. on 2nd March, 1802, and graduated at the University of Philadelphia. He moved to Alabama to practice medicine, there made the acquaintance of Miss Charlotte Rose. They became husband and wife until the fall of 1878, when during the yellow fever scourge she died. He was a member of the Church of Christ.

January 27, 1883
Died on the 12th of January at the residence of his daughter, Mrs. Wm. Gibson, near Little Rock, Arkansas, Dr. James M. Slaughter, about 80 years of age. He was a resident of Madison County for many years.

Died on the 10th Jan., 1883, at his residence near Madison Station, where he lived nearly fifty years, Mr. James S. Baskins, aged 83.

Died at Sharon, Miss., on the 22nd Jan., Mrs. Mattie Robinson, recently Miss Boles, and relict of the late John S. Robinson.

February 3, 1883
Died at her residence near Canton, Miss., on Saturday, the 27th, Mrs. Susan F., wife of Mr. E. White. The deceased was a native of this county and a daughter of the late Ephraim Wallace.

February 17, 1883
Died on the 12th day of February, 1883, Mrs. Elizabeth Monohan, of this place, in the 45th years of her age. He disease was consumption. She died in the faith of the Holy Catholic Church.

February 24, 1883
Died at his home near Sulphur Springs, on the 15th Feby., Mr. Wm. P. Bilbo, a native of Alabama, but for the last 40 years a resident of Leake and Madison counties. He was about 60 years of age. He leaves six children and a wife. He was a member of the Methodist Church.

March 24, 1883
As we go to press, we learn that Miss. Lena May, only daughter of Mr. Catlett Conway, of Virginia, and sister of Eugene and John Conway, of this place, died on the 22nd, at Nazareth, Ky., where she was attending school.

March 31, 1883

Miss Lena May Conway, aged 13 years, 11 months and 22 days, died from the effects of pneumonia, at Nazareth Seminary, near Bardstown, Ky., on March 22nd, 1883.

April 7, 1883

Died at his residence near this place, on April 3rd, Mr. John J. Briscoe, aged 58 years.

Died on the 6th, Effie Bird, aged 13 months, youngest child of Mr. J. W. and Mrs. McKie Owen.

April 21, 1883

We announce the death of Frank George, Esq., of Cleburne, Texas, which occurred on the 14th, at his home in that place, from heart disease. His devoted wife, who was in attendance on her sick mother, Mrs. John Handy, received a telegram, left for Texas. She was accompanied by her brother, Mr. Joe Handy. Mr. George was for many years a member of the Canton Bar.

On Monday afternoon our community was startled by the report that Mr. James Gould was accidently but fatally shot by Mr. John Wah__er. The parties were about one mile from town. He was removed to the residence of Mr. J. J. Gilman. He remained unconscious and between the hours of twelve and one o'clock he breathed his last.

April 28, 1883

On Sunday last the towns of Wesson and Beauregard were visited by a cyclone. At Wesson the damage to life and property was apparently confined to one particular portion of town, Peach Orchard street. The houses on this entire street were completely destroyed and the inmates buried beneath the ruins.

The town of Beauregard was totally destroyed. There was not a single house left standing. The dead and wounded were taken to Wesson.

The following is an authentic list of the dead found at Beauregard up to the present time: Miss Mary Mikell, George White, Mrs. Huber, M. Story, J. Terrell, J. A. Williams, Miss Georgia Mitchell, Miss Eula Benton, Lewis and Wm. Parker, Rev. T. Green, Wm. T. Keeting, Dr. and Mrs. Luther Jones, Wood and Johnnie Jones, William Sanford, Miss Annie Claussing, E. Bahr, George Holloway, three colored men, Jerry Smith, Caleb Ellis and Joe Hunt, three colored women and three colored children, names unknown, a child of Mr. Foote Carter, and a child of Mrs. Swett.

The following is a list of the dead at Wesson: Mrs. Saunders and son, Miss Sallie Ford, two little sons of Ed. Allen, Mrs. Causey and her daughter Bettie, Mrs. Wilkinson, Z. Loftin, S. Briston and two little boys.

May 12, 1883
Died on the 6th day of May, Mrs. Rebecca, wife of Mr. Reuben H. Gould, in the 63rd year of her age.

July 28, 1883
Charles B. Smith, son of W. H. Smith, of Vicksburg, shot and killed himself last Sunday afternoon at the residence of his father, on Cherry Street. The shooting was believed to have been accidental.

August 11, 1883
After a short illness, John P. Mumford died last Wednesday morning. The deceased was a brother of Wm. T. Mumford, Esq., one of the proprietors of the City Hotel. He was born in Baton Rouge, April 12, 1841, and was 42 years of age. He was in the Confederate Army.

Died on the 24th of July, at his residence near Sharpsburg, Mr. Robert Hicks, aged 76 years. His son, Dr. J. W. Hicks, of Goodman, attended him during his illness. He was a member of the Baptist Church.

August 18, 1883
On 12th August, 1883, the spirit of "Bettie", beloved wife of W. H. Magruder, soared to it's home on high. She was 48 years of age and had been married 23 years.

Died August 13th, of congestion, Louis, only son of L. G. and Bettie Slaughter, aged 19 months.

Died near Skipwith Landing, on the 8th of August, 1883, John Lynn Alsworth, in his 14th year.

September 15, 1883
Died at their house in this city, on the 9th, Mrs. Susan W. Handy, in the 68th year of her age, and on the 12th, Judge A. H. Handy, in the 74th year of his age. Judge Alexander Hamilton Handy was born in Somerset County, Md., December 25th, 1809; married Jan. 14th, 1835. He came to Mississippi in 1837.

Mrs. Susan W. Handy, his wife, was born in Queen Ann County, Md., Sept. 12th, 1815.

October 20, 1883
It is our painful duty to record the death of James Monroe Anderson, Sr., who expired on the 13th at his residence in this city. He was united with the Methodist Church. He was 54 years of age and had spent the greater part of his life in this community.

Died near Vernon, Miss., October 2, 1883, Henry Clifton Maynor, only son of A. H. & L. A. Maynor, in the 13th year of his age.

Died in Colorado, Texas, Oct. 1, 1883, Katie S., infant daughter of Leonard and Mrs. Sallie Snider, aged 14 months and 3 days.

May 3, 1883

Died at the residence of her father, L. W. Thompson, in this place, on the 18th, Mrs. Eugenia H. Tarry, relict of the late Edmund Tarry, of Mecklenburg, Va., to whom she was wedded in 1858, and who preceded her to Spirit Land twenty years ago. She was left with three young sons

Died in this place on the 1st, Mrs. Gidery, aged 61 years, formerly of Baton Rouge, La.

Died on the 28th of October, at the residence of Mr. John F. Hendricks, Mrs. Mariah M. Rucker, aged 74 years, relict of the late Col. John W. Rucker and mother of our townsman, W. W. Rucker.

November 17, 1883

Capt. Robert Joslyn, formerly a well-known citizen of North Mississippi, died in Austin, Texas, on the 4th. Capt. Joselyn at one time edited a paper at Holly Springs.

Died at her residence in Decatur, November 9th, Mrs. Jane V. Ward, aged 4_ years. The funeral took place at St. Patrick's Church.

December 1, 1883

Died on the 23rd, at Madison Station, at the residence of his father, Mr. James A. Dinkins, Hammle(?) Dinkins, aged 27 years.

December 15, 1883

Died at this place, December 9th, at the residence of her brother, Mr. Brad Luckett, of consumption, Mrs. Henrietta B. Sanders, in the 42nd year of her age. The deceased was the oldest child of Col. O. A. Luckett, and was born and reared in Madison County. She resided above Memphis.

December 22, 1883

Died at Little Rock, Ark., Dec. 13, 1883, Marie, only child of James T. and Fannie Noonan, aged 3 years and 4 months.

Died on the 14th, at her residence, Mrs. Drusilla, wife of E. D. Cowan and eldest daughter of Mr. John T. Cameron, of this county.

Vicksburg -- Died on the 13th, of paralysis, wife of Albert G. Cassell and daughter of ___ Sutherland, of this place.

December 29, 1883

Yazoo City - John T. Posey, of the firm of Williams and Posey, was insulted by John James, a negro butcher. Posey went off and got some of his friends and returned to the corner of Main and Jefferson streets, where James had last been seen. Without warning the Posey party was fired upon. John Posey, Carnot Posey and Jasper Posey were riddled with buckshot and instantly killed. H. O. Ellet was dangerously wounded and Fritz Halider slightly wounded.

John James, one of the leading negroes in the difficulty last night, was killed this morning while his arrest was being attempted. He fired three times and was killed by citizens who were trying to arrest him.

Hon. Robert Day, of Yazoo County, died last Monday evening, 24th. Mr. Day was elected Sheriff in November and would have taken charge on the 1st of January.

January 5, 1884

On December 30th, 1883, T. H. Weathersby yielded up his spirit to Him who gave it.

We are grieved to announce the death of Major James W. Baughn, which occurred at his residence in this place, on the 31st of December, 1883. He had been in failing health for some time. He was a native of Georgia, but came to this State when quite a young man.

Died in New Orleans, December 29th, of consumption, Mr. Herbert Thompson, about 26 years. The deceased was the youngest child of Mr. and Mrs. Lewis Thompson. He was born and raised in this county and his remains were laid beside relatives in the family burial ground.

January 12, 1884

Mr. Joseph Bernard Murphy, oldest son of the late Jeremiah Murphy, died of consumption at the residence of his mother, in this place, on the 21st day of December, 1883.

The death of Mrs. T. B. Holloman, of Yazoo City -- Her husband has been pastor of the Methodist Church in that place for the last two years. She was the daughter of Mr. T. L. Holliday, of this county. She leaves seven little children, the youngest twins only 36 hours old.

January 19, 1884

Died, Mrs. Minnie J., wife of A. T. Graham and daughter of Mr. E. S. Cobb, of this county. She was born Sept. 23, 1858; died Dec. 19, 1873 (Date as printed) with pneumonia.

Died in this place, on the 19th, at the Singleton House, Capt. Robert Fuqua, a well known railroad conductor of the Illinois Central.

January 26, 1884
Died on the night of the 15th, at the residence of her son-in-law, Mr. Henderson Alsworth, in this county, Mrs. Mary Ann, relict of the late Rev. R. N. McInnis. Mrs. McInnis was about sixty years of age.

Mr. John T. Ewing, oldest son of the late Mr. Adam Ewing, of this place, died of pneumonia at the residence of his mother, on the 21st.

Mrs. John W. Patton, a life-time resident of Jackson, Miss., died of heart disease on the 17th. He was about 55 years of age.

We chronicle the death of Mr. John W. Daney, a well known citizen of Canton, on last Saturday night, at his residence. He was a native of North Carolina, but came to Canton when a mere youth. He was forty-five years old last June.

February 2, 1884
Died on the 25th January, after a short illness, Master Lyons Harvey, aged eight years and two months. He was the oldest son of Senator Harvey.

March 29, 1884
Funeral services for the late Bishop H. H. Kavanaugh were held in the Methodist Church in Jackson, on the 23rd.

April 12, 1884
Died at her residence in this county, April 8th, Mrs. Sallie, wife of Dr. Lake Smith. Mrs. Smith was the youngest sister of Mr. Wm. Mosby, of this place. She leaves a son and daughter.

April 19, 1884
Died at her house in Harpersville, Scott County, Miss., after a short illness, January 12th, 1884, Mrs. Gert_ Yarbrough Brown, daughter of John S. and Martha Y. Yarbrough, who both died with yellow fever in Lake, Miss., 1878. She was born in Stewart County, Ga., July 1st, 1848; was married to James Landon Brown of Madison County, Miss., Oct. 25, 1865.

May 3, 1884
Died at his home April 30th, of pneumonia, James, son of Capt. Randall, age 18 years.

May 10, 1884
Died on Saturday, 3rd, in Natchez, Miss., John T. Scott, in the 23rd year of his age.

Died at his residence in Canton, May 2nd, 1884, Major A. M. Rafter. The deceased, at the time of his death, was Principal of the Male High School of Canton. He was a native of Tennessee and was educated at Miami College, Ohio. He had been a citizen of Canton about two years. He was an elder of the Presbyterian Church. Major Rafter was 54 years of age. A wife and daughter survive him.

June 14, 1884
Died in Columbia, La., May 31st, Mrs. Ada Virginia Dial, nee Miss McCarty. Mrs. Dial was a native of Fredericksburg, Va. and the youngest sister of Mrs. A. J. Br__ford, of this place.

June 28, 1884
After a protracted illness, ending in dropsy, Mr. Thad. Potter died last Sunday morning.

July 5, 1884
Died in this county on the 29th, Mr. T. W. Nicholson, a native of North Carolina, in the sixty-eighth year of his age.

August 9, 1884
We record the sudden death this week of Mary Jones Butler, a colored woman who lived on the Owens place, some five miles out. She came to town last Saturday and when passing Handy's corner she careened over and died in about a quarter of an hour. Death resulted from disease of the heart.

August 16, 1884
On Tuesday, 14th, the last tribute was paid to Mrs. Fannie Jones, from Grace Church. She was born in Bradford, Wiltshire, England in the year 1825 and came to this place in 1857.

September 13, 1884
Died at his residence in this city, after a short illness, Major W. J. Kendall, in the sixty-ninth year of his age. Deceased was a native of Maryland, from whence he emigrated to the State of Georgia during the year 1838.

David S., youngest son of Major J. R. and Mrs. Fannie Powell, was born near Madisonville, in January 1861 and died at his father's residence in Canton, Miss. on the 6th day of September, 1884, after an illness of ten days, from malarial fever.

September 20, 1884

Died August 31st, F___ Hudson Dinkins, youngest child of M. L. and Ann Mary Dinkins, aged 3 years and 6 months.

Miss Felicite Lallande, daughter of Mr. & Mrs. J. G. Lallande, of this county, died on Sept. 11, 1884. Miss Lallande died of congestion.

Died on the evening of the 14th, at Madison Station, Madge, second daughter of Mr. W. E. and Mrs. Pauline Gaddis, aged 20 months.

October 11, 1884

Died on the 10th, Albert Cage, aged 13 months, infant son of Mr. and Mrs. W. H. Powell.

October 25, 1884

On 18th day of October, 1884, J. M. Anderson breathed his last. Mr. Anderson was born and reared in Madison county, and was 36 years old on the 1st day of October, 1884. He was deprived of his father by death when he was quite young. (Author's note - a very lengthy history was included)

Died on the 19th of October, Miss Margaret Jones, a member of the Methodist Church, aged about fifty years.

November 1, 1884

Alberta Hill, the youngest child of Mrs. Margaret A. Hill and the late Judge Albert P. Hill, of Canton, Miss., died at Ward's Seminary, Nashville, Tenn., October 12th, 1884, after an illness of five weeks. She was seventeen years old. (Author's note - a lengthy report followed)

November 15, 1884

Died in the city of Vicksburg, on the 12th, of consumption, Maggie, wife of Mr. John C. McCatchern, in the 24th year of her age. She was the daughter of the late Dr. James Barnett and granddaughter of the late Dr. M. J. McKie, of this place.

On the 6th, the spirit of little Allen, infant son of Mr. and Mrs. Hartje, of this place, went to his home on High.

November 22, 1884

Dr. A. K. Davis, pastor of the colored M. E. Church in this city, died yesterday morning. His disease was dropsy of the heart. He was Lieutenant Governor of the State under Ames' administration. He abandoned politics in 1875 and soon after entered the ministry of the M. E. Church.

On November 19th, Isaac Johnson was hanged in the jail yard for the murder of Bella Booker.

December 13, 1884

Died December 7th, after one weeks illness, at his father's residence, Joseph M., son of Dr. and Mrs. A. T. Semmes, in the 13th year of his age.

Mrs. Priscilla, wife of W. R. Savage, died at their residence in this county, on the 7th, after an illness of three weeks of typhoid fever. She was 56 years old, a native of Berts(?) County, N. C. and had removed to this State in early life. She was a member of the Methodist Church. She was the mother of Mr. Emmett Savage and Mrs. Lula Ray.

January 17, 1885

Adam Weber, formerly of New Orleans but for several years a citizen of Canton, died of heart disease, on the 14th. He leaves a widow and seven children.

THE CONSERVATIVE
Carrollton, Mississippi

April 4, 1885

Died, Peter W. Johnston, at his residence in the town of Carrollton, Miss., March 10th, 1885. Mr. Johnston was a native of Scotland, born in Falkirk, August 17th, 1817. He came to America in his 17th year. He served in the Mexican War. He leaves a wife, two daughters and three sons.

Vicksburg, March 19th - Judge E. Jeffords, of Issaquena County, lately Representative in Congress, died suddenly at the Washington Hotel this morning, of heart disease.

April 18, 1885

It has been the will of God to remove within the last few months, Brothers Wm. Ewing, P. W. Johnston and Robt. Ray. The former two were permitted to enjoy God's blessing to quite an old age.

May 30, 1885

A duel occurred at Rolling Fork in Sharkey County, last Saturday morning, between Mr. W. K. McLaurin, of the firm of McLaurin & McLaurin, of Brandon, and Mr. S. F. Shelton, Chancery Clerk of Sharkey County, in which Shelton was instantly killed. The difficulty grew out of a political feud of two years ago, which resulted in their meeting Saturday morning on the rail road track at Rolling Fork, with double barrel shotguns, with no one present but the principals. McLaurin met the Marshal and told him he had shot Shelton and gave himself up. Shelton was found dead, with his gun lying cocked beside him. Fifteen buckshot had penetrated his body in the region of his heart.

Both were young men, natives of Brandon, and about the age of 28 years. Shelton was a son of Judge Wm. Shelton of Brandon. McLaurin is a brother of Hon. A. J. McLaurin of Brandon.

On last Saturday morning, near Coila Springs, ten miles south of Carrollton, a negro boy about eighteen years old, named McKinney, struck and mortally wounded a young white boy named Charlie Broadway. The particulars are: The negro was employed as a field hand by the father of young Broadway, and on Saturday quit his work and went in the creek to take a bath. After remaining in the water for some time, young Broadway told him to come out and go to work. The negro came out, picked up a stick about five feet long, walked up to Broadway and after a few words Broadway turned to walk away when the negro dealt him a blow on the back of the head, crushing the skull and causing Broadway's death the next morning. Mr. H. W. Cooley arrested the negro.

On last Saturday, a young white man named Wm. Mathews, in company with several others, went to Johnson's mill, four miles south of Carrollton, to go in swimming. Mr. Mathews, in attempting to dive from the bank, struck his head against the bottom with such force as to cause his death a few days after.

June 13, 1885

On Sunday last, a crowd of colored boys went to Judge Johnson's mill on Pelucia Creek to go in swimming. Two of the boys, Charlie Hunter, aged 15, and Wm. Keyes, aged 14, went in - one could swim and the other couldn't. One swam across and called to the other to come to him, which he attempted to do by wading. He struck deep water and cried for help, when the other went to his assistance. The drowning boy caught the other around the neck and both went to their death before assistance could reach them.

June 27, 1885

Tom Bell killed Ned Green near Newton last week. The facts were as follows: Tom Bell lived with his father. Ned Green and his wife for sometime past had been living there too. At dinner time on the day of the tragedy, Tom and Ned had a quarrel and Ned struck Tom. During the afternoon Tom threatened to kill Ned. That night the quarrel was renewed and Tom seized a brick and struck Ned in the stomach. The effect of the blow produced death in a few minutes.

July 11, 1885

Grenada, Miss., July 7th -- This evening, as the Sheriff was going to the train with Felix Williams, who had been convicted of murder and sentenced to the penetentiary for life, a mob composed of 150 men forcibly took Williams from the Sheriff and deputies. The mob then went to the county jail and took Perry McChristian, who had been convicted of murder and sentenced to by hung, but whose case had been appealled, and these two - Perry and Williams - were carried off by the mob and hung.

Felix and Perry killed, last August, a peddler who had nothing but his pack and $12.30 in money.

On Friday evening, 3rd, Mr. John M. Allen, who lived about 4 miles east from Carrollton, was called from his residence about 8 p.m. by some person or persons, under the pretense that they had a note for him. When a few feet of the gate he was fired upon by an assassin and instantly killed. Mr. Allen was an old man. His wife, who had been an invalid for many years, died about a year ago.

July 18, 1885

Died of flux at her home near Vaiden, Miss., on the 27th of June, 1885, Mrs. Mary E. E. Hoge, wife of Mr. H. J. Hoge. Mrs. Hoge was born in Giles County, Tenn., on the 25th of March, 1820 and was married on the 8th of November, 1838. She leaves a husband and nine children.

August 8, 1885

We learn that on last Monday morning, Charlie Hawkins, a colored man living on the Davis plantation three miles west from Black Hawk, was found murdered in his bed. Our informant says that Hawkins was literally cut to pieces; the wounds having seemingly been done with a pocket knife. A colored man suspected of the crime was arrested.

August 22, 1885

Died on the 17th of August, baby Summerfield, son of H. S. and Jennie G. Sanders, aged 5 months and 27 days.

August 29, 1885

Mr. James Sykes, one of the oldest and most respected citizens of Columbus, died at his home in that city on the 20th.

The *Winston Signal* says that a grand-son of Mr. Wm. Triplett, living near the line of Winston and Noxubee counties, was gored to death by a bull last week.

Maj. James Bell, Sheriff of Lowndes County, died at his residence in Columbus, Miss., on the 22nd, after a lingering illness.

September 5, 1885

Col. T. C. Everett died at his home near Vaiden last week. Col. Everett was one of the most respected citizens of our county.

September 12, 1885

John A. Duffy, the unknown man who was found sick near Chunchula a few days ago, by Mr. W. H. Tanner, died at that place Monday morning. In answer to questions before his death he said that his mother was in New Orleans.

Mrs. E. B. Oury, the aged mother of the proprietor of this paper, is lying dangerously ill at her home in Winona, and little hope of her recovery are entertained.

September 26, 1885

Dr. D. L. Smith, a citizen of Wesson, was shot and instantly killed by J. L. May, at Wesson, on the 15th. May claimed that the doctor had interferred in his domestic happiness, causing a separation between himself and wife.

Leon Cockrell, the negro who shot and killed Aaron Wazee, col'd., in a church near Canton last week, was overtaken by a posse a few days after, but refused to surrender, opened fire with a pistol and was himself fired upon and instantly killed.

Mayor Southworth held an inquest over the body of a colored woman named Rosa Harris, found lying in Pelucia Creek, near the residence of Mr. E. M. Hemphill. We learn that the water where the body was found was only about two feet deep, and that the body of the woman bore unmistakable evidence of brutal treatment. Green Harris, her husband, has been arrested and charged with murder.

Seven murderers now linger in our jail, all colored, and as follows:
Chas. Fullilove, charged with murdering a colored man, near Vaiden.
Jake Purnell, for the murder of Mark Purnell.
Wm. McKinney, killing Charlie Broadaway, white.
Green Harris, murdering his wife.
Martha, Mary Jane and Ella Hawkins, mother and sisters of Charlie Hawkins, charged with his murder.

October 3, 1885

Hon. James M. Hatham, died at his home in Sunflower County, on the 12th, aged 39 years.

Mr. Robert Ward, brother of Dr. B. F. Ward of Winona, died at his home in Montgomery County on the 19th, aged 54 years.

Mr. S. C. Anderson, of Pike County, about fifty years of age, in attempting to unchoke a gin, on Tuesday of last week, had his right arm so mangled as to cause his death in a few hours.

October 10, 1885

Mr. E. F. Kemp, one of Columbus' oldest citizens, died suddenly of heart disease, last Monday morning.

Will Hill and Arch Turner, both colored, living south of this place, went coon hunting on Wednesday night. They treed a coon and set fire to a dead tree with the intention of waiting until daylight, lay down near the fire and fell asleep. During the night the tree burned down and fell upon the sleepers. Turner was so badly injured that he lived but a few hours, and Hill had his leg broken. (Vaiden Watchman)

December 5, 1885

Mr. Albert Barr, a citizen of Leflore County, died at his home near Shell Mound, in that county, ten days ago. Mr. Barr was well known in our town.

Mr. Buck Wright and his son shot and instantly killed Mr. Eugene Melton, in Grenada, on Wednesday of last week. Mr. Melton was a son-in-law of our fellow citizen, Mr. J. R. Shackleford.

December 19, 1885

Col. John F. Vance, an old citizen of Hazlehurst, died at his residence in that town, on the 13th.

THE CARTHAGINIAN
Carthage, Mississippi

November 6, 1875

Died October 18th, Mrs. Napsy L. Cotten, in the 71st year of her age.

August 8, 1877

Died July 30th, 1877, Carlos, son of R. L. and Lucy Ratliff.

July 9, 1881

The death of Mr. C. W. Wood, of Beadles, Wood & Co., has brought sorrow to this city. (Author's note - a lengthy report followed.

April 15, 1882
On yesterday we were summoned to the funeral of Mrs. M. E., wife of Mr. J. A. Hendrick. Her illness was of several months duration. (Lena, Miss., Apri. 10, 1882)

May 6, 1882
A difficulty occurred at the grist and saw mill of Elias Edwards, April 29th, resulting in the death of one of the parties. The parties to the affray were Jeff and Jim Buck Davis on one side, and A. H. Grant and Elias Edwards on the other. Grant was killed and Jim Buck Davis received several buckshot in one of his legs. (Author's note - a very lengthy report of the trial of the Davis brothers followed.)

May 27, 1882
Died at his residence near Carthage, on May 24th, William B. Mann, aged 53 years. To the bereaved wife and eight children we offer our sympathy. Mr. Mann was a member of the Methodist Church, and also of the Masonic fraternity.

Mr. Redding was found dead near Laurel Hill in Neshoba County, on Monday last. An inquest was held and it was decided that he drowned. Mr. Redding was between 97 and 100 years old.

August 18, 1883
Mr. James Williams "Little Jim" died at his home on Lobutcha yesterday morning, of some chronic disorder. He had been sick in bed for six weeks.

Flora, the thirteen year old daughter of Mr. Robert Blailock, died at her father's residence near Thomastown, after an illness of two weeks.

We learn of the sad bereavement which recently befell Mr. & Mrs. U. S. Roberts. Within the space of a few weeks they have lost two little children -- one a boy of two years, the other an infant of six months.

July 25, 1885
After a lingering illness, Mrs. Ella Freeny, wife of Mr. James R. Freeny, died at her home, on the 23rd.

THE ARGUS
Clinton, Mississippi

March 9, 1883

The evidence before the jury is Mr. P. G. Feltus was murdered by his brother. It occurred on the night of the 22nd of February, near Woodville. Ed. Feltus has been arrested and placed in jail.

MISSISSIPPI BAPTIST RECORD
Clinton, Mississippi

April 5, 1877

Died at his home near Taylorsville, Smith Co., Miss., on the 19th of March, 1877, Joseph Martin, aged seventy-seven years, five months and eleven days.

On March 31st, 1877, little Carbelle, daughter of P. C. and Anna J. Williams, quietly passed away.

December 13, 1877

On the night of the ___, Brother James C. Wiley fell asleep in the arms of Jesus. He lost two children in Texas, and with chronic disease himself, he came to his uncle's, Dr. J. B. Gage, at this place, to die.

Died on the 31st of November, at Memphis, Mrs. Lizzie Eggleston. She leaves four sons.

January 3, 1878

Little Jennie, only daughter of William W. and Jennie E. Wiles(?), of Yazoo Co., Miss., died December 13th, 1877, aged two years.

Died near Winona, December 9th, 1877, M. D. Adaire, in the 24th year of his age.

January 31, 1877

Died on the 25th, of pneumonia, at his residence near Grenada, Bro. William Howle. Bro. Howle was a member of the Grenada Baptist Church.

Died on the 25th, Miss Lillie Long.

On the morning of the 18th, Bro. Richard Long fell asleep in Jesus.

February 7, 1878

On the 28th, little Orville Parker was badly crushed by the "turn table" at the Grenada depot, while playing.

Died on the 10th of November, 1877, Bro. John Cole, in the 80th year of his age. He was born in South Carolina and at an early age moved to Lawrence County, Miss.

February 21, 1878

Died near Cooksville, Miss., on Jan. 25th, 1878, Father Moses Fleming, about eighty six years of age. Brother F. was a deacon of Friendship Church, near Cooksville.

Died of swamp fever, near Utica, Hinds County, Miss., Oct. 10, 1877, Ezra Broadwater, age forty-five years, two months and twenty-seven days. He was a native of South Carolina, but for twenty-five years a citizen of Hinds County. He was married to Miss M. E. Cooper, March 4th, 1865. He united with New Zion Baptist Church, Nov. 11, 1875.

Died on the 7th, in her fifty-fourth year, Sister A. L. M. Bourn. She was a member of the Brandon Baptist Church.

Died on Feb. 10th, 1878, near Looxahoma, Miss., Mrs. J. A. Montgomery, in her sixty-second year.

Died of pneumonia, Jan. 8th, 1879, at the residence of his father, in Hinds County, Miss., Mr. J. H. Bass. Also on the 13th, his mother, Mrs. S. J. Bass.

Died near Cotton Gin, Miss., on the 11th, February, 1878, Maggie Harrison, consort of Sterling Harrison, and daughter of Benjamin and Martha Colther, in the 22nd year of her age. She was a member of Central Grove Baptist Church.

February 28, 1878

Died at her home near New Prospect, now Choctaw, formerly Webster County, Miss., Mrs. Jane Mariah Micow, widow of Eld. John Micow, a Baptist minister, well known in Mississippi and Virginia. She was born in Essex County, Va., March 3, 1785 and at her death was ninety-two years of age.

Died at his residence, near Port Gibson, February 13th, 1878, Samuel Mackey, aged 73 years.

Died, Mrs. Elizabeth Small, in Summit, Miss., Feb. 21, 1878, aged seventy-one years and nine days. She leaves five children.

March 14, 1878
Little James Hays Rowe, son of Eld. A. V. Rowe, of Durant, aged four months and twenty-four days, departed this life Feb. 24th, 1878.

April 4, 1878
Died at his residence near Crawfordsville, Miss., on the 17th of March, 1878, in his eighty-first year, Terrell Brooks. He was born in Warren County, Ga., December 14th, 1797, and moved to this county in 1822.

Died near Good Hope, Leake County, Miss., Feb. 2_, 1878, Mr. Alexander Leggitt, aged sixty-nine years and eight months. He was for many years a citizen of Madison County, Miss.

Died at the residence of her husband, near Sallis Station, Miss., on the 17th of March, 1878, Lou Sallis, wife of J. W. Sallis, in the thirty-third year of her age.

May 27, 1880
A most shocking thing occurred on Bogue Chitto, near the Mississippi and Louisiana state line, on the 15th. Bro. A. H. Brock, while at the steam saw mill of his brother, was lifting a scantling over the saw, when the saw struck jerking him over it and cutting his right leg literally to pieces. His body also, was much bruised by the fall. On the 19th his suffering ended in death. Bro. Brock leaves a wife and five children, a father and mother, three brothers and three sisters.

January 6, 1881
Died Dec. 28th, Noah McDaniel, little son of Thos. R. and Selena McDaniel, of Tangipahoa Parish, La.

September 8, 1881
Died of consumption, near Mountain Creek Church, Miss., Aug. 7, 1881, David Cannon, aged about 56 years.

Died at the residence of his father, four miles north of Utica, Hinds County, Miss., Aug. 21, 1881, of congestion, little Milton Jones Cartmell. He was born January 23, 1876.

January 5, 1882
Departed this life September 6th, 1881, at his home in Meridian, Miss., Deacon L. Hurlbutt, in the 71st year of his age. He was born in New York State, February, 1811. In early manhood he moved to North Carolina, thence to central Mississippi, and afterwards to New Orleans, La. While living in Holmes County, Miss., about 1850, he joined the Baptist Church at Richland. In 1863 he became a citizen of Meridian, Miss.

Mrs. Mary A. Lowe died at Terry, Hinds County, Miss., at the residence of her son-in-law, Mr. J. J. Halbert, in August, 1881. She was born in Edgefield District, S. C. in August, 1793 and at the time of her death was 88 years of age.

Died at his home in Washington Parish, La., on the 28th of Nov., 1881, Tyra Rambert, aged 76 years, 7 months and 24 days. He was a member of the Hays Creek Church.

Died near Terry, Hinds County, Dec. 27th, 1881, Edna Earle, only daughter of John B. and Mattie A. Statham. She was 8 years and 24 days.

Charles Bayliss departed this life at Clinton, Miss., Dec. 21st, 1881, aged 15 years, 11 months and 10 days. He was a son of T. A. and M. Bayliss, of West, Miss.

March 9, 1882

Gambrell, three years and eight months of age, the only son of Bro. and Sister P. C. Williams, Grenada, Miss., died on Feb. 21st, 1882.

Died at her home in Canton, Miss., February 26, 1882, Mrs. Effie Avery, wife of Thos. N. Avery, in the 34th year of her age.

Jennie Veal retired at night in usual health and died at 11 o'clock the same night. Sister Veal was born October 17, 1854 and died January 16, 1882. She leaves a husband and three children.

May 11, 1882

Died at the residence of John H. Kent, April 25, 1882, Smith H. Kent, aged 85 years and 18 days. He was born in Halifax County, Va., on the 8th day of April, 1797.

May 18, 1882

Bro. T. D. Geren, a ministerial student in Mississippi College, died of the effects of measles, May 12. Bro. Geren was born and raised in Webster Parish, La., and died in Clinton, Miss., at the age of 28. (Author's note - this was a combination of two notices.)

Died near Verona, Miss., on May 5, 1882, Mrs. Mary McMillan, wife of Capt. J.A. Brinkley. She was born January, 1844.

May 25, 1882

Died May 14, 1882, Miss Clara Latimer. She was born in Lancaster County, Ohio, and died in Copiah County, Miss., age 53 years.

June 1, 1882

Died at his residence in West Point, Miss., May 18, Wm. B. Shelley. He was born in Greensboro, N. C., August 11, 1821. He joined the Baptist Church at eighteen years of age. He was married November 21, 1854 to Miss Sallie H. Borum, daughter of Deacon R. Borum.

Died at her home in Washington Parish, La., May 15, 1882, Sister Ophelia Criel, after a sickness of more than two years. She was a member of the Franklinton Baptist Church.

Died at the residence of James Griffis in Grenada County, Miss., May 20, 1882, Miss Francis Griffis, in the 89th year of her age. The deceased was born in Edgefield Dist., S. C., November 20, 1794.

Died at his residence near Duck Hill, Miss., May 10, 1882, J. W. Wood.

Died May 21, 1882, Sister Emma Sale, aged 27 years. She leaves a husband and a number of relatives.

Died in Summit, Miss., May 20, 1882, Sarah E. Smith, in the 79th year of her age.

June 8, 1882

Died at his residence in Holmes county, Miss., on the 26th of April, John M. Nall, aged 50 years. He was the son of the late Elder B. Nall, a member of the Mount Vernon Baptist Church.

June 22, 1882

Died at the residence of her husband, Dr. Wm. Saul, in Clay County, Miss., June 14, 1882, Mrs. Fannie Saul, daughter of Eld. John Paden, aged 21 years.

Died near Aberdeen, May 20, Augusta Viola, daughter of L. J. and Mrs. N. E. Hilburn. She was 12 years, 1 month and 2 days old. Her disease was typhoid malarial fever.

July 6, 1882

Died at the residence of N. W. Hemby, in Lawrence County, Miss., on the 25th of June, Louisa Hemby, aged about seventy years. She was born in N. C., Aug. 7, 1812, and was married to S. B. Hemby June 14, 1827.

Died in Duck Hill, June 30, 1882, Mamie, only daughter of Mrs. Cornie and Lorell Rose.

July 13, 1882

Died in Durant, Miss., on the 5th July, 1882, William Hamilton, youngest son of A. and L. J. Cochran, and the grandson of J. H. Cochran, aged 4 years, 9 months and 22 days.

O. L. Johnston died in Jackson, Miss., July 9. He was sick only 24 hours. He was born in Hopkinsville, Ky., April 21, 1825; came to Mississippi in 1846; married October 4, 1848. He was graduated in medicine at St. Louis in 1853.

Died at the home of her son, Warren Andrews, with whom she was living, on the 21st of June, 1882, Louisa Andrews, aged 62 years. She was born in Abbeville District, S. C., 1820; came to Mississippi when young; was married to Lewis Lomax, elder brother of A. A. Lomax, in 1838, who died June 1844, leaving her with two girls. She married again in 1848 to F. G. Andrews, who died in the late war.

Mr. W. P. Finley was born in Madison County, Miss., December 25, 1836 and died at Fannin, Miss., May 15, 1881, of pneumonia, being 41 years of age. He graduated in the medical department of the University of Louisiana in 1859. He began practice in Kosciusko, thence moved to Greenwood. He was married during the war to Miss K. C. Carlton, of North Carolina.

July 20, 1882

Died at the residence of his son, W. H. Schilling, on the 23rd of June, 1882, Michael Schilling, aged about 77 years. He leaves an aged companion, three sons and three daughters.

August 10, 1882

Died August 3, Amite City, La., Dr. John Williams Cothron, aged 47 years. He was born in Perry County, Ala.

August 17, 1882

Died in Winona, Miss., August 1, 1882, Mrs. Rebecca Hodges, in the 89th year of her age. Her remains were carried to the family graveyard, near Lexington, Miss.

September 7, 1882

Died July 17, 1882, at the residence of P. H. Boatler, in Rankin County, Miss., Mrs. Sarinthia F. Turner, aged 25 years, 2 months, and 26 days.

Died on the 13th, Ella, only daughter of J. J. and M. J. Shanks. She was entering her thirteenth year. (Goodman)

September 28, 1882

Died on the 6th of June, 1882, of consumption, at her residence in Covington County, Miss., Mrs. Martha Harper, wife of A. S. Harper, aged 74 years, 11 months, and 6 days. She was married to A. S. Harper October 2, 1835; joined the Baptist Church at Ebenezer, Covington County, October 1, 1854.

William R., son of Dr. W. F. and Nannie P. Barksdale, was born in Hardy, Miss., January 10, 1878.

Died at his home in Simpson County, Miss., June 26, 1882, Isaac Bush, aged 73 years, 6 months and 2 days. He was born in Edgefield District, S. C. and came to Mississippi when quite young. He leaves a wife and six children.

Died at her home near Cox's Ferry, Hinds County, Miss., Mahala Oldham, aged 64 years.

October 5, 1882

Died from the kick of a mule, near Bowling Green, Miss., on the 16th of September, 1882, John Anderson Howell, youngest son of W. J. and E. Howell. He was born in Noxubee County, Miss., February 25, 18__.

October 12, 1882

Died in this city, October 1st, Mrs. Annie Storts Hackett, wife of Rev. J. A. Hackett, aged 43 years. (Shreveport Daily Times)

Died at Wesson, Miss., on Sept. 25, 1882, Mrs. S. M. Morris, wife of Samuel Morris, of Wesson, Miss. She was the oldest daughter of Stephen Sasser, of this place. She was born in Amite County, Miss., November 29, 1848. She married Samuel Morris on the 30th day of October, 1881.

Died near Brandon, Miss., Aug. 30, 1882, Robert Nelson, only son of James W. and Sue May, in the tenth year of his age.

Died of congestion on the 25th of September, Lee Wells, eldest son of W. Lum and Alice Wells, of Salem Church, aged 9 years, 2 months and 12 days.

October 27, 1882

Died at Free Run, Yazoo County, Miss., July 25, 1882, Joseph Hughes Frazier, infant son of James Frazier, aged 3 years, 9 months.

Died at Free Run, Yazoo County, Miss., July 16, 1882, Emma Shurley, wife of J. R. Shurley, aged 34 years. She was a member of Rocky Springs Church.

November 16, 1882

Died in Tallahatchie County, Miss., Oct. 25, 1882, W. H. Lay, aged 51 years, 2 months and 22 days.

Died in Tallahatchie County, Miss., Clark, infant son of W. B. Leatherwood, aged 7 months and 4 days.

Died, Jessie, daughter of Dr. H. A. and S. B. Simmons, Kossuth, Miss., Nov. 1, 1882. She was 5 months and 27 days old.

November 23, 1882

Died of scrofula at her home near Thyatira, Tate County, Miss., Nov. 7th, Mrs. F. A. Adair, aged 43 years.

Died near Utica, Hinds County, Miss. November 14, 1882, Mrs. Susan Dudley, wife of G. W. Mimms, Sr., in the fifty first year of her age. She was born 1831 near Huntsville, Ala.; married in Hinds County, Miss., 1849; joined the Utica Baptist Church, 1851.

December 21, 1882

Died near Bethlehem, Miss., Nov. 13, 1882, Eliza Greer, aged 48 years and 3 months. She was a member of the Salem Baptist Church.

Died very suddenly at her residence in Lawrence County, Miss., Nov. 12th, 1882, Mrs. Lycian Sutton, aged about 70 years.

January 4, 1883

Sister Jack, wife of Judge W. H. Jack, president of our Baptist State Convention, died December 27, after 11 days illness.

Died of pneumonia, near Bethlehem, Marshall County, Miss., Nov. 17, 1882, Mary Poe, wife of H. E. Poe, aged thirty years, ten months. She leaves a husband and four children.

January 18, 1883

Died at her home near Oxford, Miss., December 13th, 1882, Lillie Hewlett. Lillie was accidently shot by her younger brother Graves. She was 14 years old.

Brother G. W. Walker departed this life on the 9th of November, 1882. Brother Walker suffered many years from cancer on his face. He was born in this country January 22, 1835. He leaves a wife and one son.

January 25, 1883

Died in Wilkinson County, near Fort Adams, at her home, on the 4th, Mrs. G. H. Peets, wife of Dr. Peets.

Died January, 1883, neat Fort Adams, Miss., after a protracted illness, Benjamin Hosea.

Died, S. Y. Carter, Yazoo County, Miss., December 1st, 1882, aged 26 years. He was deacon of Ogden Church, Yazoo County.

Died December 11th, 1882, Miss Paralee Carter, aged 21 years. She was a sister of Bro. S. Y. Carter.

February 1, 1883
Dr. W. L. Hemphill, an eminent physician of Edwards, Miss., died at his residence on December 21, 1882. He was born in Morgan County, Ga., February 2, 1818, and in early life moved to Mississippi.

February 22, 1883
Died at the residence of her husband three miles below Durant, Miss., on the second of February, 1883, Sister Millan, aged about 65 years.

Maj. W. P. Meriwether was born in Goochland County, Va., June 7, 1806, and died of dropsy in Okolona, Miss., February 12, 1883, at seventy-six years, eight months and five days. He lived twenty years in Alabama and twenty in Mississippi. He had one son who preceeded him in death. He leaves a widow, his third wife.

March 8, 1883
Died near Chapel Hills, Hinds County, Miss., Feb. 14, 1883, Hiram, son of W. S. Slater, aged 3 years, 3 months and 12 days.

Brother John Morrison departed this life at his home near Cato, Miss., March 1st, 1883. He was a member of the Dry Creek Church.

My brother, Charley J. Williams, died on the 26th of February, 1883, from the effects of pneumonia. Signed Percy C. Williams.

March 15, 1883
Sister Kate H. Patton, daughter of T. B. Heslep and wife of W. H. Patton, of Shubuta, Miss., was born in Carroll County, Miss., January 17, 1848 and departed this life at Micanopy, Fla., February 14, 1883.

James F. Barbour, of Alabama, died at his sister's, Mrs. Helena Lytle, in Tarrant County, Texas, December 26, 1882. The deceased was born in North Carolina in 1827.

April 5, 1883

Sister T. Lancaster, aged 83 years, died at her residence four miles from Clinton, March 31st, and buried the same day. She was born in Virginia in June 1800.

April 12, 1883

We are called to mourn the death of I. E. Varnado. More than thrity years ago he became a Baptist. He fell asleep in Jesus on the 30th of March and was buried in the family burial ground.

Mrs. Fanny Deupree, wife of J. I. Dupree, of Deerbrook, Miss., and daughter of Gen. B. M. and Martha Bradford, of Aberdeen, Miss., died on January 30, 1883, at the residence of her husband. She was born in Pontotoc, but reared in Aberdeen, Miss.; professed religion in 1866, and married in October 1867.

April 19, 1883

Died in his home in Copiah Co., March 21, 1883, Elijah F. Bailey was born Nov. 26, 1819; married Sept. 7, 1843 to Martha Allred who survives him. He united with the New Providence Church in the year 1850.

Died at Judge Robt. Leachman's, Meridian, Miss., April 10, 1883, Mrs. L. B. Rushing, widow of the late James M. Rushing. She was a member of the Lauderdale Baptist Church. Her body rests in the McLemore cemetery.

Died at Wesson, Miss., March 22nd, 1883, Mrs. Martha Nelson, wife of James Nelson. She was born in Hinds County, Miss., Aug. 10, 1883, was baptised into the fellowship of the Good Hope Baptist Church, Newton Co., Miss. She was at the time of her death a member of the Wesson Baptist Church.

Died at his residence in Pike County, Miss., March 31st, Mr. H. Washington, after an illness of sixteen days. He was thrity four years, four months and twenty seven days old. He united with the McGee's Creek Baptist Church in 1871. In 1883 he joined Smyrna Church. He left a wife and four children, two brothers and two sisters.

Died at his residence near Sardis, Miss., of consumption, J. M. Brown, April 1st, 1883, age about 18 years.

J. J. Higginbotham died at his home in Dublin, Texas, March 22, '83, aged 59 years. For many years he was a Deacon of the Baptist Church at Water Valley, Miss. He left Mississippi over a year ago and moved to Dublin, Texas, where he died of consumption.

David Olinger died at the residence of his son, J. D. Olinger, Water Valley, Miss., April 3, 1883, at the age of 77 years. He died after a long illness of dropsy.

Miss Bettie Herring died of pneumonia, March 17th, 1883, at the residence of her brother-in-law, Capt. Israel W. Pickens, near Shreveport, La., aged 47 years, 1 month and 15 days. Miss Bettie was born in Carrollton, Carroll County, Miss., February 2nd, 1836 and removed with the family to Caddo Parish, La. in 1848. After the death of her parents she returned to Mississippi and resided in the family of her brother-in-law, Dr. Askew. In 1857 she went to live with her brother, Capt. M. D. Herring, a prominent lawyer of Waco, Texas.

April 12, 1883, at Bowling Green, Holmes County, Miss., J. H. Cochran died of pneumonia. He was born in Abbeville Dist., S. C. on August 9, 1822, moved to Oktibbeha County, Miss. in 1833.

April 5, 1883 Miss Barbery Jones fell asleep in Jesus. She was a member of the Goodman Baptist Church. She was a constant sufferer of lung affection.

April 26, 1883

On the 17th of April, 1883, Miss Emily V. Briggs, aged 14 years, was drowned by accidentally falling into a well on G. W. Harrison's plantation, near Mountain Creek, Rankin County, Miss.

Died on the 5th of April, John G. H. Baugh, in the 67th year of her age. The deceased has been a member of the Baptist Church 46 years and a Baptist preacher 42 years. About a year ago a cancer appeared on his face, from the effects of which he died.

September 27, 1883

Died at home near Cherry Creek, Pontotoc County, Mississippi, August 14th, Ella, only child of J. H. and Jennie Cobb, aged twelve years, eight months and seven days.

Sorrow in the house-hold of Hon. J. H. Downer, of this county, because of the death of his little grandson, Walter J., son of John D. and Martha E. Eads, aged 7 years.

Mr. Lewis Howell was born in South Carolina, July 26th, 1799; moved to Louisiana in childhood; to Mississippi in 1826; and in Simpson and Rankin counties he lived until death. He died at his home near Dry Creek Church, Rankin County, August 18th, 1883, aged 81 years, 1 month and 27 days. He was three times married, was the father of ten children, four sons and six daughters. Two of his sons were Baptist ministers.

Mary Gordon, oldest daughter of Rev. C. M. Gordon and Mrs. Ida I. Gordon, died of diptheria in Amite County, Miss., September 12, 1883.

Died at Bloomfield, the residence of Mrs. Mary J. Inge, in Amite County, Mississippi, on the 15th, Herbert Inge Gordon, aged 4 years, 6 months and 6 days.

November 6, 1884

Died near Winden, Webster Parish, La., Sept. 17th, 1884, Kinchen Monsingo, aged seventy-seven years. He was born in Darlington Dist., S. C., February 1807.

Died on the 19th, Sister M. L. Henderson. The Macedonia Church has lost a faithful member.

November 13, 1884

Died at his residence, L'Esperance, four miles east of Rodney, Miss., October 21, 1884, Mr. Charles L. McGill, in the twenty-ninth year of his age. He was the son of Mrs. S. McGill.

Died October 20, 1884, in Floyd, West Carroll Parish, La., of congestion, Archie Thames, aged nineteen years, one month and six days.

November 20, 1884

Mrs. Annie Durham, daughter of N. J. and S. A. McMillan, was born 31st of May, 1860; married Mr. W. H. Durham, December 6th, 1883; died November 9th, 1884, aged twenty-four years, five months, and eight days.

November 27, 1884

Died on 2nd of November, 1884, Oscar Norris, son of Marshall and Adeline Norris, aged 6 years, 2 months, 2 days, after an illness of four days of hemature.

Mr. J. B. Alexander, night operator of W. U. Telegraph line, Union City, Tenn., died of typhoid fever at his parent's home, Booneville, Miss., October 9th, and was buried in Booneville cemetery.

December 4, 1884

Died in Shelby County, Texas, on September 25, 1884, Mattie A. Craddock, consort of W. Y. Craddock, aged thirty-three years and eight months. She was born in Keachi, La., on 25th January, 1851; married on 10th December, 1872.

Willie E. Purser, son of D. I. and D. J. Purser, was born in Franklin County, Miss., on September 27, 1872 and died November 12th, 1884.

December 11, 1884

Died at the residence of Mrs. R. E. Fancher, Attala County, Miss., on the 15th of November, 1884, J. W. Fancher, son of H. H. and P. H. Fancher, aged seventeen years, five months and eleven days, of apoplexy.

Died near Terry, Miss., on November 21st, after a brief illness of congestion, Thomas Adde Therrell, only son of Benjamin E. and Sarah J. Therrell. Born April 11th, 1881 and died Nov. 21st, 1884, aged 3 years, 7 months and 10 days.

Died November 23rd, 1884, near Abbeville, Miss., Tyler Logan, aged eighty-one years, seven months and three days. He was born near Abbeville, South Carolina, April 20th, 1803; joined the Baptist Church in 1826.

December 18, 1884

Miss S. L. Black, daughter of S. L. and Elmirah Black, was born in Attala County, Miss., on September 1st, 1867 and died December 4th, 1884.

Died October 21st, 1884, Lizzie Ruple, eldest daughter of J. H. and E. Ruple, aged fifteen years. She was attacked with typhoid fever and lingering more than four weeks.

After a protracted illness, Miss Mary F. Brooks died in Starkville Female Institute, November 24th, 1884.

Died at Magnolia, Pike County, Miss., September, 1884, Mrs. Mary Lee, in the 64th year of her age.

On the morning of the 28th, near Brownsville, Miss., Mary M. Chapman, wife of W. C. Chapman, breathed her last. At the time of her death she was connected with Beulah Church, Hinds County.

January 22, 1885

Died January 11th, 1885, at the residence of Mr. J. F. Jenkins, Edwards, Miss., Moses Brock, son of Moses Brock, in the forty-first year of his age. He was buried in the family plot of the Utica City cemetery.

On the evening of the 8th, just two months after the demise of Robert M. Whitfield, son of Dr. R. H. and Emma Whitfield, their daughter, Edith, in the 14th year of her age, passed away.

January 18th was our marriage anniversary. It is memorable now because death came and took Louis Alfred, our little four year old son. We have given up four. Alex. A. Lomax.

February 5, 1885

Miss Laura N. Robbins, daughter of S. L. Robbins, died at her father's home near Meridian, Jan. 13th, 1885, at the age of twenty-two, her body laid to rest at Oak Grove Church.

Mrs. Adaline Galtney departed this life, Dec. 16th, 1884, at her late residence, in her sixty-fifth year.

February 12, 1885

Died of pneumonia at his home in Longtown, 25th of Jan., 1885, Mr. A. O. Askew, in the 81st year of his age. He was born in Bertie County, N. C. in 1804, moved to Tennessee with his parents while quite young. He married first Miss Hewlett, who lived only six years. Later he married Miss Susan ___, who survives him. He leaves a wife and one son, Hon. J. O. Askew.

February 19, 1885

Died in Clinton, Miss., Jan. 31st, 1885, in the sixth year of her age, Marrin, daughter of G. M. and Hattie Lewis.

Little John, infant son of John F. and Eudora Jackson, has fallen asleep in Jesus.

Robert L. Riggin was born in Hinds County, Miss., Dec. 15th, 1818 and died in Hinds County, Dec. 6th, 1884.

Mrs. Jane Crawford, daughter of Moses Harvey and wife of Hon. N. R. Crawford, was born May 4th, 1811 and died January 27th, 1885.

Mattie Means Munn, youngest daughter of R. R. and Eliza Riggs, departed this life the 25th day of December, 1884, at her father's residence near Kingston, La. She was born 22nd of May, 1854. The 30th of January, 1879, she was married to Mr. W. S. Munn, whom she followed to the grave.

February 26, 1885

Died near Hazlehurst, Miss., Feb. 16th, 1885, Mrs. F. James, in her thirty-eighth year. She leaves a husband and several children.

Died of consumption on the 15th, Miss Annie Laurie, daughter of I. H. and Anna Davis, aged twenty years.

Died at the residence of his father, Choctaw County, Miss., on the 8th of January, 1885, Thompson Bruce, aged fourteen years, six months, and ten days. The cyclone of 1883 reduced his father's house to broken fragments, his mother was instantly killed, and he received a head wound from which he suffered as long as he lived.

Theodore and Alice Sturges are deeply bereaved by the death of their little daughter, Nellie, Feb. 11th, at the age of five years.

Died at her home near Clinton, La., on Feb. 8th, 1885, aged twenty-one years, Mrs. Ella Smith Norwood, eldest daughter of J. C. and Matilda Smith, and wife of A. J. Norwood, Jr.

Died at his residence near West Station, Holmes County, Miss., January 9th, 1885, Burwell B. Wilkes, age seventy-five years, three months, and five days. He was born in Charlotte County, Va., 1809; came to Mississippi about the twentieth year of his age; spent several years in the counties of Warren and Yazoo; came to Holmes in 1834; married Elizabeth Caster, Nov. 24th, 1836; united with the County Line Missionary Baptist Church about 1851. He leaves an aged wife, three daughters and two sons to mourn their loss.

Sister H. W. Rockett had been sick some time at Harrison, Miss., their new home, and on the 8th her spirit took it's flight.

March 12, 1885

Elisha Williams Henderson was born in Walton County, Ga. on the 10th of February, 1831, on the 2nd day of May, 1850 he was married to Miss Ann Eliza Webb, of Tallapoosa County, Ala., who bore him eight children, four of whom have already gone to heaven. His wife died on the 29th of May, 1865. In June 1855 he was licensed to preach by the Bethel Baptist Church, Tallapoosa Co., Ala. In 1857 he removed to Scott County, Miss., remaining only one year. In 1858 he removed to Ala., settling in Maine County. On the 14th of September, 1865 he married Mrs. Eliza Emmie Henderson, of Troup Co., Ga., who bore him two children, one of whom died in infancy. She died August 3rd, 1873. On the 1st of January, 1884, he was married to Miss Beulah Eunice McCoy, of Panola County, Miss., who bore him three children. She survives him.

Near Goodman, at the residence of Mrs. N. Bell, Emma, daughter of T. W. and Joan Bell, died suddenly on Jan. 30th, 1885, being only one year, nine months and twenty-five days old.

Mrs. Mary L. Bolls, daughter of Pulaski and Susan Dudley, was born in Hinds County, Miss. in 1833; was married to Mr. P. R. Bolls in 1856, and fell asleep in Jesus on the third, at her home in Utica. She leaves a husband and four children.

Mary E. Boon was born the 6th of July, 1852, in the town of Minden, Webster Parish, La., where she was raised and educated. She was the daughter of Mr. R. A. and Mrs. Melvina Lancaster, and departed this life at her home in Webster Parish, the 21st of February, 1885. She was married to W. J. Boon on the 11th of October, 1870.

Died at his son's residence in Lawrence County, Miss., near his old home, April 9th, C. C. Butler. He was born October 1817. He married Miss S. A. Longino, Aug. 29th, 1831. He joined the Baptist Church at Hebron in May, 1855.

Died at her home in Lawrence County, Miss. on the twenty-fifth day of February, 1885, from the effects of the measles, Miss Mary W. Cannon, in the forty-eighth year of her age.

Died on March 1st, 1885, at Woodburn, on the Sunflower river, Mr. A. P. Sale. His body was laid in the Bell graveyard, two miles from Goodman, beside his wife.

Died, Mrs. Calista Biles, February 13th, 1885, at the residence of Mr. Alfred Miller, Marshall County, Miss., of pneumonia.

Died at Abbeville, Miss., Feb. 24th, 1885, Mrs. Hattie E. Mason, in the forty-fifth year of her age.

March 26, 1885

Miss Amelia Hallos was born Feb. 17th, 1858; joined the Baptist Church at Uitca, Hinds County, Miss., 1873, and died Dec. 11th, 1884.

Miss Mary W. Cannon died of measles, Feb. 25th, 1885, near Monticello, Miss., aged forty-seven years. She was born in Lawrence County, Miss. in 1838.

T. J. Murray died of heart disease, on the 19th of January, 1885. He was born in Simpson County, Miss. about 1829.

On the 10th of March, 1885, Thos. Nicholas Faulconer fell asleep in Jesus. He was born Oct. 30th, 1869, at his death being 15 years, 4 months and 10 days old. "Tommie" was the oldest son of Capt. W. H. Faulconer of Ebenezer, Holmes County, Miss.

After a brief illness, James M. Moss fell asleep Feb. 9th.

Albert Byron Milton died March 7th, 1885, after an attack of pneumonia, in the 20th year of his age.

Mrs. Martha Didlake died at the residence of her son, Jno. M. Didlake, March 17th, 1885, after a protracted illness. She was born in King and Queen County, Va., April 5th, 1812, seventy-two years, nine months and thirteen days. She was married in 1832 and was the mother of ten children.

July 16, 1885

Bettie Childers Clayton, of Tupelo Baptist Church, and wife of A. J. Clayton, died in her forty-first year, June 28, 1885. She was born in Virginia, but lived the greater part of her life in north Mississippi.

After a lingering illness of several weeks, Mary E. Yarborough, wife of John Yarborough, fell asleep in Jesus on the 2nd day of June. She was born in Copiah County, on the 12th day of August, 1846. The 20th day of September, 1866 she was united in marriage.

Mrs. Lucy Martin died on the second day of June, 1885. She joined the Salem Baptist Church, in Smith County, in 1865. After her husband died she moved to Simpson County. She leaves three sons and two daughters.

October 15, 1885

Died on the night of the 18th, of congestion, at her home near Holmesville, Miss., Laura A. Brent, wife of W. J. Brent. She leaves her husband and four small children.

Fanny Reed departed this life on the 15th day of September, 1885.

Died at his residence near Brushy Fork Church, Copiah County, Aug. 31st, W. J. Bailes, born in Copiah County Oct. 29, 1816, age 67 years, 10 months and 2 days.

THE CRYSTAL SPRINGS MONITOR
Crystal Springs, Mississippi

July 29, 1875

Died July 22nd, 1875, Sallie, daughter of R. C. and E. Fulks, and wife of Willie Hall, in the twenty-second year of her age.

Alex Wilson (col.) stabbed his brother, Bill Wilson, fatally with his pocket knife, at the negro church, on Saturday night last.

September 2, 1875

Died August 19, 1875, Etna, aged one year and ten months, daughter of Marcus H. and Elmira S. Robertson.

September 9, 1875

Died at his residence in Hinds County, Miss., July 22nd, 1875, of hemorrhage of the lungs, E. F. Dean.

October 7, 1875

A most horrible murder was committed in Washington County a few days ago. Two young men, Mr. Wm. Morgan and a son of Mr. Pope Erwin, had made a crop together in Washington County, and had taken some of their cotton into Greenville for sale. Having affected the sale they started for their home. They had not proceeded far when they were waylaid by some ruffians, brutally murdered and robbed. Their bodies were found the next day, with their skulls split open with an axe.

October 14, 1875

Our community was startled last Saturday morning at the news of the sudden death of Joseph Moseley, a mulatto grocery merchant, who had been a resident of Crystal Springs for many years. It appears that on Friday night a number of negroes were in the restaurant kept by Moseley, and that whiskey had been furnished them until they became troublesome. Joe undertook to eject them and a quarrel ensued, in which a colored man named Henry Barker, from Utica, Hinds County, took a prominent part. Moseley slapped him and pushed him off the gallery, enraging Barker so that he drew his pistol and fired three shots, two of which took effect, one in the leg and the other in his right breast, penetrating the lung and causing almost immediate death.

October 21, 1875

Died in Copiah County, Miss., at the residence of her parents, Sept. 26th, '75, of congestion of the brain, Lillie May, infant daughter of W. T. and F. A. Matheny. Lilly was born June 7, 1875.

On Friday 15th, at Edwards, Mr. Sid Whitehead was accidentally killed by a bar keeper named Chas. McMullen. It appears McMullen was drunk and a brother of his was attempting to take a gun out of his hand, when he fired it off, the ball penetrating Mr. Whitehead's head, behind the left ear, which caused his death in about half an hour. Mr. Whitehead was standing in the door talking with a negro man, unconscious of any approach of danger.

December 2, 1875

Died near Hazlehurst, on the 21st, Mrs. Catherine, wife of Mr. A. R. Granberry.

The sudden death of Elisha Sumrall on Monday last, cast a gloom over our community. It appears that he has a son who has for some time shown marks of aberration of mind and who was very hard to manage. The boy is about 13 years of age and in the habit of carrying a pistol. The cause of the quarrel between him and his father was of a trivial character. The father resolved to whip him, and taking him out to the woods walked off in search of a switch. No sooner was he back than the son leveled his pistol at the father's head and fired. The ball entered at the base of the skull on the back of the head. The father fell and expired instantly. The boy is held as a prisoner.

March 30, 1876

Francis M., son of F. M. and M. T. Holliday, was born in Louisiana Feb. 15, 1858. He removed with his mother to Mississippi neart Crystal Springs, in July, 1858, with whom he resided until he departed this life on the 8th of March, 1876, of typhoid fever.

June 1, 1876

Died May 25th, in Vicksburg, Miss., August, oldest son of Joseph Piazza.

July 13, 1876

On the 3rd, in Crystal Springs, Mrs. E. J. Summers passed from life to death, a resident of Hinds County, aged 59 years, 6 months, after about 3 weeks illness.

The killing of young Leffingwell at Dry Grove -- After supper Carballo commenced using profane language and without any provocation he stepped up to Leffingwell and grossly insulted him. Leffingwell made a mild reply, but before the words were well spoken, Carballo stabbed him on the left breast with his pocket knife. Leffingwell died in an hour. Leffingwell was seventeen years of age and Carballo will be 21 in October. The latter was a printer by trade and formerly worked in this office.

Died on 8th, Charlie, infant son of R. A. and E. C. Lugenbuhl, aged 7 months, twin brother of little May, who was called away about two weeks before.

Died on the 12th, Charles C., youngest child of C. Appel, aged eighteen months.

Died on the 8th, aged 2 years and 4 months, Edna Maude, oldest child of D. P. and Augusta Barnes.

July 27, 1876

Died on the 23rd July, at Crystal Springs, Miss., Helen Lear, infant daughter of D. B. and Mattie B. Packer, born March 30th, 1875.

Died 28th June, 1876, near Brown's Wells, Copiah County, Miss., Mrs. Elizabeth Rains. The deceased was born in East Louisiana, on the 15th day of March, 1813, on the Shenochlaha river. She removed to Copiah County in her youth, and then to Natchez, in which place she lived thirty years, then returned to Copiah County.

August 3, 1876

Died July 27th, 1876, James Prentiss, son of O. P. and Augusta Barner, aged 4 months.

August 17, 1876

Willie, son of J. W. Mathis, who resides about six miles east of Crystal Springs, met with a fatal accident on Sunday last. The child, who is about nine years of age, was visiting a neighbor's house (Mr. Henry Hyland), when he and a little son of Mr. Hyland were left alone. The fatal accident occurred in handling a loaded gun. The ball passed completely through the child's head, killing him instantly.

Died near Crystal Springs, on the 14th, Jabez Ford, son of J. J. Ford, Esq. He leaves a wife and infant child.

September 7, 1876

Died on Thursday morning, 7th, Otto, son of H. N. and H. C. Tyler, in the fourth year of his age.

Died on 1st, Jacob, son of Hiram and Ella Callendar, in the fifth year of his age.

October 5, 1876

Died 4th October, Minnie, daughter of J. M. Newton, of this place, aged about 9 years. This is the second little loved one taken from their parents, Mr. & Mrs. J. M. Newton, within the last few weeks.

Died on the 4th October, little Andrew, infant son of J. W. Murney, aged 11 months.

October 19, 1876

On Saturday a difficulty occurred between two young men named Fortenberry and McElmore. A misunderstanding in regard to some young ladies seems to have been the cause. Both were armed with pistols, and drawing their weapons they both fired at once, each wounding his antagonist fatally. One of them died on Sunday night and the other on Monday.

October 26, 1876

Died on the 20th, Theodore, son of Wm. M. and E. A. Priestley, aged 3 years and 10 months.

Died on the 22nd, Laura Augustus, daughter of A. J. and C. A. Martin, of pneumonia, aged 13 years. A few weeks ago Laura mourned the loss of a little brother.

Died on the 23rd, of pneumonia, Como, infant daughter of H. C. and Beatrice O. Stackhouse, of Utica.

J. A. Signaigo, formerly editor of the *Grenada Sentinel* and for many years connected with the Mississippi Press, died recently in Jackson.

November 30, 1876

Died of consumption, 25th, near Crystal Springs, T. M. Alford, in the 25th year of his age. At the time of his death he was Chancery Clerk of Copiah County.

March 8, 1877

Thomas Eddie, eldest son of T. D. and M. J. Clement, departed this life in Copiah County, Miss., February 21st, 1877. He was six years, five months and six days. He died of diptheria.

Died on 5th, near Crystal Springs, Alex. McIntosh, in the seventy-eighth year of his age.

April 12, 1877

Died on 11th, at Utica, Hinds County, after a short illness, Dr. H. C. Stackhouse, in the 33rd year of his age.

May 31, 1877

Died on the 27th of May, of typhoid pneumonia, at his residence near Auburn, Hinds County, Geo. H. Horne, aged about 29 years.

Walter Dorsey, son of T. D. and M. J. Clement, died at the home of his parents in Copiah County, Miss., March 26th, 1877. He was five years, two months and fifteen days old.
Also, Oliver Cromwell, infant son of T. D. and M. J. Clement, died March 7th, 1877, aged ten months and 11 days.

July 26, 1877

Died at the family residence near Baldwin's Ferry, July 16th, 1877, Mrs. Olivia C. Newman, wife of Mr. Charles Newman, and daughter of Mrs. Olivia H. Small, aged 21 years.

July 26, 1877

Utica, Miss. -- Henry Barker, the colored man who killed Joe Mosely, of your city, in 1875, was killed here Saturday night, by Elijah Davis, colored, while in a drunken brawl.

It seems as if death will visit every family in our midst. Mr. Mike Adkins and Mr. Jordan Corbin were both buried this week.

September 27, 1877
Died at his home four miles east of Crystal Springs, September 20th, 1877, Wirt LeRoy Dees, son of John and Mary Dees, aged 4 years, 2 months, 15 days.

Agnes Jane Bailey died at her home in Crystal Springs, August 26, 1877. She was born in this place October 28, 1864.

October 18, 1877
Died in Hazlehurst, Oct. 5, 1877, of diptheria, Lucy Roseland, daughter of Mr. & Mrs. J. M. Norman, aged 5 years and 8 months.

Died on the 10th, at her residence near Pine Bluff, in this county, Mrs. Elizabeth Fatheree, in the 71st year of her age.

Died Sept. 30th, 1877, Eulah, infant daughter of Elbert and Sarah Bordeaux, aged 1 year, 11 months and 15 days. She died of diptheria.

December 6, 1877
We announce the death of Muke Owens, the youngest son of widow Owens, of this place, formerly of Lexington, Holmes County. Muke took a freight train for Terry, was unfortunate enought to get on top of the train, in attempting to pass from one car to another he missed his step, falling between the cars and was instantly under the train. Eleven cars passed over his body, mangling it shockingly.

January 24, 1878
Mrs. A. P. Horne, wife of Geo. W. Horne, died at her residence in Hinds County, Dec. 27th, 1877.

January 31, 1878
Mrs. A. P., wife of G. W. Horne, was born in Nashville, Tenn., Jan. 1, 1817, and died Dec. 27, 1877. She was married in March 1837.

August 12, 1880
At Beauregard, Dr. Moses Ferguson shot and killed a negro named Parker Jones, on the 9th. The negro was attempting to strike him with an axe when he committed the deed.

Macon, Miss., Aug. 10 -- John B. Buck, United States enumerator for Noxubee (Co.) drowned himself in the Tombigbee (river), near Gainesville, Ala., Sunday. While enumerating the county he was much exposed to the sun, which, it is thought, affected his brain.

October 1, 1880

A difficulty occurred on the 28th of Sept., between Ben Grantham and his son-in-law Mr. Duffy, both living near Pearl River. Duffy shot a load of buck-shot from a double-barrelled gun at Grantham, twelve or thirteen of the shot taking effect in Grantham's shoulder. The latter grappled with Duffy and succeeded in killing him with a pistol. Grantham is dangerously wounded.

October 28, 1880

Maggie Bell, little daughter of Mr. & Mrs. E. D. Elliott, died on the 10th, at the residence of D. B. Lowe, in Hazlehurst, of diptheria.

Rev. W. F. Green died suddenly at his home in the Rose Hill neighborhood, in this county, on the 9th. He had been a citizen of this county more than forty years, during which he was a minister of the Baptist Church.

December 2, 1880

We record the death of Joseph H. Miller, our late Town Marshall, at the age of 38 years, of disease of the heart and liver. He leaves a wife and three children.

December 22, 1880

Died of hemorrhage of the lungs, on the 20th, Mrs. Mary J. Commack, in her 38th year. She leaves a family of four little children.

We record the death of Jane N. Gibson, on the 21st of pleuro-pneumonia, at the advanced age of 63 years.

April 2, 1881

We announce the death of Mrs. Fannie A. Pearson, wife of Rev. B. T. Pearson, of this place. She died of heart disease, March 30, 1881.

We learn of the death of Hon. Hiram Cassidy, which occurred at his home in Summit, Miss., the twenty-sixth. Judge Cassidy was a northern man by birth, but has been a resident of Mississippi for nearly forty years. He settled at Meadville, Franklin County, in early life.

April 9, 1881

Died April 6th, 1881, in Crystal Springs, Mr. Myron E. Lee, of paralysis, aged 33 years.

August 20, 1881

Departed this life October 13th, 1881 (copied as printed), Charles Edgar, youngest son of Bryant M. and Luis E. Keithley, aged 9 months and 21 days.

September 8, 1881

The intelligence of the death of Dr. Wm. R. Hooker reached town on Wednesday. He had been out Tuesday night attending a professional call, and on returning, from some cause fell from his horse or was thrown from him, and while lying in the road a heavily loaded wagon ran over him and so crushed him that he died in twenty minutes. Dr. Hooker was comparatively a young man, the son of the late Col. Zadock Hooker, of Copiah County, and brother of Hon. C. E. Hooker, member of Congress from this State, and a native of South Carolina. He married the daughter of Mr. Bardee Segriest. Dr. Hooker was in the 40th year of his age.

September 17, 1881

Gen. Wm. F. Tucker was assassinated at his home in Okolona, last Wednesday night, by some one who called him to the door and shot him dead. An 18 year old negro has been arrested and jailed.

January 14, 1882

We announce the sudden death of Mr. William S., eldest son of Col. J. L. Power. Young Mr. Power came to his death by the accidental discharge of a pistol, in his own hands, when showing it to a young lady.

January 28, 1882

Mrs. A. V. Davis, wife of Dr. R. M. Davis, was born in Miss., Jan. 5th, 1852, was married to Dr. Davis, Jan. 16, 1878, and died Jan. 18th, 1882.

April 15, 1882

Dr. Jack Wharton, U. S. Marshal, N. O., died on Monday evening of apoplexy. Col. Wharton was a native of Maryland and was born on the 1st December, 1832. He was a son of Dr. Thomas Wharton who resided, a few years ago, near Terry. (Author's note - a lengthy report of his Civil War service in the 4th Texas Cavalry followed).

April 22, 1882

On the 6th, while Mr. Alex. Henson was absent from home, a negro, George Hughes, who lived on the place, went to the well where Mrs. Henson was washing, and it is believed, after committing that darkest of all crimes, murdered his helpless victim, after which he threw the body into the well, where it remained until night when it was discovered.

CRYSTAL MIRROR
Crystal Springs, Mississippi

March 18, 1876
Col. J. M. Sublett, of Yazoo County, was killed at Austin, Texas last week.

April 8, 1876
The Angel of Death visited our community on the 30th and bore away the spirit of Mrs. Myra Willing Osterhaut.

Col. Martin Keary, of Vicksburg, killed Christy Jones, his son-in-law, one day this week. The coroner's jury rendered a verdict of justifiable homicide.

May 20, 1876
Austin Ferguson was murdered at Beauregard by some unknown party or parties. Suspicion at once rested upon H. E. Dunbar and Robert F. Bostwick. Ferguson had walked into the saloon of W. C. Loving, and while standing at the counter he was fired upon by someone concealed in the back room, the load taking effect in the head, killing him almost instantly. Just afterward two men left the saloon and were supposed to be Dunbar and Bostwick. Dunbar and Ferguson had a difficulty two years ago in which the latter was shot and wounded by the former.

Since the above was put in print, Bostwick has been captured and Dunbar killed.

August 19, 1876
Mr. Jobe Ford, residing near this place, died on Monday last, after a brief illness.

We learn of the death of Young Will N. Beauchamp, which occurred at Auburn, Hinds County, on Sunday evening last.

August 26, 1876
Jimmie Thompson, nephew of our townsman S. D. Robinson, was drowned near Helena, Arkansas, on Monday last.

Died August 12th, 1876, Minnie, daughter of J. M. and Emma E. Girault, aged one year and two months.

THE METEOR
Crystal Springs, Mississippi

March 17, 1883
A. J. Tillman, of Gallman, an old citizen of this county, died of pneumonia last Sunday morning.

April 21, 1883
No occurrance has given birth to more comment than the Chapel Hill tragedy of last Saturday culminating in the killing of Dr. E. W. Crume by Mr. J. T. Rumph. Our informant states that Dr. Crume was unarmed. He proceeded to Chapel Hill under a bond imposed by Mr. Rumph. Upon his arrival he was met by Rumph armed with a shot gun and opened fire on Crume. Dr. Crume died Saturday night.

May 12, 1883
William Dudley, of Canton, Miss., a brakeman on a freight train, was killed Tuesday morning north of Gallman, by accidently falling between the cars. His body was terribly mangled.

October 6, 1883
Died at Cherry Grove, near Crystal Springs, Lilly, eldest daughter of the Hon. and Mrs. G. W. Miller, Oct. 4th, 1883.

October 13, 1883
Died at Brown's Wells Thursday morning, Robert D. Osburn, aged 37 years, 3 months and 3 days.

October 2, 1883
Died at Chatawa, Mississippi, in the fourth year of his age, on the 5th September, little Willie, infant son of Mr. & Mrs. W. H. Taylor, of this city. (Ft. Worth, Tx. Gazette)

November 10, 1883
Tuesday morning the report spread through town that Print Matthews was killed at the poll by E. B. Wheeler. The origin of the difficulty is obscure.

Prince Matthews was killed this morning by E. B. Wheeler, with a shotgun. Eye witnesses state that Matthews drew his pistol on Wheeler. (Author's note - part of a lengthy report of the local disturbance resulting.)

March 15, 1884
Eva Aubrey, youngest child of W. R. and Pearle Smith, born in Crystal Springs, Miss., June 3rd, 1882, died March 5th, 1884.

June 21, 1884
Died Monday noon, after a protracted illness, Mrs. Alice Allen, nee Siebe, wife of C. E. Allen.

October 25, 1884
Tuesday night, Col. Jno. T. Holt passed away, after an illness of a few days.

Daisie C., daughter of A. and C. E. Baccher, born July 13, 1877, died Oct. 13th, 1884.

December 6, 1884
O. C. Crum passed away after a lingering illness, in New Orleans, last Thursday the 27th. His remains were brought here and buried in the cemetery at Old Crystal Springs.

March 7, 1885
Mrs. Ella Smith Norwood, eldest daughter of James C. and Matilda Smith, and wife of A. J. Norwood, Jr., died at Norwood, La., Feb. 8th, 1885, buried at Crystal Springs, Miss. Feb. 10th, aged 21 years.

March 14, 1885
On the evening of the 3rd, John W. Fortner was caught by a falling tree and crushed to death. Mr. Fortner was born on Dec. 7th, 1811 in what is now known as Warren County, Miss. Mr. Fortner was married three times. There are three children living of his first marriage, but one by his second wife who died young, by his surviving wife there were three, two of whom preceeded him to the grave.

Died in Carrollton, La., on the 9th, Christian Kerner, youngest son of the late Rev. John Williamson, and the grandson of Bishop Kerner, aged 13 years.

April 4, 1885
Rubie Lucille, daugher of Mr. C. D. and Mrs. Emma Rhymes, was born the 28th of May, 1882, and died the 9th of February, 1885, aged 2 years, 8 months and 12 days.

September 5, 1885
In the Editor's household this week, two grandsons seriously ill, one of whom died on Thursday morning - Henry Monroe, son of R. G. and Selina M. Harris, of New Orleans.

October 24, 1885
We chronicle the death of Miss Emma Gramling, daughter of Mr. & Mrs. A. D. Gramling, which occurred at the home of her parents on Gum Grove plantation, this county, October the 5th. She was a

member of the Methodist Church. She was buried near her old home on Gum Grove.

October 31, 1885

Mrs. V. V. Fairman, nee Witherspoon, died at the residence of her husband, L. Q. Fairman, Esq., near Crystal Springs, on Oct. 16, and was buried the 17th at Old Crystal Springs cemetery. She was a native of Copiah County, the daughter of Jno. G. And Sarah Witherspoon, the neice of J. H. and Jesse Thompson. For seventeen years she was an invalid. She died in her 47th year.

THE EDWARDS CITIZEN
Edwards, Mississippi

September 27, 1876

A negro named George Banks, living on the Mallett place near Cayuga, was shot and instantly killed by an unknown party, on Saturday night last. Banks and some other negroes were playing cards, when the assassin fired through the cracks in the wall, and made his escape without being discovered.

We learn of the death of Dr. S. Davis, of the Forrest Register. A noble man has gone from among us.

October 4, 1876

Gen. Braxton Bragg, of Confederate fame, died in Galveston, Texas last week, of heart disease.

December 2, 1876

We regret to learn of the death of Troy M. Alford, late Chancery Clerk of Copiah County. He died on Friday of last week.

July 21, 1877

Died near Baldwin's Ferry, Hinds County, Miss., on the evening of the 16th, Mrs. Olivia C., consort of Mr. C. D. Newman.

September 15, 1877

Died Sept. 13, 1877, at the residence of Mr. Geo. D. Nixon, Edwards, Miss., Thomas Quinn, son of G. D. and Laura Nixon.

September 29, 1877

Died at the residence of Mrs. Susan Collum, near Edwards, Hinds County, Miss., on September 8, 1877, Mrs. Mahala Norwood, aged 40 years.

Died near Queen's Hill, Hinds County, Miss., on September 19, 1877, Mary Elizabeth, youngest child of C. K. and N. E. Farr, aged 2 years, 9 months and 27 days.

December 8, 1877
Died near Edwards, Miss., December 4, 1877, Mrs. Lize Drummond, wife of T. W. Drummond.

THE FOREST WEEKLY REGISTER
Forest, Mississippi

June 13, 1877
On the 7th Jno. G. Owen breathed his last, surrounded by all his family. He was a few days past seventy-seven years of age and had been a prominent man in Scott County many years.

May 5, 1880
Capt. W. T. Ward departed this life on the 30th day of April, 1880, at his home in Raleigh, Miss. He spent many years in Smith County, where he raised his family. At the time of death he was Clerk of Circuit and Chancery Courts. His mortal remains now lay buried in the old Raleigh graveyard beside his mother and several of his children.

FRIAR'S POINT GAZETTE
Friar's Point, Mississippi

May 13, 1881
Mr. C. Canfield lost his little daughter May, of Shufordville, with inflammation of the brain.

July 1, 1881
Last Tuesday, Mac McKinney, a colored man living on the N. B. Leavell place, was shot and killed in a somewhat mysterious manner. He was sitting on the gallery of the house, only one small boy being present with him. While sitting in a stooping position the pistol dropped out of his pocket and discharged, the ball striking him directly under the shoulder, and lodged near the opposite side. No person was known to be present, but certain matters connected with his death lead to the suspicion that he was murdered. McKinny was an old resident.

July 15, 1881

Last Sunday morning came news of the sudden death of Capt. W. N. Brown. He lost his wife nearly a year ago, leaving two orphan children.

August 19, 1881

Died on August 16, 1881, at the family residence of J. W. Shipp, George Stovall, infant son of Mr. and Mrs. J. N. Bond, aged 2 months.

August 26, 1881

The "Comet" announces the death of it's editor, Col. F. T. Cooper. His death causes deep sorrow among the editorial fraternity.

September 16, 1881

On Wednesday morning an Irishman named Isaac Dickerson, was found dead sitting on the top of a fence, upon Old River. The deceased had been at work at Miller's Point recently, and was in town on Tuesday. The curious part of it was that he set his carpet sack on the ground while he got on top of the fence and died, and was found in a sitting position, -- death from natural causes.

September 30, 1881

Died at Friar's Point, Miss., September 26, 1881, Yerger Harris, infant son of Mr. and Mrs. R. N. Harris.

October 7, 1881

Died at Friar's Point, Miss., on September 30, 1881, Mary Aurea, infant daughter of Mr. and Mrs. T. W. Carter.

November 11, 1881

Died at Meldon, Tenn., October 1, 1881, James Crowley, infant son of Mr. F. C. and Mrs. Lou F. Johnson.

November 18, 1881

A colored man named John Rhodes, living on the Carson place, was killed by a shot in the head last Saturday night in his cabin, by two masked men. John Jacobs, the one who killed him was an old hand on the place and was regarded as peaceable.

December 2, 1881

At a festival on the J. D. Brown place, on the 5th ult., a difficulty arose between Fineese Brown and Jack Barnhard, during which Brown drew his pistol and killed Barnhard. He made his escape and was not heard of until the 28th, when Mr. J. D. Brown heard of his lurking place in the neighborhood and proceeded to Mr. Will Cammack's place and discovering him secreted in an outhouse, he arrested him and brought him to town.

December 23, 1881
Died on the 18th of December, 1881, on Capt. John Daley's boat at the landing at Friar's Point, Miss., Mr. Wm. Grace, of Rising Sun, Ind. He was about twenty years of age, a nephew of Capt. Daley. He was taken down with typhoid fever.

January 20, 1882
Died at the residence of his father, on the 8th of January, 1882, Mr. James Harris, in the 22nd year of his age.

February 3, 1882
Died at Friar's Point, Miss., February 2nd, 1882, at the residence of Mrs. Dudley, Mr. W. S. Russell.

February 10, 1882
Died at the residence of her father-in-law, Mr. J. G. Chism, on the 31st of January, after a brief illness, Mrs. Angie Chism, wife of Mrs. S. B. Chism, of Friar's Point, aged 22 years.

March 30, 1882
A colored man named Wm. Henry was drowned in the overflow on the Barbee place, about two weeks ago. He and his son were out in a dug-out. The young man barely saved his life, but the father was lost.

June 15, 1883
Died at her home on the Mound place, Yazoo Pass, May 28th, 1883, Mrs. Josephine Stovall, wife of R. G. Stovall. She leaves a family of five children, 4 girls.

August 10, 1883
On Tuesday last, Capt. D. W. Pressell, one of the most influential citizens of Mississippi, was arrested at Mayersville, Miss., charged with outraging the person of Miss Julia Neilson, at that place, a girl of nine years. Yesterday his trial took place and the girl having testified to Pressell's guilt, he was remanded to jail without bail. Even though Capt. Pressell was guarded by a special posse of officers, the jail door was battered down, the prisoner taken with a rope around his neck and hanged from an oak about half a mile from the prison. He breathed his last at 12:30 last night. Capt. Pressell was sixty-five years of age, and brother-in-law to Judge Jefferds. (Author's note - this was part of a lengthy report).

August 17, 1883
Mrs. Alice W. McClure, wife of Dr. J. W. McClure, died at Danvers, Ill., her former home, on the 2nd. She had been suffering for a number of years from consumption.

August 24, 1883

In the death of Mr. J. M. Clindining, our town has lost one of the most useful citizens. He was getting old and feeble, and over-exertion in the extreme heat of the season no doubt rendered his system liable to the disease of bilious dysentery, which ended his life.

October 19, 1883

Died at the residence of his father in the town of Friar's Point, Mississippi, October 7th, 1883, James R. Cooper, son of J. J. and Elizabeth Cooper. The deceased was born August 5th, 1850 in Fayette County, Tenn., and during early boyhood removed with his family to this State.

November 23, 1883

Died at the residence of C. G. Bobo, near Clarksdale, on November 10, 1883, T. G. Bobo, of congestion

Died at the residence of his parents, on the 21st November, 1883, General Regulus Brady, son of Mr. C. C. and Mrs. S. A. Caldwell, aged 15 months.

November 30, 1883

(Letter) Hazlehurst, Miss., Nov. 9, 1883
To: The Second Assistant Postmaster General -

Sir -- I write to know what I shall do in regard to mail on route No. 18,282 from this place to Westville. The contractor, J. P. Matthews, my brother, was on last Tuesday morning brutally murdered. The day previous - Monday, and armed mob came to town and gave him orders not to vote, if he did they would kill him. On Tuesday they came to the polls with shotguns, and when my brother voted and turned from the polls, he was shot twice with a shotgun, twenty-four shot taking effect in his breast, and he died instantly. Respectfully, G. E. Matthews, P. M.

January 25, 1884

Died January 14, 1884, Maggie, daughter of the late J. T. Rucks and Sallie B. Rucks, aged 24 years.

Hon. Wm. R. Spears, Senator for Warren County, died on Saturday night, of consumption.

February 22, 1884

The Hon. Benjamin King died yesterday at his home in Beauregard. He had been in a low state of health for the past two years. He was about sixty years of age.

February 6, 1885

On Wednesday night Mr. Ed Meany, an Irishman employed on the levee, was killed by Capt. Harvey, at Capt. Sullivan's camp, some ten miles below this place. Meany was walking boss, and had been drinking, and his attention to business did not seem satisfactory to Capt. Harvey, who had some words with him during the day. During the night the quarrel was resumed, and resulted in the death of Meany from a gun shot wound. His body was shipped to Memphis, where his family resides. Harvey made his escape.

February 27, 1885

Deputy Sheriff Charles Parmore informed us of the death of Mr. A. B. Foster at Jonestown, on the 22nd, of pneumonia. Mr. Foster is the nephew of Mr. J. A. Laughridge, postmaster at Jonestown.

March 13, 1885

Died at his father's house, near Dublin, Miss., after a brief illness of pneumonia, John N. Sandifer. Deceased was born September 21st, 1862, expired January 7th last, and was just entering his twenty-fourth year. He joined the Missionary Baptist Church, July, 1878.

March 27, 1885

Jacob Thompson died at his residence in Memphis last Tuesday, in the 74th year of his age.

Mr. W. H. Viers, the old and well-known barber of our town, died of pneumonia, the 23rd.

May 1, 1885

Died at Ensley, Tenn., of membranous croup, April 23, 1885, Camille, child of D. B. and Maggie Maynard, and grandchild of F. C. and E. C. Stephenson, aged 1 year and 6 months.

May 29, 1885

Died at his residence in this county, May 22nd, 1885, of congestion, Mr. Samuel Edwards, aged 72 years. Mr. Edwards was born in Iradel County, North Carolina, and was well known as one of the oldest residents in this vicinity.

June 26, 1885

Lake Charles, Miss., June 13th -- A cruel and cowardly murder took place at Malone's on Wednesday last. F. H. West, manager for J. W. Eldridge, on Lake Charles, for some trivial offense, attacked a negro woman with a hoe. She being very strong, took the hoe from him and threw it into the lake. He then drew his pistol, again she proved her strength and succeeded in getting his pistol and threw it into the lake. She got him down and made him promise to let her alone. In the struggle she cut him several times in the face and neck.

As he prided himself on his physical strength, he was teased considerably. The matter rested for near a week, when he determined to kill her. He cut a heavy stick, got W. S. Campbell to go with him and rode up to where she was plowing and commenced his work. She avoided his licks by dodging under his mule, when the stick slipped or he threw it at her, she gathering it, made for him. West deliberately drew his pistol and shot her down, then emptied every chamber in her body while she was on the ground pleading for mercy.

A colored man named Geo. Smith, living on the Hunt place, on the Yazoo Pass, last Saturday, in company with his mother-in-law, proposed to go down to the Pass to fish. Getting a small boat they proceeded. Later in the day Smith returned to his home and reported that she had fallen out of the boat and was drowned, that he had fastened the body to a tree where it could be secured. Neighbors went to get it and found it as he had described. Upon examining the body several wounds on her head and one of her arms broke, showed that she came to her death by violence instead of drowning, and that he had murdered her. The neighbors at once marched the murderer to town and had him lodged in jail.

THE GREENVILLE TIMES
Greenville, Mississippi

January 9, 1875
On Thursday last a difficulty arose between Mr. Will Stone and Mr. T. L. Brown, in which Mr. Brown was shot and killed instantly. Mr. Stone was arrested. The killing occurred in the hardware store of Weatherbee and Brown, and grew out of a disagreement concerning the purchase of a lot by this firm from Mr. Stone. Mr. Brown, taking up a small iron bar, advanced, when Mr. Stone shot him. Only one shot was fired.

January 16, 1875
Died at her residence in Greenville, of pneumonia, on the 13th January, Mrs. L. A. Kirkland.

March 6, 1875
On Sunday night last, on the Courtney place, a colored man named Allen was shot and killed by some person as yet undiscovered. A colored man named Albert Carson was azrrested as the assassin but after examination was discharged.

March 13, 1875

We learn that Mr. R. T. Hardy, proprietor of the Riverton drug store, died at that place March 2, 1875. Mr. Hardy was a native of Glasgow, Scotland, and was about thirty-one years of age. He had resided in Bolivar County for ten years.

March 20, 1875

The Herald brings intelligence of the sudden death of Captain R. M. Brown, of Water Valley, and editor of the *Mississippi Central*, published at that place.

April 3, 1875

Colonel Lewis A. Middleton, editor of *The Times*, was killed by D. L. Love, editor of *The Citizen*, at West Point, Mississippi, on the 25th of March. Middleton had published a paragraph intended as a joke at Love's expense, but the latter took it seriously, and a fight ensued, in which Middleton was killed.

We announce the death of Mrs. Narcisse Lucille, widow of General Wiliam Barksdale. Mrs. Barksdale died at the residence of her son, Ethel, in Yazoo City, on Tuesday morning last, of pneumonia.

We have the painful intelligence of the murder of Colonel D. A. Butterfield, at Hot Springs, Arkansas. Col. Butterfield was a manager of a street railroad and line of stages, and was reproving one of his employees for abusing the animals under his care when another one came up behind the Colonel and struck him on the head, killing him instantly.

May 22, 1875

Hon. John Watts died at Newton, Mississippi on the 19th, aged seventy years. He had been District Attorney for eleven years, Circuit Judge twenty-one years, and had served in both branches of the Legislature.

Entered into rest on the 10th, Mrs. Elizabeth F. Bott, in her fifty-second year. she was born in Chesterfield County, Virginia, March 25, 1823 and resided in Tennessee until her removal with her husband to this State in 1840.

Died at Barnardiston, Washington County, Mississippi, May 6, 1875, Mrs. Mary A. Chotard, widow of the late J. C. Chotard.

Died at the residence of her grandmother, Mrs. Ann Halsey, last week, Hattie, daughter of Dr. D. C. Jackson.

Major John P. Strange, well known as Ajutant General of Forrest's cavalry brigade, died at his residence in Memphis on the 17th. He had been an invalid for some weeks.

June 12, 1875
Died in Greenville on the 8th, Dr. Fox. The deceased was a native of Warren County, Miss. and a son of the Rev. J. Fox, of that county.

Died at the LaGrange place in Washington Co., on the 8th, Mr. N. Merrill, of Lake Providence, Louisiana.

June 26, 1875
Died at the residence of his brother, L. J. Comstock, at Bergen Point, New Jersey, on June 13, 1875, Elisha J. Comstock of Greenville, Miss., aged 31 years, 8 months and 10 days.

July 10, 1875
Died at the residence of Dr. J. A. Morson, on Deer Creek, on July the 4th, Mr. John B. Aickman.

July 17, 1875
Died in Greenville, Mississippi, after a lingering illness, on the 14th day of July, 1875, Mrs. Mary A. Beck, wife of J. G. Beck.

July 24, 1875
Died at Glenora place in this county, on the 17th, Grant Williams, of paralysis.

By the *Carrollton Conservative* we learn of the death of Dr. Liddell, at his home in Carroll County.

Brutus Johnson was shot and killed by Jerry Myers in Issaquena County, July 14th. The deceased was the employer of Jerry Myers and the trouble grew out of a squabble concerning the crop. Myers was arrested; both colored.

August 21, 1875
Died near Washington City, on the 11th of August, Major Robt. H. Archer. The deceased is the father of W. H. Archer and Mrs. Mary Brown, of our town.

October 2, 1875
Died in Greenville, Miss., on the 28th of September, 1875, Mr. William J. Davis, aged 42 years. The deceased was born in Wellsburg, Virginia. He served as a soldier of the Confederate Army, first in the 21st Mississippi regiment, and afterwards in Rice's Battery.

On Wednesday night last two men from the "colony" named Wm. M. Morgan, aged 35 years, and W. Luther Ervin, aged 22 years, were murdered near Fish lake bridge. The murder was committed with an axe whilst the men were asleep, they having camped out on their way home. Suspicion at once attached to a negro man named Columbus Vernon in the company of the murdered men frequently.

October 9, 1875

Died in Washington County, Miss., September 29, 1875, Nellie Virginia, eldest daughter of J. C. and R. C. Estill, aged one year, ten months and 24 days.

October 16, 1875

Died at her residence near Greenville, October 15th, 1875, Mrs. Laura Sutton, wife of J. M. Sutton, for many years a resident of this county.

Died October the 7th, at the residence of his father, Col. J. N. Collier, Payton Knox, eldest son of J. N. and S. C. Collier, in his 23rd year.

December 11, 1875

Died at his residence at Auburn, Dr. Peters, on the 10th. He will be buried from his house the 12th, at 11:00 A. M.

December 18, 1875

On last Tuesday morning the notorious colored lawyer, J. D. Werles, drowned himself from the Greenville wharf-boat. He walked on the boat and asked a couple of dray-drivers "if they ever saw anyone commit suicide?" They replied "No" when he said, "Well watch me," and leaped into the river. He was in domestic and financial difficulties.

Died after a short illness, December 10, 1875, at her late residence, Deer Creek, Miss., Mrs. R. C. Estill, wife of James C. Estill, aged 28 years, 7 months and 14 days.

December 25, 1875

A man named Patrick Murray was killed in front of Kennedy & Hanway's saloon on Thursday last. He was one of a party of Irish laborers, as was James Cooney, who killed him. The stabbed man died immediately. Cooney was arrested.

February 12, 1876

Died on the 7th, J. J. McMurry, of this place.

May 27, 1876

Died at the residence of her uncle, Leon Moyse, in Greenville, Miss., May 24, 1876, after a short illness, Harriet Moyse, aged 20 years.

Died March 29th, at his residence in central Montgomery Co., Virginia, of pneumonia, Captain J. R. Hammet.

June 17, 1876

On Judge Buckner's place, near Auburn, one day this week, a colored man named Sam. Morton was drawing a seine through water near the levee, when he stepped into a deep hole and was drowned.

On Sunday last, a negro woman named Patterson, living on W. M. Worthington's place, was thrown from a wagon and killed.

July 15, 1876

Died on board the steamer *Capitol City* at Memphis, on the 7th, A. W. Webber.

September 2, 1876

Died on the 29th of August, in his 24th year, after a short illness, at Stoneville, Washington County, Miss., Sigmund Mayer. When a child he came with his parents to America and lived until some three years since, in Vicksburg.

Died in Greenville, August 30th, Lula C. Yager, only daughter of Andrew and Margaret Yager.

Died in Greenville, August 28th, Cam. M. Robinson, son of Mrs. J. H. Young, of Riverton, Bolivar County, Mississippi.

Died in Greenville, August 24th, Bettie Archer, infant daughter of Rev. S. and Anna P. Archer.

Died in Greenville, August 31st, Davis B. Trigg, infant son of W. R. Trigg.

Died in Greenville, August 30th, Wm. H. Small, aged about 12 years.

September 9, 1876

On Wednesday afternoon, September 6, 1876, sorrowing friends conveyed to the tomb the body of N. B. Johnson. (Author's note - a lengthy obituary followed).

Died on the 5th, Mr. Jno. S. Hudson, of this county, who has lived for several years in Sunflower County.

Died on the 9th, in Greenville, J. L. Quinlan, for several years an officer on the wharf-boat.

September 18, 1876

Died on September 5th, in Jackson, Mississippi, Hon. Ephraim G. Payton, late Chief Justice of Mississippi, aged 74 years. For forty years he lived and practiced law in Copiah County.

September 23, 1876

Died in Greenville, Miss., on September 20, 1876, Mrs. S. J. Rucks.

September 30, 1876

Died on 21st, at Hot Springs, Arkansas, George B. Medley, of Liverpool and the Greenville Cotton Seed Mills. Mr. Medley was a native of Liverpool, England and came to Greenville about six months ago after purchasing the seed mill and ginnery of J. B. Cole.

Died at his residence in this county, on 28th August, Henry Melchor.

October 7, 1876

Died at his residence near Greenville, on the 4th, Mr. W. P. Montgomery, in the 27th year of his age. Mr. Montgomery was born in 1800 in South Carolina. He came to this county in 1828, where he has ever since resided. He leaves a widow and a large family of children.

Died at his residence near Greenville, October 6, 1876, Mr. John Kanatzer, who for ten years has been a citizen of this neighborhood.

October 21, 1876

Died in Greenville, October 20, 1876, Isadore, infant son of L. and H. Schlesinger, aged twenty months.

December 2, 1876

Died in Greenville, 22nd November, Rachel, infant daughter of Louis and Huldah Schlesinger, in the third year of her age.

December 16, 1876

Died at his residence in Washington County, after a long illness, on the 11th, John B. Mosby.

January 6, 1877

Several weeks ago an account was given of the tragic end of Captain James B. Harvey, a few moments after he debarked from the steamer *Cheek*, near Austin, Tunica County, Mississippi; also how he had received a decoy letter and had at once taken passage on the vessel destined to Austin.

Some days ago John M. Ragan, who keeps a saloon at Austin, also Dr. P. E. Chapman, who married a neice of Mrs. Manning, and one Harold Christenstein, were arrested at Austin on suspicion of having been accessory too the murder. All three confessed to the fact of their presence at the scene of the murder, but state that Manning fired the shot that laid Harvey low, that they had been summoned as a posse and that they did not suspect his design to kill Harvey. The impression in Austin is that an intimacy had previously existed between Harvey and Mrs. Manning. Mrs. Manning has also been arrested on a charge of being implicated in the taking of Harvey. Sheriff Manning was arrested in Jackson, Miss.

The death of John McMecklin occurred in Greenville on the 5th of January, 1877. Mr. McMecklin was a merchant in old Greenville before the war. Mr. McMecklin fell a victim to pneumonia.

January 13, 1877
Hon. Wm. R. Barksdale, Representative from Grenada County, died at his residence in that county, Jan. 10.

February 10, 1877
Died at his residence at Omega Landing, Madison Parish, La., February 4, 1877, Capt. W. R. Stone, aged thirty-seven years.

George L. Potter is no more. He died suddenly of apoplexy, at Lexington, Holmes County, Mississippi, whither he had gone to attend the Chancery Court. Judge P. was a native of Vermont, but for the last thirty years a citizen of Jackson, Miss. He leaves one daughter, who is married, and three sons. He was at the time of his death, probably near sixty years old.

March 3, 1877
Died in Greenville, March 1, 1877, William H. Harrison, aged about fifty years, and for five or six years past a resident of this place.

April 28, 1877
Died on the 16th April, 1877, at the plantation of J. Q. Wills, Mr. C. H. Burt, aged 37. He was a native of New York, but for many years a resident of Mississippi.

Moses B. Black, founder and pastor of Mount Horeh, colored Baptist Church in Greenville, died at his residence on the 26th.

James M. McKay, an old man from Winston County, Mississippi, died in this town yesterday. He was a blacksmith and had been at work on some of the plantations near town.

May 26, 1877
The Harrodsburg (Kentucky) Observer of May 18th contains the announcement of the death of the wife of Mr. Ed. V. Ferguson, formerly of Greenville. - Died in Harrodsburg, May 15th, Willette, wife of E. V. Ferguson. The death of Mrs. Ferguson was an unexpected shock.

August 4, 1877

A letter from our former townsman, Mr. Lee Hexter, now of Cleveland, Ohio, we learn of the death of his little daughter, Clara Estella, under circumstances of a peculiar nature. At eight o'clock in the evening Mr. & Mrs. Hexter left their house to visit a neighbor, leaving their children in perfect health; and on their return at ten o'clock found little Clara in a dying condition. The parents can form no idea of the cause.

August 11, 1877

Died at the residence of Mr. John Manifold, in Greenville, Miss., on August 9th, 1877, Mr. Robert Davenport, in the 47th year of his age. "Uncle Bob", as he was affectionately called by those who knew him, was for many years a citizen of Jefferson Co., Miss. moving there as early as 1832. He came to this county in 1855. He was a contractor and builder.

August 23, 1877

Died at Refuge, Washington County, Mississippi, August 20th, 1877, Walter E. Davis. The deceased came to the United States from London, England, and had resided in this county for nearly three years.

September 1, 1877

Died at Skipwith, August 24th, of congestive chill, Leon Goldstein, in the 21st year of his age. The deceased was born in New Orleans, where his mother resides. He was the eldest son.

October 27, 1877

Died in Greenville, October 26th, 1877, Esther, youngest daughter of Jacob Alexander.

November 3, 1877

A telegram from Richmond, Va. announces that our fellow citizen, Hon. Geo. T. Swann, died very suddenly in that city yesterday morning, of apoplexy. The Judge and his wife went to Virginia a few months since in quest of health.

November 17, 1877

Died at his home on Deer Creek in this county, Mr. W. F. Smith, on the 3rd. Mr. Smith was one of the oldest citizens of this county.

December 1, 1877

Died at the residence of Dr. D. C. Montgomery, in this county, November 29, Charles Montgomery, aged 19 years. The deceased was the son of Eugene Montgomery of Bolivar County, and the grandson of Ex-Governor Charles Clark.

December 22, 1877
Died at his plantation in Bolivar County, on the 18th, Ex-Governor Charles Clark, a native, we believe, of Ohio, but a resident of this State since his early manhood, first in Jefferson, afterward in Bolivar County.

December 29, 1877
Died, Mrs. Jane E. Courtney, at her residence at Oakland plantation on Deer Creek, December 25th, 1877. Mrs. Courtney was the widow of the late Jno. Courtney, a respected citizen of this county.

January 5, 1878
Died in Greenville, Miss., on the 2nd of January, 1878, after a lingering illness, F. X. Schmalholz, in the 48th year of his age. He was formerly a merchant tailor in New Orleans, but for six or seven years engaged in business here.

Died at his residence on Deer Creek in Washington County, on the 25th of December, 1877, of pneumonia, Mr. George P. Waine.

February 9, 1878
Died at Skipwith, in Issaquena County, on the 7th, H. A. Glidden. Doctor Glidden, as he was commonly known, was a native of Malta, and about sixty years old. For nearly twenty years past he has lived here, and served in the war in a company raised here.

On last Saturday evening, at Clarksdale in this county, a man by the name of Jordan, assaulted Bud Ellis, beating him over the head with the butt end of a pistol. It was reported to a younger brother of Bud, that Jordan was killing his brother, whereupon the lad rushed in and shot Jordan dead. (Coahomian)

April 27, 1878
Died at his residence in Rosedale, Bolivar County, the 22nd, W. R. Campbell, in the 37th year of his age, of inflammation of the bowels. Mr. Campbell was a native of this county, where his mother and sisters now live, and at the time of his death Sheriff of Bolivar County. He leaves a wife and five children.

May 4, 1878
Died at Linden Place on Lake Washington, in this county, the 3rd, Miss Anna Fitzsimmons Hampton, only child of Mr. Christopher F. Hampton.

May 11, 1878
Among the passengers on the *James D. Parker*, when she left Memphis last trip, was a young man named Dr. J. W. Rogers, who came from some point in Mississippi. He appeared to be in good

health, the first morning he was suddenly taken with a congestive chill. During the spell of vomiting he ruptured a blood vessel and before the boat reached Cairo he was a corpse. The gentleman is believed to be Dr. J. W. Parker, of Deer Creek, in this county.

June 22, 1878

Died at the residence of her husband, Dr. Gerdine, on Deer Creek, Mrs. Sallie West Gerdine, on the 17th. On the 2nd of September last she stood by the altar, a blushing bride. She died in the communion of the Methodist Church.

Died at Blount Springs, in Alabama recently, Maj. Charles Edmondson, of Bolivar County, (Miss.), formerly of St. Louis. Maj. Edmondson served during the late war on General Bowen's staff.

Died at her father's residence near Greenville, on the 21st, Kate, infant daughter of S. W. and M. A. Montgomery.

July 6, 1878

Isaac Freeman, drayman for L. Wilkowski & Co., while endeavoring to dip a bucket of water from the river on Tuesday evening last, fell in and drowned. His body has not been recovered. He was an old colored man.

July 13, 1878

Died at the Peabody Hotel, in Memphis, on the 6th, Mrs. B. T. Worthington, of Leota, in this county.

Died at Loughborough plantation, on Williams Bayou, in this county, on the 7th, Mr. L. H. Mosby. The deceased was a native of this county.

Died at Beersheba Springs, on the 4th, Mrs. Morgan, of Lake Washington.

Dr. Jackson, a physician in the neighborhood of Bernard, Arkansas, was shot and killed there on Saturday last, by a man named Hollis, a hotel keeper. Jackson was drinking and wanted to borrow Hollis's horse. Being refused, he became insulting, and Hollis shot a load of buckshot into him. Hollis has been arrested.

September 14, 1878

List of Deaths to Date (Yellow Fever epidemic)
Aug. 23 - Mabry, girl, 4 years old, white
    25 - Dave Woodruff, colored
    30 - Perry, boy, white
    31 - Pat Finnegan, man, white
Sept. 1 - Wm. Marshall, man, white
    2 - Mat Fox, man, colored

2 - E. J. Eyrne, young man, white
2 - John Simpson, man, white
2 - D. E. Brooks, man, white
2 - Mrs. D. Morris, white
2 - Rebecca Morgan, girl, col.
3 - Pryor, girl, child, white
3 - Jonas Houston, man, col.
3 - Maria, cook at Newman's
4 - C. Bathkee, white
4 - Mrs. Fannie Brooks, white
4 - J. A. Chiesa, Mrs. Storey's child, girl, 5 years old, white
3 - Fred Perry, boy, white
4 - Mrs. James Perry, white
4 - Sow Lee, chinaman
- Mark Kyle, man, colored
5 - Ed McKenzy, man. col.
5 - Scott, girl, white
- Josephine Fox, girl, white
- Mrs. Thos. Mowbry, white
- Mrs. Hattie Jones, colored
- Lyman Stowell, man, white
- Hiram Pulman, young man, white
5 - W. A. Haycraft, man, white
6 - Mrs. M. Morris, white
6 - Elijah Gray, man, colored
6 - Jerry Strather, man, col.
6 - Philip Barnet, man, white
6 - Miss Willie Scott, white
6 - Milton Jones, man, white
6 - Caroline Zeigler, woman, col.
7 - Eliza Belfield, colored
7 - Col. C. E. Morgan, white
7 - Mrs. A. Cox, white
7 - James Perry, white
- Capitola Harris, colored girl
7 - Wm. Telfer, white
7 - Emma Duvall, white
8 - Chas. Huntley, white
8 - Jas. Young, colored
8 - Julius Ratchlitz, white
8 - Maj. Alexander, colored
8 - Beontine White, girl, col.
8 - Mrs. Nellie Gray, colored
8 - J. Winker(?), in country
8 - Richard McCullough
8 - Jas. Carney, white
8 - Chas. Irving, colored
8 - Winnie Smith, colored

8 - Griffin Guy, colored
8 - Mrs. Young, white
9 - Dave Harris, colored
9 - Edward Calfall, white
9 - Mrs. Geo. Sanford, white
9 - Mrs. J. S. Ballard, white
9 - Burden Balm, colored
9 - Mrs. F. P. Smith, white
9 - Geo. Stream, white
10 - Mrs. Shorey, white
10 - Geo. Bird, white
10 - Mrs. K. A. Ballard, white
10 - Henry Harris, colored
10 - Fred Pryor, white
10 - Chas. Shaws, colored
10 - Boynton Houston, colored
10 - Dr. Stafford, white
10 - Aleck, butcher, white
10 - Luis Ware, colored
11 - Willie Caffall, white
11 - Mrs. Julia Pogle, white
11 - Louisa Massey, white
11 - Lizzie Johnson, colored
11 - Mrs. T. P. Perry, white
11 - Abe Smith, man, white
11 - Emma Hawkins, colored
11 - Eva Weatherbee, girl, white
11 - Elliott Dodge, man, white
11 - John Bannion, man, colored
11 - Wm. Brown, man, colored
11 - George Dorman, man, white
11 - Steve Sutton, man, white
12 - Louis Coffall, man, white
12 - Louis Radjesky, man, white
12 - Mrs. Beck, woman, white
12 - Mrs. Fletcher, white
12 - Mrs. Trammel, white
   - Theo. Harbicht, man, white
12 - Mrs. L. P. Wetherbee, white
13 - Mrs. E. Hasberg, white
13 - Walter Quck, man, white
13 - Steinberg, man, white
13 - Wash Walker, man, colored
13 - Mrs. S. A. Platt, white
13 - Willie Ebles, child, white
13 - H. B. Putman, man, white
13 - Mrs. Wm. Eblers, white
13 - Dr. V. F. P. Alexander, white

13 - Robt. Cooper, man, white
13 - James McCann, man, white

September 21, 1878
List of Deaths, cont'd. (Yellow Fever epidemic)
Sept. 14 - Raphael Marshall, white
14 - Jas. Miuzles, white
15 - Rev. D. C. Green, white
15 - Walter B. Butler, white
15 - Thos. McLean, white
15 - Frank Wagner, white
15 - J. Radlesky, white
15 - Long Hon, chinaman
15 - Jake Husk, colored
15 - Bennie Diggs, white
15 - Wm. Taylor, white
15 - Henrietta Rogers, colored
15 - Toll Underwood, colored
15 - Chas. Bigelow, colored
16 - Ella Jones, child, colored
16 - Mrs. Ballard, white
16 - Chas. Boswick, white
16 - Jas. H. Buckner, white
16 - Jas. Davidson, white
16 - Stephen Green, white
16 - Jas. Connell, white
16 - Mary Jones, colored
16 - Thos. Kyle, white
16 - Mrs. F. Pryor, white
16 - Mrs. H. Bathke, white
16 - Joe Badwick, white
16 - Jackson Hayes, colored
16 - Bigelo, child, white
16 - Mrs. Habichi, white
16 - Henry Laurens, white
16 - Gus Forrester, white
17 - Frank Gallagher, white
17 - John Ballard, baby, white
17 - D. E. Young, colored
17 - Mrs. M. Slevers, white
17 - Anna Platt, white
17 - Gus Coughler, white
17 - Geo. Brown, colored
17 - Helen Finley, white
17 - Frank P. Smith, white
18 - Henry Freundt, white
18 - Willie Harris, boy, colored
18 - Mrs. L. Polle, white
18 - Wm. Ehlers, white

18 - W. L. Porter, white
18 - John S. Ballard, white
18 - Willie B. White, white
18 - Nellie Warden, white
18 - John Ralph, white
18 - Margaret Williams, colored
18 - N. J. Nelson, white
18 - M. Morris, white
18 - W. P. Kretsehmar, white
18 - Leonard Phillips, colored
18 - Abe Wall, white
18 - W. J. Mauley, white
18 - T. P. Perry, white
18 - Tom Sylvester, white
18 - Mary Jarvers, colored
18 - Caroline Marks, colored
18 - Chas. Williams, white
18 - Fanny Diggs, white
18 - Calvin Kelter, colored
19 - Lou Hanian, colored
19 - Don Shannahan, white
19 - Elvira Blackburn, colored
19 - Mrs. J. S. Barnhurst, white
19 - Dave Morris, white
19 - Ben Sands, colored
19 - M. Duffy, white
19 - Alex Moray, colored
20 - Albert Wheeler, white
20 - Mrs. T. B. Shaw, white
20 - Mrs. John Small, white
20 - John Siinpendorter, white
20 - L. Welizenfeldt, white
20 - Thos. Miggins, white
20 - John Barchurst, white
20 - Julius Lochman, white
21 - ___ Tremble, white

September 28, 1878
List of Deaths, cont'd. (Yellow Fever epidemic)
Sept. 22 - Jas. McLean, man, white
22 - Margaret French, colored
22 - Jas. Kinstler, man, white
22 - A. B. Trigg, man, white
22 - Jacob Watts, man, colored
22 - Eliza J. Clark, girl, colored
23 - Arthur R. Yerger, white
23 - Annie Berry, girl, white
23 - Adolphe Fleischer, white
23 - L. P. Weatherbee, man, white

110

23 - Amelia Kiastler, girl, white
23 - Helen Bailey, babe, colored
23 - Lorenzo Griffin, man, colored
23 - Henry Vaughn, man, white
24 - Emma Pernel, woman, col.
24 - Chas. Griffin, man, colored
24 - ___ Perry, child, white
24 - Anderson Greathouse, col.
24 - Mrs. L. M. Flournoy, col.
24 - Fanny Kelly, woman, white
25 - J. Gossett, man, white
25 - Garrett Scott, woman, white
25 - Steve Stewart, woman, colored
25 - A. Fleischer, woman, white
25 - Mrs. G. W. Elliott, white
25 - John Manifold, man, white
25 - Abe Hamburger, boy, white
26 - ___ Pryor, child, white
26 - Bertha Morris, girl, colored
26 - Forest Barr, man, colored
26 - C. F. Melsner, man, white
26 - Rachel Radjesky, girl, white
26 - Mrs. A. Ward, woman, white
27 - Alice Grant, woman, col.
27 - Dick Cheatham, man, col.
27 - Nancy J. Smith, woman, col.
27 - Louisa Bodky, girl, white
27 - Gus Gregory, man, colored
28 - L. E. Morgan, man, white
28 - Geo. W. Claiborne, child, col.
28 - Pat Burnes, man, white
28 - Rachel Amberg, colored
28 - Infant child of W. J. French

October 5, 1878
List of Deaths, cont'd. (Yellow Fever epidemic)
Sept. 28 - Sophia Yocum, white
28 - Geo. Brazier, man, white
28 - W. Tilley, Jr., man, white
28 - T. B. Speaks, man, white
29 - Mrs. L. Weisenfeldt, white
29 - John H. Nelson, man, white
29 - Eliza Kress, white
29 - Helen Shaw, girl, white
30 - Wes. Weatherbee, white
30 - J. M. Sanders, colored
30 - Marshall Woodson, colored
30 - Henry Thornton, colored
30 - Mary White, colored

Oct. 1 - L. M. Langley, white
1 - Mrs. Mitchel, white
1 - J. H. Sanders' child, colored
1 - Minnie Kielher, girl, white
1 - Mrs. Stafford, white
1 - Mary A. Cook, colored
2 - Rev. T. Page, white
2 - Lena Herman, girl, white
2 - Jake Bier, white
2 - Louisa Clarke, colored
3 - Dr. J. S. McCall, white
3 - Alex Johnson, colored
3 - Milton Kelter, man, colored
4 - M. W. Johnson, white
4 - Cesar Manger, colored
4 - Walter S. Berry, child, white
4 - Rosa Edingburg, colored
4 - Mrs. James, woman, white
4 - Monroe Fletcher, colored
5 - G. W. Elliott, man, white
5 - Nancy Keene, woman, col.
5 - King Hinds, man, col.

Deaths in the county:
Stoneville - Henry Monk, man, white
Henry Lemler, man, white
Blanche Marainski, child, white
M. J. Morzinski, man, white
___ Morzinski, baby, white
Mrs. Marcella Hartman, white
D. L. Stone, man, white
Dr. A. S. Gerdine, man, white
Winterville - John Winter, man, white
C. K. McAllister, man, white
Mrs. A. W. McAllister, white
Sherisy Whiter, boy, white
Mrs. Wm. Montgomery, white
Dr. Wm. Montgomery, man, white
Pat McKeon, white
Mrs. Dan Shannahan, white

October 19, 1878
List of Deaths cont'd. (Yellow Fever epidemic)
Oct. 5 - Dan Johnson, man, colored
5 - Thos. McMorris, colored
6 - Dr. Archer, man, white
7 - Mary Ann Barr, girl, col.
7 - Mable Wetherbee, white
7 - Inf. child of D. Morris

    8 - Mrs. Greenfield, white
    8 - Perry Ellis, man, colored
    8 - Infant child of Eugene Johnson
   10 - Oscar Smith, man, colored
   11 - Wm. Myers, man, white
   11 - Geo. R. Clark, white
   12 - Fred Johnson, boy, white

Deaths in county:
Winterville - Dr. Kirby, man, white
           Frank Lawson, colored
           J. E. Everitte, man, white
Colored man at C. H. Smith's
Ida, child of Sam Brown
Mrs. Ph. McLean
Mrs. Rebecca Melvin, white

October 19, 1878
List of Deaths, cont'd. (Yellow Fever epidemic)
Oct. 15 - John Cotrell, man, white
     15 - Infant child of John Rice, col.
     15 - Infant child of Dan Wilson, col.
     15 - Thos. Johnson, boy, white

October 26, 1878
List of Deaths, cont'd. (Yellow Fever epidemic)
Oct. 19 - Philis Carter, colored
     20 - Emma Childs, white
     21 - Loyd Talibert, colored
     21 - Margaret Freeman, colored
     22 - Ah Ways, chinaman
     24 - Addaline Geinelle, white

Deaths in county:
Stoneville - Mrs. Lamkin, white, at Burdett's
Winterville - Eddie Winters, boy, white
           Robt. Bolding/Holding, colored

Sam Crocket, white
B. F. Foley, at Refuge
John Byrne, white
Dr. Oden, white
J. W. Hill, white
Henry Jones, white
Chany Edmondson, colored

November 16, 1878
Died in New Orleans, during the recent epidemic of yellow fever, John Hampton Sims, aged 17 years and 8 months. The

deceased was a son of Mrs. Sims and a brother of R. L. Sims, formerly of Greenville.

November 23, 1878

We regret to announce the death, during the week, at his residence on Deer Creek, of Mr. O. C. Rives, senior.

January 25, 1879

Died near Greenville, Miss., on the 17th of January, 1879, Caleb Mennifield, a mail agent of Warrenton, Warren County, Mississippi, but for the past two years a resident of Greenville.

Died at Leesburg, on Deer Creek, in Washington County, Mississippi, January 11th, 1879, a white man, pauper, by the name of William Gilmore, said to be from Giles County, Tennessee.

February 1, 1879

Yesterday morning, Mr. A. B. Heslip, Sheriff of Claiborne County, breathed his last, after a week of severe illness.

February 15, 1879

Died in Greenville, on the 8th, R. A. Farmer, of pneumonia.

April 23, 1879

At Austin, Tunica County, Mississippi, on the 16th, Mr. W. A. Granthal struck M. J. Jones, City Marshall, with a bridle. The latter drew a revolver and shot Granthal, killing him instantly. Jones was arrested.

Vicksburg Herald, 19th -- A fatal shooting affray occurred this morning. Mr. John Dent and Captain Jack Brereton, of the city police force, has some words, which resulted in a resort to arms. Three or four shots were fired, one took effect in Mr. John Dent's head causing death almost instantly. Captain Brereton received a ball in his right shoulder.

May 17, 1879

Pascagoula Star -- Last Tuesday, during the rain and thunder storm, Mr. John Williamson met his death. During the storm Mr. Williamson and seven other men were moving timber of some kind on Dog river at Moss Point. Lightening struck a tree near by and all the men were more or less shocked by the electricity. Mr. Williamson received a severer shock than the rest, fell into the river and sank. Whether he was killed by lightening or drowned no one knows.

July 12, 1879

We regret to learn of the death of the oldest daughter of Major H. J. Feltus, at his home on Deer Creek, on the 10th.

Last Sunday evening Julius Fleetwood shot and killed Dock Owens at Fern Springs, in Winston County. He took Owen's pistol from him and shot him twice, the second time in the head, inflicting a fatal wound.

August 23, 1879

Died at Woodstock, in this county, August 14th, 1879, in the 7th year of her age, Mary Thurston Randolph, daughter of W. F. and Nannie B. Randolph.

September 20, 1879

Died on London plantation, Washington County, Mississippi, the residence of W. M. Worthington, September 17, 1879, Miss Carlile Stone, formerly of Richmond, Kentucky.

November 22, 1879

Dr. J. S. Walker was recently called to Richmond, Kentucky, by reason of the illness of his father, who is now, as we learn, dead. Mr. Walker was quite an old man.

Our citizens regret to learn of the death of Mr. Augustus Davis, who came here during the epidemic of 1878 in charge of the New Orleans nurses. He died recently in New Orleans.

Died on the 5th of November, 1879, at Duncansby, Issaquena County, Miss., Mary B. Turnbulll, widow of the late Frederick G. Turnbull, aged 73 years.

December 20, 1879

Died at Woodstock, in this county, on the 16th of December, W. F. Watson. Mr. Watson was a son of Judge Watson, of Montgomery, Alabama. He had planted on the Mississippi river for several years.

January 3, 1880

On Christmas Day a negro man named Marshall Cross made an assault upon Mr. Phil Buckner, in the store of Mr. Jewell, where he is employed as clerk. Mr. Buckner shot and killed his assailant with a pistol. The magistrate, J. H. Robb, decided the killing to be self-defense.

January 10, 1880

Died on the 5th day of January, at his home on Bogue Phalia, in this county, in the 60th year of his age, of pneumonia, Nathan A. Heard. Mr. Heard was a native of Georgia, but for nearly half a century had been a citizen of this State.

January 31, 1880
W. Allen, aged 19 years, son of D. A. Love of this county, died suddenly of congestion, on the night of the 26th.

Died on the 14th, at the Wildwood plantation of General Hampton, on Lake Washington, Mr. W. G. Tutt, aged 70.

February 14, 1880
Cowles Meade Vaiden, one of Mississippi's most public spirited citizens, died after a lingering illness, at his home in Carroll County, February 6.

March 6, 1880
Died in Minneapolis, Minnesota, on the 19th of February, 1880, Mrs. H. Mary Irish, widow of the late Henry T. Irish, and mother of Mr. Henry T. Irish, of Greenville, Miss., aged 73 years.

March 27, 1880
Early Thursday morning the boiler in Morgan's mill discovered the dead body of Albert Otterbein. He was a Swede and had been in the employ of the mill. It is supposed that he had climbed up on top of the boiler to sleep, and had rolled off and broke his neck by the fall.
Amongst the curious who went to examine the body of Otterbein, was Charles Schephner, a Swede also, but an old citizen of the county. After leavng the mill, Mr. ___ walked upon a raft near by, and finding a colored man there dipping a net, he asked if the water was deep; and being told that it was, took off his hat, bade the colored man "good bye" and plunged into the river. He was seen to swim or float for some distance, then deliberately bury his head in the water and disappear from sight.

April 3, 1880
The soul of Joseph Cassing, was on April 1st, 1880, wafted into the presence of his Creator, in his third year.

Died on the 27th day of March, 1880, in the city of Brooklyn, New York, John S. Penrice, in the 69th year of his age; over fifty years of which was passed in this county. He was widely known for the excellant character of the hotel he long kept, first at Princeton, then at old Greenville.

April 10, 1880
Died in Greenville, April 8th, 1880, of abcess of the liver, William G. Andrews, of Salem, Alabama.

New Orleans, April 5 -- Mrs. Elenora Hennen, widow of the late Duncan N. Hennen and mother of the late Mrs. J. B. Hood, died today, aged 62 years.

April 24, 1880

Died on Keystone plantation, near Egg's Point, in this county, on the 21st, Mr. Samuel Able. The deceased's father was an old citizen of the county.

May 15, 1880

Died in New Orleans, on the 13th, Adedese Farrar Lee, wife of John M. Lee, of this county.

May 22, 1880

A special dispatch to the *Vicksburg Herald*, dated at Starkville, Mississippi, May 17th, says that an old Baptist preacher, by the name of Jim Henry (colored) was shot and killed near that town, on the 16th, by a colored gentleman named Scott Bell. Cause: the "gospel sharp" had loved, "not wisely, but too well," the charming Mrs. Bell. Mr. B. didn't like the arrangement and so he emptied two loads of buckshot into the old sinner, and hid his carcass in the brush.

June 19, 1880

Died at Northwood, Washington County, Mississippi, June 12, 1880, Alice Maude Mary Ede, only daughter of Joshua and Eliza Ede, aged 5 months and 1 days.

This morning, from Hinds County, we glean particulars of the lamented death of Governor Brown. It appears that his wife was quite unwell and needed the services of a physician. The Governor mounted a horse and rode into Terry, some two miles distance, and secured a physician, who returned with him. Reaching home, he told the doctor to go on to the house and that he would ride to the pond, water his horse, and follow him in a few minutes. In a short time the riderless horse passed the house, and search being made for the Governor, his lifeless body was found in the water where he had fallen. He had twice before had slight attacks of apoplexy, and the rapid ride of four miles under the intense heat, no doubt caused a more severe attack, in which he fell from his saddle and perished.

June 26, 1880

Died at his home near Arcola, in this county, June 23rd, 1880, Levin Henry Collier, in the 51st year of his age. The deceased was a native of Worcester County, Maryland, but for thirty-four years a citizen of Washington County, Mississippi.

Died at Friar's Point, Mississippi, at the residence of her son-in-law, D. A. Scott, on the 16th, Mrs. E. B. Yerger, the wife of Col. Alex Yerger, of Rosedale, Bolivar County, Mississippi, aged 51 years and 11 months. Mrs. E. B. Yerger had a sister, Mrs. F. Valiant, and a brother, Mr. L. T. Rucks.

October 8, 1881

Died in Greenville, October 4th, 1881, Mrs. Mary E. Gildart, wife of Town Marshall W. K. Gildart.

Died, Mrs. Amanda Worthington, aged 76, at her residence on Lake Lee, Wayside plantation, October 5th, 1881. She was the mother of Messers. W. M. and S. Worthington, Mrs. Jas. Stone and Mrs. Davis Buckner.

Mr. Jas. C. Moore died at the residence of Mr. Jno. McCutchen, on Deer Creek, October 6th, 1881. The deceased was a brother of Mr. John Moore, of the firm of A. B. Finley & Co.

Ruby Anderson, daughter of Mr. & Mrs. Lomax Anderson, aged 7 years, died at their home on Deer Creek.

Died at the Glenmary plantation, on the 7th, Mrs. Wright, wife of Mr. G. M. Wright.

October 15, 1881

Died October 10th, 1881, William Jason Walker, infant son of Dr. J. S. and Belle Orville Walker, aged 1 year and 17 days.

October 29, 1881

Died in Gainesville, Texas, October 22nd, William P. Green, in the 24th year of his age. Mr. Green had but a short time since removed from Greenville to Texas. Mr. Green was a native of Port Gibson.

November 28, 1881

Fulton, Miss. -- A fatal accident occurred on Saturday last, six miles north of this place. Two young men, J. W. Chilcote and R. T. Senter, neighbors and freinds, were out turkey hunting, neither knowing the others whereabouts. Mr. Chilcote had killed a turkey, but hearing, as he supposed, another yelping, began to call, at the same time standing behind a fence and placing the turkey he had on top of the fence. Mr. Senter supposed the "call" to be a turkey, approached carefully to within shooting distance, and seeing the turkey on the fence, fired. It fell. When he reached the place he saw that he had not only hit the turkey, but the ball had passed through the body of the game and struck the head of his friend who lay there dead. No one attaches any blame to Senter, as we learn from Mr. W. H. Rouse, brother-in-law of the deceased.

December 10, 1881

At the store of Ford & Peak, in Arkansas, a few miles below here, on Saturday night last, Dr. McGavock has a difficulty, amounting to blows, with a negro man who lived on the Sunnyside plantation. The negro armed himself with a shot-gun and went to the store where the deceased was; and as soon as he appeared at the door shot him fatally in the breast. Dr. McGavock was a native of Tennessee and had lived near Sunnyside for several years. His remains have been taken to his father's home in Tennessee.

Woodville, Miss., Nov. 25 -- Dr. David Holt died today, aged 89. He was a veteran of the War of 1812, and for 81 years was a physician in this county.

The *Lexington Advertiser* gives particulars of the assassination of Mr. Catlin, on Yazoo river in Leflore County. It seems that when the merchant Lowenstein was murdered five or six years ago, Mr. Catlin had the river dragged and Lowenstein's body found. The murder of Catlin was a direct sequel to that of Lowenstein. Craig Jordan had stolen Mr. C's skiff and anticipated prosecution for that offense.

Parker Jordan, who was Craig's uncle, told Craig that Catlin had hunted up the evidence on which the two negroes were hung for killing Lowenstein, and that he had received a part of the goods taken from Lowenstein's store and had promised those two negroes that if they were hung he would see that Catlin was killed for the part he had taken in prosecuting them.

December 17, 1881

Died at Wayside plantation, in Washington County, on the 15th, Davis Buckner, Esq. Mr. Buckner had been an invalid for a long time.

December 31, 1881

Died in Greenville, December 30th, 1881, Clemmence, daughter of Jacob and Henrietta Hirsch, aged about two years.

January 7, 1882

On last Tuesday night Mr. Chas. Soens shot and killed a man named Bates, at the Landau store on Deer Creek. Bates came to the store, of which Soens was in charge, somewhat intoxicated. There were a number of negroes present and Bates conceived some offense against one of them. He drew his knife, striking the negroes and cursing Soens, who was endeavoring to quiet his troublesome customer. Bates finally, after night, left the store. But just as Mr. Soens was going to bed, he returned and knocked for admittance. Soens was afraid of his life if he let him in. Bates began breaking down the door, threatening to kill him when he got in; Soens prepared for the worst, securing a Winchester rifle and warning Bates not to enter. He came through the demolished door, Soens fired, the bullet entering the breast and coming out in the back. Bates staggered off the gallery and fell to the ground a dead man.

January 21, 1882
We announce the death of William S., eldest son of Col. J. L. Power. He had just obtained his majority.

We have just been informed that Mr. J. E. Bryan, a merchant of Chicot County, on the river a short distance above here, committed suicide a few days since, by taking morphine. Financial embarrasment was the cause of the deed.

January 28, 1882
Entered into rest, Oct. 5, 1881, Mrs. Amanda Worthington, in the seventy-sixth year of her age.

February 11, 1882
Died at the residence of his father, on Deer Creek, Washington County, Mississippi, on the 29th day of January, 1882, Andrew H. Myers, son of Mr. J. S. Myers, in the 26th year of his age.

February 25, 1882
Died in Greenville, Mississippi, on the 20th of February, Mr. Patrick Dunn. Mr. Dunn was an old citizen of Port Gibson, Mississippi, and came here some three years ago.

Mrs. Flora F. Anderson died at the residence of Col. Jas. D. Stewart, on Wednesday night. She was in her ninety-eighth year. Mrs. Anderson was the widow of Judge Wm. E. Anderson. She was a native of Kentucky.

March 4, 1884
Died at his residence near Greenville, Washington County, Mississippi, February 27th, 1882, in the 58th year of his age, Mr. J. B. M. Lawson. The deceased had been for many years a citizen of this county.

Died at his home in Tallahatchie County, aged 74, Mr. Shields, father of Jno. W. Shields, of Greenville. Mr. Shields resided formerly in Jefferson County, Miss.

May 20, 1882
The most distressing death of the Monticello cyclone was that of Mrs. Cannon. Hearing the storm approaching Mrs. Cannon, with her baby in her arms, rushed to her husband, Dr. Cannon, who threw his arms around her neck. At the same moment the wind blew the timbers of the house down upon them, crushing them to the floor, the mother with the infant in her arms, the husband with his arm around his wife's neck, and there he choked her to death. The falling timbers did not seem to hurt her, but locked the doctor's arm so closely about her neck that he could not move it. All his efforts to throw off the timbers were futile. The babe was also

killed, whether by the falling timbers or was pressed to death by it's mother we did not learn.

June 3, 1882
Died in Greenville, on the 30th, Carrie Penny, aged 16. She was the daughter of the late Dr. B. F. and Mrs. A. C. Penny and was born in Greenville.

June 17, 1882
Died June 10, 1882, at the residence of W. D. Ferris, of Westburg, Washington County, Mississippi, Mr. W. M. D. Kefauver.

June 24, 1882
Died at the residence of her father, J. H. Robb, on Lake Lee, Washington County, Mississippi, June 18th, 1882, of congestion of the brain, Mattie Thompson Robb, aged 6 years, 7 months and 16 days.

July 1, 1882
Died at Eureka Springs, Arkansas, on the 27th, LeRoy Pope Percy, aged 58 years.

Died at Eureka Springs, on the 28th, Fannie Percy, wife of Alfred Downs Pace and daughter of Col. and Mrs. W. A. Percy, aged 23 years, 5 months and 4 days.

July 8, 1882
Judge J. P. Walker, the father of the Walker boys recently murdered near Aberdeen, was shot and killed at Goodwin, Arkansas. Judge Walker had been furnishing a saw mill owned by Mr. Shoddy. Mr. Shoddy owed Judge Walker a good amount and was not disposed to let the Judge get his money. One word brought on another, and Mr. Shoddy shot Judge Walker with a large pistol through the bowels. After being shot, Judge Walker got his gun and killed Shoddy on the spot. Judge Walker lingered until Sunday. He was a native of Alabama and had raised a large family.

July 15, 1882
Died at Arcola, Washington County, of brain fever, on the 10th of July, 1882, Rev. S. G. Jenkins.

July 27, 1882
Telegraphic dispatches here to the children of Mrs. Grafton Baker informed them of the death of their mother at Grand Junction, Tennessee, on the 26th. She had been in ill health for some time, and went to Tennessee in the vain hope of recovery. She was the widow of the late Judge Grafton Baker, and for ten years a resident of Greenville.

August 5, 1882

Died at Hot Springs, Arkansas, on the 29th July, 1882, Mr. William A. Cleaton, of Washington County, Mississippi. Mr. Cleaton was for many years a citizen of Yazoo County.

Died at their residence on William's Bayou, Washington County, August 3rd, 1882, Augusta, daughter of Captain A. B. and Hallie Baugh, aged about 18 months.

August 19, 1882

Died at his residence in G'ville, August 12th, 1882, Mr. Eugene W. Lawson, late publisher of the *Mississippian*. He was born in Vicksburg.

Died August 11th, 1882, at the Arkansas City Hotel, Mr. Joseph S. Wallace, a levee and railroad contractor.

September 2, 1882

Died at Niagara Falls, August 22nd, 1882, Willie, son of Mr. & Mrs. John W. Shields, of Greenville, Mississippi.

Died in McKinneyville, Sharkey County, on the 23rd August, Susie, daughter of Rev. J. H. Shelton.

September 9, 1882

Mrs. T. G. Walcott died at her residence on Deer Creek, in Washington County, September 3rd.

September 30, 1882

On Sept. 23rd, Merrett Hinds, colored, living on Bear Garden plantation, was drowned in Steel's Bayou, on the Lake Washington and Deer Creek road, while attempting to cross the ferry.

Eugene Smith was stabbed and killed at Eureka, in a drunken fray, on last Monday, by a man named Welborn. The deceased was a brave soldier, a member of Company I, 21st Mississippi regiment, during the late war. His slayer escaped.

October 7, 1882

Died in Cincinnati, September 28th, 1882, Kinnie, son of the late Tim. and Mrs. Josephine O'Connor, of Greenville, Mississippi, about 8 years of age.

October 28, 1882

Died at her home in Claiborne County, Mississippi, October 16th, 1882, Mrs. Emma E. Evans, wife of Louis de N. Evans, and daughter of Mrs. S. F. Buckner of Washington County, Mississippi.

Died in Greenville, October 25, 1882, Adele, aged one year, daughter of Mr. & Mrs. Jas. Robertshaw.

November 4, 1882
Died in Greenville, Rennah, aged 12 years, daughter of Mr. and Mrs. Whitehead, of this place.

November 11, 1882
Died in Greenville, November 9, 1882, Gustav Witkowski, for many years a merchant and planter in the river counties of Louisiana and Mississippi.

December 9, 1882
Died at the residence of her parents on Lake Lee, Washington County, on the 3rd of December, 1882, Fannie Gwyn Robb, aged 11 years and 11 months, daughter of Eugene A. and Carrie B. Robb.

We get the particulars of the killing of W. H. H. Tison, Speaker of the Mississippi House of Representatives, at Baldwin, Tippah County, on the 5th. Domestic troubles in the family of Col. Tison's brother culminated in an attack on Ed. Saunders, a merchant in Baldwin, by the two elder Tisons and a son of each, which resulted in Saunders being badly beaten and injured. During his confinement he was repeatedly informed that Colonel Tison had threatened to kill him. Going out for the first time he carried his shotgun and shot Tison on sight, killing him instantly.

December 30, 1882
The death of ex-Governor and General B. G. Humphreys (also written as G. B. Humphreys), born near Port Gibson in 1812, was a classmate of Jefferson Davis at West Point Military Academy but left the academy before graduation. He lost his first wife early. (Author's note - a very lengthy report followed)

January 20, 1883
Died at his residence on Deer Creek, on the 15th, F. A. Metcalfe.

Died at his home near Nebletta, in Bolivar County, recently, Wm. Cook. The deceased was one of Bolivar's oldest inhabitants.

We learn of the death, at his home in Bolivar County, recently, Dr. J. L. Richardson, an accomplished physician.

January 27, 1883
Died in Greenville, January 26th, John Wilson.

February 3, 1883
Died at her residence near Greenville, on the 31st, Mrs. John Kanateer.

February 10, 1883
Died at Longwood, February 8th, Merritt Williams, son of C. P. and Anna Williams, aged 3 years and 11 months. Mr. Charles P. Williams was until recently, a resident of this county, and was on a visit with his little son to the home of his brother, Merritt Williams.

March 3, 1883
Died in Greenville, Mississippi, on the 2nd of March, 1883, Mr. Joseph P. Foster. Mr. Foster had been a citizen of Greenville for the past ten years.

March 10, 1883
Died at the residence of his father near Egg's Point, in Washington County, Mississippi, on the 8th of March, 1883, of pneumonia, Jefferson Scott, son of Mr. J. W. Scott, aged 18 years.

Died on the 6th, at her residence in Greenville, Mississippi, Mrs. Ernestine Lewy, wife of Mr. B. M. Lewy.

March 31, 1883
Died at his residence in Greenville, Mississippi, March 28th, 1883, Jacob Hirsch, in the 44th year of his age. Mr. Hirsch was one of the first settlers of the town. He was a member of the Jewish congregation. He was a private in the 9th Louisiana Infantry. He leaves a widow and several children.

Died in Greenville, March 24, 1883, of protracted meningitis, Samuel, son of Mr. Marx and Mrs. Julia Ginsburger, aged about 8 years.

April 7, 1883
Died in Chicago recently, Harriet Byrne Ousley, daughter of the late Major Byrne, of Greenville. At the time of her death she was residing in Chicago.

April 14, 1883
Died at Seauvin, Georgia, March 31, 1883, of cancer, Oliver J. Head, aged 38 years. He had been a citizen of this county for several years past.

June 2, 1883
Died at his home near Greenville, after a long period of ill health, Mr. Robert Cleary, an old citizen of this county.

June 9, 1883

Woodville, Miss., June 6 -- William Goddard, the leading builder of this place, took two ounces of chloroform today, in the presence of his wife, who endeavored to prevent his doing so, and in two hours he was dead. It is difficult to assign a reason for the rash act. The deceased was a soldier in the 21st Mississippi Regiment during the war and was severely wounded at the defeat of Cedar Creek.

Died in Sunflower County, May 27th, Mrs. A. M. Champion, wife of Mr. Champion of the Georgia Pacific Railroad. She was a native of Georgia. Her remains were laid to rest on Mound, the graveyard near Stoneville.

June 30, 1883

Died at the store of Mr. Julius Landau, on Deer Creek, Washington County, Mississippi on June 26th, 1883, Mr. Charles M. Sowens. He had for several years past been in the service of Mr. Landau.

August 18, 1883

We learn of the assassination near Jackson of Mr. Pearson, a citizen of Rankin County. And the fatal shooting of Mr. Ike Bonham, a merchant of Vicksburg, who was shot by Harry Moore, who intended to slay John Coleman, a newspaper reporter. Moore is the same "killer" who some years since killed Mr. Hazelett, an old citizen of Vicksburg.

August 25, 1883

Woodville, August 20 -- At Kionstra's store, above Fort Adams, Charles Sims and Moseley, clerks, got into a fight. Sims got Moseley down and was beating him, when Moseley drew a pistol and fired, killing Sims instantly. Chas. B. Sims was a native of Wilkinson County and formerly lived in Greenville with his mother. His brother, Robbie Sims, now employed at Messrs. Faison & Smith.

September 1, 1883

Died at the residence of Mr. James Archer, in Jefferson County, Miss., James Archer Finlay, infant son of Mr. & Mrs. John P. Finlay, of Greenville, aged 7 months.

September 15, 1883

Died on Deer Creek, near Overby Station, on the 10th, Mrs. Caroline O'Neal, wife of Mr. R. T. O'Neal.

September 22, 1883

James M. Sutton, Esq., one of our oldest citizens, died at his home near town on the morning of the 21st, in the 79th year of his age. He was a native of the State of Illinois, but had resided in this State more than fifty years.

Little Janora, only daughter of G. B. and Janie P. Shelby, who was born at Sardis, Miss., March 29, 1879, died at Sunny Side, Ark. on Saturday last. The remains were brought up on the *City of Vicksburg* on Sunday, and interred in the City Cemetery.

October 6, 1883

Deaths in Greenville in September:
- 2 - Robert Thomas Whiteway, white, age 13 months, 2 days, flux
- 3 - Sarah A. Riley, white, 35 years, childbirth
- 12 - John Johnson, colored, consumption
- 12 - Mrs. J. E. Smith, white, flux
- 13 - Mike Kernan, white, flux
- 16 - Elenora Crockett, colored, age 8 months, remittent fever
- 18 - Maria Bird, colored, infant, bronchitis
- 18 - Keziah Buchanan, colored, age 25, consumption
- 19 - Nancy Smith, colored, syphilis
- 21 - James M. Sutton, white, age 77 years, 3 months, ulcerated bowels
- 22 - English Davis, colored, 29 years, dysentery
- 27 - Clara Carthy, colored, 1 year & 9 months, cholera infantum

H. M. Snowberger, Undertaker & City Sexton

October 20, 1883

Died at his home on Graniens Bayou, on the night of the 18th, Mr. Ben James, a young man, native of this county.

Died in Greenville, Mississippi this morning, October 20, 1883, Mr. Henry T. Saltziger. Mr. Saltziger came to this city about 5 years ago from Memphis, Tennessee.

Mr. John Bergman, for many years a merchant in Chicot County, Arkansas, but whose family residence is in Greenville, was buried here on Sunday morning, the 14th.

October 27, 1883

With regret we note the death of Captain Ike Shelby, which occurred at his residence about ten miles east of Concordia, in this county, on last Sunday. For several days he had been confined to bed with malarial fever. During the late war he served in the army as a lieutenant in Mayson's dragoons, from this county. After Dr. Mayson was wounded and became surgeon, his brother, Evan Shelby, became captain and he first lieutenant.. Evan Shelby was killed on the retreat of Hood from Tennessee, and Captain Ike became a captain of Stark's regiment, 28th Mississippi. (Rosedale Leader)

On last Saturday at Arcola, Grafton Baker shot and killed Benjamin Williams. After examination of many witnesses and consideration of the facts, the Justices concurred that the homicide was justifiable, having been committed in the necessary defense of his younger brother, Percy Baker.

The death of the veteran statesman, jurist and soldier, Gen. Samuel Jamison Gholson, at the advanced age of 76 years, occurred at his residence in this city, on the 16th. (Vicksburg Herald)

Died at the residence of his mother-in-law, Mrs. Nannette Switzer, in Washington County, Mississippi, on the morning of the 18th of October, 1883, Mr. B. F. James, aged 26 years. He fell a victim to the fatal hematura brought on by undue exertion and exposure.

Died of hematura, on the 4th of October, at the residence of his grandmother, Mrs. Nannette Switzer, Willie B. Wells, aged 10 years. Willie was the only child of his mother, Mary Wells.

November 3, 1883
October Death List:
4 - Robert Hibler, col., 1 year, 6 months, natural causes
5 - Stillborn child of Lena Butler, col.
7 - W. H. Showse, white, congestion of the brain
10 - Coley B. Gray, col., pauper, 1 year, 10 months
17 - John Smith, col., 10 years, congestion of the brain
19 - Son of C. Booker, 2 months, inflammation of bowels
20 - Henry G. Salzinger, white, dysentery
22 - Rebecca Brooks, col., cancer of the breast
24 - Jennie Blackburn, col., consumption
28 - Irvin Turner, col., 1 month, convulsions
28 - Angeline Green, col., 75 years, chronic dysentery
31 - Moses Latham, 1 year and 7 months, malarial fever

November 10, 1883
Print Matthews, leader of the Republican of Copiah County, was killed at Hazlehurst yesterday morning, by Mr. E. B. Wheeler, with a shot gun. A difference of political nature was the cause of the affray.

Killing at Vicksburg -- Last night, a few minutes after the time for the curtain to rise at the Opera house where the John F. Ward Combination is playing, the audience was startled by the discharge of two pistol shots, followed in a few minutes by two more. For a few minutes there was danger of a panic but order was soon restored. A reporter of the *Herald* rushed behind the stage and learned that D. R. Allen, one of the managers of the company, had been shot by Frank E. Stark, the advance agent of the company. Allen was pronounced dead.

December 1, 1883

Dr. W. E. Backner died of dysentery at Arcola, Saturday night and was buried on Monday, Nov. 26, at Col. A. J. Paxton's. He was only 25 years of age.

We have just learned that Dr. Chas. Dadly, an old citizen of Lake Washington, died suddenly at his home yesterday.

December 8, 1883

Death Report of November:
Susie Baker, col., died Nov. 1st, age 25 years
Alfannce Smith, col., died Nov. 2nd, age 2 years
Jordan Dines, col., died Nov. 5th
A. Sumell, white, pauper, died Nov. 8
Jake Bennett, white, pauper, died Nov. 10
Sylvester Lyttle, col., died Nov. 21, age 9 months
Fannie Sheppard, white, died Nov. 25, age 3 years
Albert Holmes, white, pauper, died Nov. 26

December 22, 1883

Homicide -- We learn by the *Vicksburg Herald* of Thursday, that Howard, a negro, struck Pat Flynn, manager on the Mr. Joe Wilezinski's Lake Washington plantation, with a billet of wood, breaking his neck. Howard was captured. Cause, a woman.

A woman named Lila McGee, killed and brutally mutilated another woman on the plantation of Mr. H. T. Ireys. Cause, a man.

December 29, 1883

Steve Jackson shot Joe Ross on Monday night, both laborers on Mr. Pollock's plantation on Lake Bolivar. Jackson stole a mule and came to Greenville to take a boat. M. B. Brown pointed him out to policeman Johnson, but whom he was apprehended. Ross is not dead, but badly wounded.

Yazoo City, Miss., Dec. 25 -- Last night Mr. John Posey was passing a butcher shop near the post office and was grossly insulted by John James, colored. Posey went away and got several friends and started back. In the meantime, the negroes armed themselves with shot guns and placed themselves in the shop.

When Posey and his friends got to the corner they met Wm. Foote, who also insulted Posey, and they got into a fuss. It was so dark they could not see each other a foot apart. At the first shot the negroes killed two of the Posey's and a man named Nichols, about eighteen years of age, son of Capt. Nichols. No negroes were killed.

This morning the citizens went out to the slaughter-house and found John James, a negro, who was armed and fired three shots. The citizens killed him. Fritz Halder was shot and badly wounded, as was Henry Ellett.

The Poseys were sons of Gen. Carnot Posey, who was killed at the head of his brigade, in Virginia, in 1863. Their family was an old one of Wilkinson County.

January 5, 1884

Jackson, Miss., Jan. 1 -- Fritz Halder, who was wounded in the affray at Yazoo City, Christmas Eve, died last night. He has been County Treasurer for the past four years. Halder was ruthlessly shot down while interposing to prevent the affair.

Died on Dec. 28, 1883, at the residence of J. D. Britton, this city, Herbert Thompson, of Washington County, Miss., in the 26th year of his age. The deceased was the son of Julius Thompson, of Deer Creek.

January 12, 1884

Jesse James was killed at Rosedale, Bolivar County, because of craps. The amount of controversy was 25 cents. Both negroes.

Mr. James M. Buckley, Deputy State Auditor, died of an eptileptic fit on Anguilla planatation on Tuesday last. His remains passed through this city yesterday for Jackson, where they will be buried today. They were accompanied by a daughter and two sons of the deceased. (Vicksburg Herald)

January 19, 1884

Died at his residence on Black Bayou, in the 64th year of his age, Grant A. Bowen. The deceased was a native of Lebanon, Tennessee, though he lived in this county for near fifty years. He leaves a widow and two children, and was brother of Mrs. Shall Yerger.

January 26, 1884

Harry Moss died at the residence of Mr. R. H. Henry, Wednesday evening, of pneumonia.

A negro man named Charles Johnson was shot and killed on the outgoing train yesterday by another negro named Joe Bell. The cause of the dispute was trivial, and the slain man was the aggressor.

February 9, 1884

Died at his home in Greenville, the 5th, Noah Huny Leavenworth, in the 58th year of his age. Mr. Leavenworth was a native of Ste. Genevieve County, Missouri, where his remains were taken for burial. He has lived in this vicinity for a number of years, with his brother Mr. J. H. Leavenworth, and conducted a saw mill and lumber business of Leavenworth Bros.

February 23, 1884

Little Harry, young son of Mr. & Mrs. T. H. McGowen, of Magnolia, was accidentally shot in the face on the 7th, by a boy named McCarty, and died from the wounds last Saturday. (Author's note - a lengthy report followed).

Died the 17th, in Greenville, Harriet Theobold, infant daughter of Dr. and Mrs. S. R. Dunn.

Died the 17th, in Greenville, Helen, daughter of Rev. and Mrs. S. Archer, aged 15.

March 15, 1884

Died in Greenville, at the residence of his parents, the 9th, Jas. Mosely, son of Mr. and Mrs. J. D. Smith, in the 4th year of his age.

March 22, 1884

Newton West Atterbury, infant son of Dr. J. T. Atterbury and wife, was born July 28th, 1883 and died March 12th, 1884, it's little body laid in the cemetery at Arcola, Miss.

Columbus, March 19 -- Bishop H. H. Kavanaugh, of the Methodist Episcopal Church, South, died at this place this morning. He came here on a visit from New Orleans and was taken ill with bladder affection. He was eighty three years old. His remains will be taken to Louisville, Ky.

March 29, 1884

Baoyu Sara, March 19 -- Dr. John G. Archer died on the 17th, after a long illness. His remains will be interred at Saint Stephen's cemetery, Williamsport, La. A wife and two grown sons survive him. The deceased was the father of Dr. Archer, who died here while devoting himself to our citizens in 1878.

April 19, 1884

On last Wednesday night Joe McCaffrey, the second mate on the steamer *Will S. Hays,* was fatally stabbed by a rouster while the boat was lying here. There was a quarrel, the rouster refusing to work and asking for his discharge money. The murderer escaped.

April 26, 1884

Died the 25th, Sam'l. R. Dunn, Jr., son of Dr. and Mrs. S. R. Dunn, aged 3 years and 5 months.

May 5, 1884

Skipwith, Miss., April 28 - Samuel T. Wilson, a white convict guard on Col. Ed. Richardson's Rustic plantation on Washington Bayou, was lynched by a negro mob last night. The facts: Wilson, with a crew of four convicts, was hauling lumber on a flatboat. They landed near where a negro named Ned McDanniel was fishing. Wilson and McDanniel had some words. Two negroes testified that Wilson took McDanniel on board the boat and beat him, then ordered them to throw him overboard, which they did. Wilson plead not guilty. The white people condemn the action of the negro mob, as the man was tried by a negro, convicted by the evidence of two unreliable negroes, and hung by a negro mob.

May 10, 1884

After an illness of several weeks, Col. Thos. H. Hunt died yesterday morning.

Died in Greenville, after a long illness, on the 7th, Mrs. Cattonhead.

The *Meridian Mercury and Observer* says: Yesterday a negro named Jack Smith was sitting in front of the switch engine, while moving along the track. The engine threw a calf off the track, which struck the negro, knocking him to the ground. His head came into contact with a cross tie and was crushed.

May 24, 1884

Our community was startled by the death of Col. J. F. H. Claibourne. He had been ill a long time. Col. Claibourne was born on the 24th of April, 1807. (Natchez Democrat)

Died in Greenville at the residence of her sister, on the 22nd, Orville Blanton, wife of Dr. J. S. Walker and daughter of Dr. O. M. and Mrs. M. R. Blanton, in her 27th year.

Died at his home in Greenville, on the 20th, after a long illness, Barney Cahn, a native of the province of Lorraine, aged about 45 years. The deceased was an old citizen of this town. He leaves a widow and a large family of children.

Memphis, May 19 -- C. B. Robinson, a merchant doing business at Polk's Landing, near Commerce, Miss., committed suicide here today by taking morphine. His wife came here yesterday seeking him, alarmed at his long absence from home.

May 31, 1884

On last Thursday, C. J. Teal and W. B. Reeves were tried as accessories to the killing of Winfield Ivey, in Sunflower County, on the 15th. Winfield Ivey was reported to have slandered the sister of Mr. Reeves on the 14th. (Author's note - a lengthy report followed)

Died in Jackson, on the 23rd, at the residence of Mrs. Buck, Richard Burdett, aged 44. The deceased was a native of Fauquier County, Va., though a resident and large planter of this county for nearly 20 years.

June 7, 1884
Died June 2nd, at his residence on Bayou Granicus in Washington County, Miss., Francis Jerome Craig, aged 57 years, of congestion of the brain. Mr. Craig leaves a wife and infant son, besides his neice and nephew, who looked to him as a father. He was a native of South Carolina, having moved to this State about 27 years ago.

Died, Alfred Holt, infant son of Dr. O. W. and Mary H. Stone.

Died, Corrine, infant daughter of W. W. and Ella Stone, aged three months and sixteen days.

July 5, 1884
Yesterday morning on Col. Richardson's Hollywood plantation ten miles south of here, Frank Steward was shot and killed by Lee Brady, both negroes. A woman with whom Brady had lived, on last Monday married Steward. She owned a row of potatoes which Brady had given her; and Steward was pulling vines from them as the property of his wife. He was ordered by Brady to desist, and upon refusal was shot twice with a pistol, and instantly killed.

July 19, 1884
William Franklin Paxton, in the 25th year of his age, died on the 14th July, 1884, at the residence of his parents, A. J. and H. M. Paxton, near Arcola, Washington County, Mississippi.

Died after a brief illness, July 14th, 1884, at her home near Overby Station, Washington County, Mississippi, Mrs. Laura M., wife of Vastine C. Slater, and daughter of E. V. and E. M. Barwick, formerly of Madison County, Mississippi.

THE WEEKLY COPIAN
Hazlehurst, Mississippi

October 10, 1885
Purser Lard, son of Mr. L. H. and P. J. Lard, born in August 1879, died February 8th, 1885.

THE COPIAH SIGNAL
Hazlehurst, Mississippi

March 17, 1882
Died in this place, this morning, Rev. Dr. W. E. M. Linfield, for many years minister in the M. E. Church, South.

May 5, 1882
Elinor Martin, infant child of Mr. Harley and Mrs. Maggie Page, of Martinsville, was taken by the Good Shepherd on the 1st of May, 1882, aged 1 year, 8 months and 13 days.

Joseph A. Horne was born in Montrose, Jasper County, Miss., Dec. 4, 1842. His parents moved to Handsboro, this State, and there he grew up. He entered the Confederate service in the 20th Miss. Regiment and rendered service until severely wounded in July 1864, near Atlanta, Ga. After the war he resided in East Mississippi, and about 1882 located in Hazlehurst. He was twice married - to Miss Maggie B. Smith, of Forest, and Miss Myra Oatis, daughter of C. R. Oatis, of Hazlehurst. The latter and a little three year old daughter survive him. His disease was consumption. (Author's report - a lengthy report followed)

July 21, 1882
Mrs. Mary M. Brown was about 43 years of age at the time of her death. She was a resident of the county; her husband proceeded her to the grave several years ago. She was stricken with paralysis two months ago from which she never fully recovered. A few days since she sustained a second attack and on the 11th passed away. She leaves three sons, all grown.

September 1, 1882
Died on Sunday morning, Mary Belle, daughter of Charles P. and Emily A. Cook, age 7 years, 11 months and 8 days.

October 27, 1882
Died at Hazlehurst, Miss., on the 17th of October, Roswell B. Gilbert, in the 53rd year of his age.

January 12, 1883
Mrs. Mattie E. Rogers was born near Holmesville, Pike County, Miss., August 18, 1851; married Mr. G. W. Rogers, February 20, 1873, and died after a lingering illness December 25, 1882, aged 31 years, 5 months, 5 days. The deceased leaves a husband, two children, a mother, brother and sister, Mrs. Hartwell of Wesson.

The death of Mrs. Capt. Oliver last Wednesday cast a gloom over our town. Funeral took place from Presbytarian Church.

February 23, 1883
Died on the morning of the 17th, the infant of E. G. and Sallie F. Baker, aged twelve days.

March 2, 1883
Mr. Samuel J. Wood, a citizen of Copiah County, died at his residence about three miles northeast of this city, on the morning of February 25th, 1883.

March 16, 1883
Death claimed our brother, M. Faler, on the 24th day of January, 1883.

March 30, 1883
On Monday morning last, Mr. J. W. McLemore, a citizen of the neighborhood of Learned Station, on the Natchez and Jackson Railroad, was returning home from his neighbor Mr. Brock, is supposed to have died of heart disease, as he was found dead in the road and his horse grazing in a field nearby. The discovery was made by two school boys - his own sons. He leaves a wife and several children. (Clarion)

Leon McLemore was raised in this county and is the brother-in-law of our townsman, Mr. Berry Wilson. He had been living in Hinds County a few years.

April 13, 1883
Mrs. Kate Massengill was the daughter of Mr. James C. Redus of this county, and was born in Sumter County, Ala., Sept. 11, 1842. Her mother died when she was three years of age. At the age of 22 she connected herself with the Hazlehurst Presbyterian Church. April 5, 1866, she was united in marriage with Mr. M. J. Massengill, who died June 8, 1878, leaving in her charge six children, two of them mutes. In 1880 the disease which finally terminated her life, manifested itself. On Sunday, the 8th April, 1883, she peacefully passed away.

April 27, 1883
Last Sunday morning a wind storm struck the towns of Beauregard and Wesson and continued but slightly abated fury until afternoon. About three o'clock a dull heavy roar seemed to fill the air with but an instants warning, all was midnight darkness. Three seconds it had passed and left rain and desolation. Those who saw the cyclone say it seemed like a dense volume of smoke.

In Beauregard, Dr. Lampkins residence was razed to the ground; he was not injured but his wife and little son were painfully wounded - the latter dangerously so. In the house at the time were John S. Terrell, D. Jones, his wife and two sons, all dead. Mr. George Holloway was fatally wounded. Ham Moody and his wife were out walking and ran to a box car, the car was thrown a hundred yards.

Mr. Moody was dangerously wounded. Seven negroes were in the car playing cards - three were killed. Mr. J. W. Ross and wife were painfully injured and their little baby is so badly crushed it cannot live. Miss Eula Benton was found dead. Miss Georgiana B. Mitchell, of New York, had her brains crushed. Caleb Ellis, colored, had his skull split open. Mrs. H. F. Carter was seriously wounded and her baby was blown from her arms.

We copy below a correct list of the wounded and dead. (Author's note: wounded not included in this book) At the house of W. C. Loving, J. A. Williams and William Sanford, dead. At the house of Elam T. Robertson, Miss Eula Benton, dead. At the house of J. L. Crawford, dead, William Parker, Louis Parker, child and Julia Schrett, 10 years old.

There were twenty-four houses down in Wesson, occupied entirely by the Mississippi Mills operatives. Many of the houses contained as many as fourteen or fifteen people. Below is a list of the dead and wounded. (Author's note: wounded not listed in this book) Miss Sallie Ford, Mrs. Wilkerson and son, William Blackburn's child, Ram Benion, Nathan Loftin's child, four nephews of J. T. Gibson, Mrs. Duncan's child, Mrs. Cancey and child - total killed 13. Anna Clauding, nurse of S. Lowenberg, died tonight. Mr. Blackburn's face so mangled that it was unrecognizable, his little child was killed outright. Mrs. Beard is suffering from concussion of the brain. She is expected to die. Joe Williams in insensible and is not likely to recover. Four of Mr. Turner Gibson's nephews were killed on the spot. Mrs. Finch has been unconscious since her injuries; she will hardly live 48 hours. Mrs. Allen has a six inch incised wound across the abdomen and another on the scalp equally large. She is now in a precarious condition.

At Georgetown on Pearl river most of the people were assembled in the Methodist Church. Three colored people were killed and ten injured. John Crawford, wife, daughter, son, grandchild and one servant were killed instantly and so crushed and mangled as to be scarcely recognizable. Mrs. Ryan's children were also killed, as also were those of Mr. John Beasley. Mrs. Fowles three sons and one daughter were instantly killed and Mrs. Fowles was carried by the wind 150 yards and thrown into a tree and died from her injuries. On the opposite side of the river, James Bass and family of 10 persons were seriously injured, only one killed.

At Tillman Station a Mr. Beggett was killed. At Caledonia, Mr. Jack Stephenson was instantly killed. At Red Lick there were several lives lost.

At Starkville, two negroes were killed. Twelve persons were killed at Aberdeen.

At Beauregard, the body of Mrs. Carter's child, eight months old, was found 500 steps from the house. Miss Walker, who has been blind for years, has the scalp torn up over her entire cranium. Mrs. Keating, a lady 75 years old, is frightfully wounded, her husband was killed.

A correct list of the killed: Misses Mary Mickle, sister of Capt. White's wife; Georgiana Mitchel, M. Benton, daughter of the tax collector of Claiborne County; Annie Clossing, of New Orleans; Ermira Terrell; her sister not before reported; Mrs. Luther Jones; Mrs. Huber, who leaves four orphan children; Mrs. Westerfield, Capt. Wies wife, James A. Williams; John S. Terrell; Wm. Sanford; Wm. Parker; R. Keating; Rev. Theophilus Green, Baptist minister; Dr. Luther Jones; Lewis Parker; Milton Story; George White; Earhest Bahr; Dr. Jones' two children; H. F. Carter's child; the child of Mrs. Shrett; the child of John W. Bass, and the following named colored people - Jerry Smith, Joseph Hunt, Caleb Ellis, Melissa Burtis' child and J. Easterling's child.

A large party took shelter in Mr. John N. Crawford's house on the Hazlehurst and Rockport Rd., and all were killed, as follows: John N. Crawford and wife, Celia A. Crawford, Jennie Crawford, Mrs. Julia Read and baby, Mr. Frank Moore and wife, Willie Read. Mr. Reed and baby and Mrs. Moore and baby are mortally wounded and will die. Mr. Hennington will die.

May 4, 1883

The Cyclone - reports still being received. At Mr. Nash's, little Mary Beasley, daughter of John Beasley, was killed, skull being crushed. (Author's note - This is a very lengthy article relating what was seen in the aftermath by L. G. Bird. Many wounded were named.)

July 27, 1883

Mrs. Fannie Mayes Harris, wife of Judge W. P. Harris, died at her residence the 17th. Mrs. Harris was the daughter of Hon. Daniel Mayes of Kentucky, and was born in Versailes in 1828. In 1843 she came to Mississippi.

Died in Hazlehurst, Miss., July 21st, 1883, of typhoid fever, after an illness of thirty days, Lewis O'amblis, aged 10 years and 2 months, eldest son of W. J. and Ellen Smith. Thus a second time within thirteen months these parents have been called upon to give up one of their treasures.

August 10, 1883

Fannie, daughter of G. B. and Margaret Nelson, was taken very suddenly, on the 26th of July, 1883, aged four years and three months. Her disease was congestion.

September 7, 1883

Ella Eudora died on the 2nd, of congestion, daughter of Mr. David Brewer, residing six miles northwest of this place. She was aged 8 years, 1 month and 18 days. Her remains sleep in the cemetery at Damascus Church.

A special from the *Vicksburg Herald* of the 4th says: The grave of Mrs. Hattie Howell, who died two years ago and was buried in the Auburn cemetery, that county, was robbed by two negroes, Jim Kiog and George Gaddis, their object being to secure the arm bones which they used in carrying out their purposes in conjuring. George Gaddis attempted to escape and was shot in the giblets. Jim King was hung last night near Auburn.

On Monday, while Mrs. Annie Coughlin was proceeding to the Wilson Railroad camps twenty-five miles east of Edwards, when descending the hill the coupling pin of the wagon in which she was seated broke, and the wagon started down the hill, throwing the lady out and falling on her, crushed her to death. Her sons had a sub-contract on the Wilson Railroad.

October 11, 1883

Mrs. Mary Walker, who died in Wilkinson County recently, was one hundred and three years old. She lived in Natchez when there was only one residence in the place, and it a log cabin. She was one of the first settlers of Wilkinson county.

October 18, 1883

Last Saturday night two negroes had a difficulty in which one was hit by a brick and has since died. The report is that Levi Redding and Leroy Smith, the parties in the affray, had a quarrel during the night but were separated. A short time afterwards Levi and a policeman were seen looking for Leroy to arrest him. On approaching him he picked up a brick and struck Levi on the head, knocking him senseless. The policeman arrested Leroy. Levi died and Leroy was charged with murder. (Meridian Observer)

November 15, 1883

Died September 14th, 1883, Mattie, daughter of Dr. Jos. B. and Martha Catchings, aged twenty years.

December 6, 1883

Jas. A. Redus, a nephew of Capt. J. C. Redus, who was breaking on a freight train, was killed on the 21st, at West Pearl River, thirty miles from New Orleans. His remains were carried to Greensboro, Ala., for interrment.

One day last week, Henry Swan, living a few miles from Magnolia, was thrown from his wagon and so badly injured as to paralyze him from his head to his heels, which resulted in his death.

An attempt was made to rob the express agent at Corinth, on the 1st. Alonzo McWilliams had placed in his safe, money received, when a masked man with a drawn pistol, demanded the safe key. Without waiting for a reply, he fired upon McWilliams, striking him just below the right nipple. McWilliams, though desparately wounded, dashed his lamp at the robber. McWilliams died from his wounds next day. The murdered has escaped.

January 17, 1884

Minnie Christine Moble, child of Mr. H. and Mrs. A. J. Moble, of Hazlehurst, was called by the Good Shepherd, on the 31st Dec., 1883. Had she lived until the 18th of March, she would have completed her 3rd year.

The *Brookhaven Democrat* records the death of Mike Suttel, which took place on last Thursday. In company with friends he went to the swamp, four miles below town, duck hunting. The parties separated and no more was seen of Mike until he was found dead. He was lying by a log with his gun between his knees and a duck he had killed near by. A jury decided he died from heart disease.

January 24, 1884

Another murder was added last night to the long chapter that disgraces the history of Vicksburg. Jack McKenna, a notoriously bad character, killed Ed. Wilson, in a gambling saloon.

Shade Allen shot and instantly killed Dan Rea, about five miles from Brookhaven last week. Both parties were colored. Allen surrendered to authorities and claims the killing was done in self defense.

A row occurred near Water Valley last Thursday, resulting in the killing of Evans Harmon, and fatally wounding of Wm. Harmon and Robt. Larnar, and the serious wounding of many others.

January 31, 1884

Died at Glen Wood, near Hazlehurst, on the 6th of January, Martha Gordon, daughter of E. G. and Sallie F. Baker, in the 16th year of her age.

March 13, 1884

Died on February 29th, at the age of 18 years and 7 months, J. Pinkney Bass, youngest son of Capt. J. A. Bass.

April 3, 1884

On Wednesday last, Oscar Jones, son of Lafayette Jones, an old citizen of Bolivar County, was fatally shot at Bolivar Landing. He was shot three times with a pistol by ___ Wilson, who resides in that vicinity. We have not heard any particulars, other than Jones was trying to use a knife upon his slayer.

Bishop H. H. Kavanaugh, one of the oldest of the Methodist Bishops, died at the residence of T. C. Billups in Columbus, Miss.,

March 18, 1884. His remains were carried to Louisville, Ky., for interrment.

April 10, 1884

Mr. Zack Rembert, an old citizen of this county, died at his home, seven miles west of here, on Tuesday morning last. He had been in bad health for a long time and was partially paralyzed. He leaves a wife. He never had any children.

On Tuesday a difficulty occurred between H. B. Penn and R. B. Rials, in which the latter was killed. An affadavit was made against H. B. Penn, R. G. Penn and L. D. Yates, charging them with the killing. A coroner's jury found that R. B. Rials came to his death by four pistol shot wounds, two stabs with a dirk knife and one blow on the head, fracturing the skull.

On the night of April 31st, a negro, aged seventeen years, named Geo. Lee, committed a brutal outrage on the four year old daughter of N. Mandel, of McComb City, and made his escape. About midnight he was captured. The next evening about two hundred citizens proceeded to the county jail at Magnolia and demanded the keys from the sheriff, who refused to give up the prisoner. The crowd was too strong however, the keys secured and the negro brought back to McComb City. He confessed his crime and was swung up to a limb and lynched.

April 17, 1884

On Tuesday morning, Mr. Jno. Murrah's two children, a boy thirteen years of age and a girl of eleven, were on their way to school, and while crossing Copiah Creek on a foot log, both fell in the creek. The boy managed to get out, but the little girl, named Myra, was drowned. Mr. Murrah lives about seven miles northwest of town.

November 20, 1884

Rice was the son of T. E. and Mrs. Jolie Groome, of this place. He was born June 13, 1874 and died Nov. 10, 1884, aged 10 years, 7 months and 27 days.

November 27, 1884

Sunday morning three little white boys were accosted by a young negro named Anderson Green, who cursed them and started at them with an open knife. One of the boys, a lad named George Shields, drew a pistol and fired at Green, severing his windpipe and inflicting wounds that may prove fatal. The boy surrendered himself but was released. Young Shields is an orphan boy, having come to Natchez from Wesson, where his parents were killed by the great cyclone of 1882, and he has been engaged in the Rosalie mills. (Natchez Democrat)

May 21, 1885

A duel took place on the 16th, at Rolling Fork, Sharkey County, between, W. K. McLaurin, an attorney, and S. F. Shelton, Chancery Clerk, in which the latter was killed. It seems the duel was the culmination of an old feud.

May 28, 1885

Last week, Bill McGowan, colored, who was working for James Russell, in Lawrence County, about five miles from Monticello, made a dastardly assault upon Miss Russell during the absence of the family. She gave the alarm and the negro was arrested and while being carried to Monticello, about sixty men took him from the guard and hung him to a tree.

June 11, 1885

Dr. J. M. Bird, who killed Capt. Brame, Sheriff of Jasper County, on May 18, 1883, was acquitted at the Jones County court.

July 2, 1885

Ben Holt, colored, was hung on Monday evening at Adams, Miss., by a mob of colored people. He was charged with having murdered his wife on Wednesday night of last week.

August 6, 1885

The trial of Jos. E. Lofton, at Monticello, Lawrence County, began on July 23 and concluded on the 30th. Lofton killed his brother Moses, in August 1884, and fled to Navarro County, Texas, from whence he was brought back last January. The guilty man was sentenced to be hanged Sept. 3.

A difficulty occurred on the 30th, near Union Church, Jefferson County, between Albert McKay and James Nevels, resulting in the death of the former. The weapons used were double-barrelled shotguns and pistols. The revival of an old feud was the cause.

August 27, 1885

Meridian Miss., August 20 -- a cruel murder in Newton County, near Garlandville, yesterday. A negro boy named Adam Horn was stealing watermelons from the patch of Henry Jones, when the daughter undertook to drive him off; whereupon he stabbed her in the breast with a knife, producing instant death. The boy fled but was afterward captured.

September 3, 1885

Mr. Walter L. Birdsong, second son of Capt. L. F. Birdsong, died on Saturday and was buried on Sunday evening. He leaves a wife and one child.

Died at Carpenter, of congestion, Miss M. Henryetta Jones, daughter of J. C. Jones.

Died in this county, August 30th, C. K. Swinney, aged 69 years and 10 days.

October 22, 1885
Mr. R. W. Carr, familiarly known as Uncle Bob, died at the residence of his son-in-law, Rev. J. W. McNeil, near Crystal Springs, on last Thursday. He lived at Handsboro, this State, many years. At the time of his death he was ninety-two years of age.

November 26, 1885
Silas Russell, of this neighborhood, committed suicide on Wednesday evening by shooting himself through the head with a pistol. The young man was a well to do farmer, but had fallen behind with his crops, and besides was involved in a love affair that preyed upon his mind.

December 3, 1885
Edmund Graves was found guilty of murder in the Copiah Court last week, and sentenced to be hanged. (Natchez Democrat)
You have that a little mixed, Luke Miller was convicted of murdering Edmund Graves and is sentenced to be hung.

December 17, 1885
After several months of suffering, Col. J. F. Vance died on Saturday night of dropsy and heart disease. The Col. leaves no children, but a devoted wife and step-daughter, Mrs. S. F. Massengill.

Died near Pine Ridge, Copiah County, Miss., June 4th, 1885, Georgia A., youngest daughter of J. B. and Elizabeth Middleton, aged 10 years, 10 months and 21 days.

Miss Fannie, daughter of John B. and E. Middleton, departed this life in Copiah County, Miss., July 12, 1885, age 18 years, 6 months and 10 days.

THE HOLLY SPRINGS REPORTER
Holly Springs, Mississippi

August 22, 1878
Died in LaGrange, Fayette County, Tenn., August 27th, 1878, Col. A. Fenton Tucker, formerly of Holly Springs, Miss.

The following is an official list of the deaths from yellow fever at Grenada, up to Sunday last.: Mrs. Field, Harry Field, Mr. & Mrs. Young, Mrs. Wilson, Mrs. Davidson, Alice McSwine (col'd.), Thos. Peacock, Mamie Peacock, W. A. Shankle, Robt. Shankle, Jas. Shankle, Miss Sallie Huffington, Miss Mary Huffington, Miss Marion Huffington, Mr. Welch, Cydny Welch, Miss Annie Lake, Mr. & Mrs. Geo. Lake, Gus Lake, Mr. & Mrs. McMillen, Mrs. McLean, Miss Lula McLean, Miss Rosa Saddler, Walter Saddler, Mrs. Chas. Coffman, Dr. Hawkins, Mayor J. L. Milton, Mr. & Mrs. Dyrrick, Mrs. Ingram, Miss Lizzie Ayers, Miss Mollie Poitevant, Mrs. Peter Kirby, Mrs. French, Joe Cromwell, Col. Geo. Cromwell, Barry Roes, F. K. Hall, Fox Eskridge, Capt. W. C. Eskridge, Willie Bauchamp, Minnie Lacock, Misses Angevine, Robt. Mayhew, Joseph Sherman, Mrs. Dr. May, Thos. Powell, Joe Morrow, David Moore, Sallie Dejournett, D. C. Crowder, Mrs. W. A. Belew, R. Stephenson, Dr. May's nurse (col'd.), Miss Kate Coffman, Miss Kate Clark, Maj. M. Conly, Langdon Conly, Mr. Moore, Dr. Galespie.

November 21, 1878

Death toll in Holly Springs to Nov. 18th, 1878.

Aug. 25 - E. L. Downs and Miss Lake, from Grenada
  31 - A. W. Goodrich
Sept. 1 - A. T. Wiltshire, from Grenada
  2 - Wm. Mackin, from Memphis
  3 - Isaac Tandler and James Chism
  4 - A. F. Brown's child, H. A. McCrosky, Frank Ganter and Robert McLain
  5 - James Fort, Mrs. James Nutall, B. P. Oliver, Bateman's child, Mrs. Stephen Knapp, Wm. Hogan and Mrs. E. A. Thomas
  6 - Gus Smith, Herman Snider's child, B. D. Nabers, A. F. Moore, Mrs. Leak, W. R. Todd, John Chenoweth, Sam Abernathy and Sam Crockett
  7 - B. S. Crump, Dr. Charles Bonner, James Walker, Chas. Ginsey, James Nuttall, Sam Bonner and R. L. Watson
  8 - Miss Julia Waite, Bateman's child, and Mrs. Blank
  9 - R. G. Campbell, Thomas A. Falconer, George Wing, Virginia Lynch and W. H. Ross.
  10 - Wm. Crump, Mrs. J. R. Dougherty, Miss Corilla Record, Hal Johnson, Clem Read, Victor Smith, W. J. Marett, Mrs. S. H. Pryor, Willie Wooten, Charles Chenoweth, E. T. Brinkley's child, Alex Seyple, J. C. Potter, R. W. Fort and A. A. Armstrong
  11 - Clarissa Davis, Father Oberti, Charles Schneider, Winfield S. Featherston, Jr., Mrs. Richard Daniel and Richard Daniel

12 - Minerva Lynch, Miss Read, Henry Epps and Scott Epps
13 - Mr. Brannon, Lizzie Lane (colored), E. T. Brinkley's child, E. W. Upshaw, Mrs. John Potter, Mrs. R. Hastings, Sam Kimball, and Dina Ingram (colored)
14 - Mariah Anderson (colored)
15 - George Kimball, Ben. Casey, Pat McGuire, George Johnson (colored) and Em. Jones (colored)
16 - Laura Demmey, Lewis Thompson, Mr. Dunn, James M. Kean, Lotta Ingraham (colored), O. J. Quiggins' child, and Mrs. Geo. Kimball
17 - Mr. E. D. Miller, Caroline Washington (colored), Ben Boyd (colored), Mrs. R. L. Watson, Peter Webber, Miss Mary Stewart and Mrs. W. S. Featherston
18 - Mrs. John Foreman, J. W. Webber, J. H. Stone, Mrs. Martin Knable and Jane McGary
19 - Stephen Knapp, Mrs. Louis Thompson, child of Rebecca Lea (colored), Wm. Collins (colored) and Col. H. W. Walter
20 - E. T. Brinkley, Capt. John Fennell, Dr. Manning, Miss Lizzie Butler and Howard Falconer
21 - Hugh Winborn and Julia Stojowski
22 - Sister Stanislas, Avant Walter, John Larouche, Eugene Leidy, Jr., Charles Harris (colored), Jim Fowler (colored), Mollie Cox's child (colored), Henry Harris (colored), Mary Gholson, Henry Carter (colored)
23 - Miss Liza Allen, Albert Rollins (colored), Henry Morton (colored), Mrs. Stone, Maj. Kinloch Falconer, Miss Darthnia Allen, Miss Nancy Allen, Dr. F. M. Fennell
24 - Thomas Henderson's child, Margaret Glassey, Mrs. Gaitley's son, Willie Castello, Dr. J. W. Fennell, Amelia Maughan
25 - Dan Phillips (col.), Jacob Berry (col.), John Power, Miss Annie Stewart, Mrs. Hutchinson
26 - Mrs. Harrington, Wm. Yancy's child, Jim Wells, Dr. Lewis, Mrs. Yancy, James R. L. Hunt, Frank Walter, Mrs. Jeff McGowan, Jimmie Walter, Gordon Allen, Sister Stella, P. Hobdon, J. M. Lumpkin
27 - Mr. Johnston, Glenn Fant, John Banks, John Hastings, Mr. Gholson at Depot, Mrs. Kate O'Gray, Jim Wells' wife, Mrs. Archie Straws, Corvan Roxy
28 - Thos. Wade, Mrs. M. Ghery, Alex. Hohenwurt, Agatha Saunders, Mrs. Crown McGuire, Miss

            Lucy Fort, Sister Margarette, Martin Thomas, Mollie Virginia, Eli Walker, Guy Allen (colored child), Miss Georgia Featherston

      29 - C. H. Walker, Dr. W. O. McKinney, Mrs. McDermott, Dan Oliver, Wm. Washington (col.), L. P. Parish, Jno. German, Jno. Pearson, Eli Chew (col.), Lucinda Sims (col.)

      30 - Strauss' infant, Herrs' infant, Rufus Howard (col.), Doctor Raymond (col.), Henry Elliott (col.), Flora Anderson (col.) Smith Barker, Randall Moore (col.), Miss Christina Carlson

Oct. 1 - Mrs. J. C. Herr, Mrs. Parish, A. C. Henderson, Mike Tiernan, Haywood McKissack, Henry Cowan, Joseph Herr

      2 - Sister Corinthia, Peter Stineman, Maughon's child, H. J. McKeugh, Amanda Sutton (col.), Martin Kuable, Jane Hill (col.), Webber's child, Augustus Bowman, Martha Walker, Mrs. Julia Roberts, Col. A. J. Hess of Philadelphia

      3 - Seldon Fant, Daniel Gray (col.) Mrs. B. A. Myers, Jim Wells' child (col.), Hal Johnson's child (col.), Thos. Gilbert (col.)

      4 - Mr. Daily, E. H. Crump, Miss Lizzie Maler, James Henry

      5 - Sister Victoria, Millie Bradford's child (col.), Mr. Miller, Lucius Boxley (col.), Henry Edmundson (col.), John Hawkins (col.), Mr. Diller

      6 - Miss Allen, G. Strather (col.)

      7 - Jake Malci, Dow Craft's wife (col.)

      8 - Allen Brogden (col.)

      9 - John G. Adams, James McHugh, Geo. Parks

      10 - Child of Chas. Harris, Paton Edmundson (col.), Mrs. Haley

      11 - Jeff McGowan (col.), Sister Lorentia

      12 - Ida McGowan (col.), Mrs. James Miller, G. Thomas

      13 - Jacob Kraus, Alsey Lea (col.)

      14 - Mrs. Lane, Millie Shotwell (col.), Willie Price (col.), Edward Brim

      15 - Wife of Paton Edmundson (col.), son of Skoesburg

      16 - John Ellis (col.), Joshua Watson

      17 - Child of Paton Edmundson (col.), Charity Gains (col.)

      18 - Joel Luckey, Dennis Lane, Ed. Willis

      19 - James Calvin, Barton Connington, Willis Edwards

      20 - Rachel Cochran (col.), Henry Vandive, Polly Martin

      21 - Robert King, Squire Yewell, Lula Lesseur, Mr. Mooney

22 - Peter Gealer's son, Alf Rogers (col.), Mrs. Compton, Amelia Martin (col.), Thos. Dressler
23 - Harriet Moseley (col.)
24 - Dr. Compton, Josephine Martin (col.), John Kimbrough, John Tiernan
25 - W. J. L. Holland, Mrs. Dr. McKinney, Mrs. Peter Gheelan, Dennis Gilwood
26 - Mrs. Gutheries, Mrs. Byers
28 - Mrs. Sam Coffin (col.)
29 - Miss Cora McWilliams
30 - Tede Nelms

Nov. 1 - R. A. McWilliams twins
2 - Thomas Hebdon, Henry Armstead's child
5 - Robert Adams, Eugene Cochran
14 - W. T. Barry's child
15 - James Donahue
18 - J. E. Tobin

January 9, 1879

Died at her home near Waterford, Miss., Mrs. Martha A. Bowen, wife of R. A. Bowen, aged 60 years, 8 months and 22 days. She was the wife of Rev. J. A. Bowen. (Author's note - husband's initials as given)

Died in Arkansas on December 30th, 1878, Mrs. Martha Worsham, sister of Mrs. Mary Finley, of this city.

Died in Holly Springs, Miss., Sept. 7th, 1878, Samuel W. Bonner. Born and raised here, his days were spent among us.

Died at Holly Springs, Miss., on September 29th, 1878, Howard Falconer, in the 43rd year of his age.

Lizzie Georgia, eldest daughter of Gen. W. S. and Elizabeth A. Featherston, was born in Holly Springs, Miss., on the 5th of June, 1861, and died of yellow fever on the 28th of September, 1878.

April 24, 1879

Died in Memphis, April 18th, 1879, of consumption, Miss Cinderella Williams, col'd., of Holly Springs, aged 20 years. She belonged to the Baptist Church.

Mr. John M. Dent, a clerk of the Parisot Line of steamers, was instantly killed by Police Capt. Jack Brereton. (Vicksburg, April 20)

THE COMET
Jackson, Mississippi

August 9, 1879

Died in Chicago, Ill., on the 1st of August, 1879, after a lingering illness, Hon. H. Musgrove, for a number of years a resident of this city.

Died at the residence of his father, on White Sand, Lawrence County, Carl, infant son of Scott and Susie R. Hathorn, aged one year, nine months and twenty-two days.

August 30, 1879

Col. D. A. Holman, indicted for the murder of Dr. W. L. Lowry and Mr. John Arnold, at Johnsonville, last winter, has made application to Judge B. F. Trimble for a writ of habeas corpus, which has been granted. (Vicksburg Commercial)

On Thursday night a young man named Charles Henly, living a few miles north of Cumberland, cut down a tree for the purpose of catching a mink. The tree fell on Henly killing him instantly. Henly was a young man just grown, and the son of highly respected parents. (Walthall Pioneer)

Henry M. Dixon, who was shot and killed at Yazoo City, Mississippi, by James Barksdale, seems to have come of violent stock; his father, Major Henry Dixon, having been killed in an encounter at Alexandria, Va., about the close of the war, with Dr. T. Clay Maddux, of this city. (Baltimore News)

September 13, 1879

Many will be surprised to hear of the death of Mrs. Mary Withers, nee, Miss Mary Peyton, for several years a resident of this place. She graduated at Fair Lawn Institute and had been married but about three years, and we believe, was the mother of a beautiful little cherub.

October 11, 1879

Another horrible and cold-blooded murder was committed in this county at Cawthon's steam mill, on September 26th, by one Sumling, on the person of D. H. Lewis. They were brothers-in-law and at work together, when Sumling struck Lewis on the posterior portion of the cranium with a handspike. One blow was sufficient to fell the victim to the ground and prove fatal in five or six hours. When he struck the fatal blow he exclaimed to Lewis, "you called my little girl a liar." (Holly Springs South)

October 18, 1879

J. S. Mason, Jr., son of Maj. J. S. Mason, of the Port Gibson Reveille, and local editor of that paper, died on the 4th inst. The deceased was born on the 2nd day of March, 1848. In the summer of 1864, when he had hardly reached the age of 16 years, he entered the Confederate army and remained there till the close of the war.

We regret to learn of the death of Mr. G. P. Farley, one of the oldest citizens of Jefferson County. Mr. Farley died at Rodney, and must have been nearly 75 years of age.

October 25, 1879

Died on the 9th, at the residence of the late Dr. W. W. Liddell, in Carrollton, Miss., Miss Rachel Thompson, a native of Virginia, in the 102nd year of her age.

We announce the death of Col. S. Threlkeld, which occurred at his residence at LaFayette Springs, a few days since. Our county has lost one of it's most honored citizens. (Oxford Eagle)

We learn of a difficulty at Air Mount last Saturday, between Mr. Frank Durret and Mr. Sam Murphree, in which the former was killed. We do not know the particulars. (Water Valley Standard)

On Wednesday night of last week, Mr. Alexander Milstead died at his residence on Turkey Creek, in this county, from the effect of a gun shot wound in the arm, which he had received some days before. By some means, Mr. Milstead accidentally discharged a shot gun, the load lacerating his arm in a terrible manner. (Water Valley Courier)

November 1, 1879

Mrs. E. W. Howcott, who has been prostrated by serious illness for several months, is sinking daily and her demise is expected at any moment. (Canton Mail)

We chronicle the death of Mrs. Florence Mimms, wife of Mr. Sam Mimms, which occurred on Wednesday last week, at her late residence at Utica.

Mrs. Lucinda McMackin, widow of the late Gen. T. C. McMackin, for many years a citizen of Vicksburg, died at the residence of her nephew, Mr. McAlpine, at Christianburg, Ala., on the 18th, in the eightieth year of her age.

We are in receipt of the sad news of the death of our associate, Capt. W. B. Yowell, at Oakland. (Coffeeville Times)

The sad news reaches us of the death of Mr. E. B. Drane, formerly of Enterprise, and son of the late Judge W. Drane. His death, which occurred in New Mexico, was caused by the accidental discharge of a pistol in his own hands.

From Perry county we learn that Thomas P. Hinton, an old citizen of that county, aged about 54 years, was bitten by a rattlesnake on the 11th, from the effects of which he died in a few hours. He was in the woods hunting at the time, but lived to get home. He leaves a wife and several children.

Mr. L. J. Lampley, a brakeman on the M. & O. R. R., while in the act of coupling the cars at Whistler, the 21st, was caught between the cars and badly mangled, one arm and leg being nearly severed, from the effects of which he has since died.

On the night of the 19th, a mob of ruffians went to the residence of Dr. E. F. H. Johnson, a citizen of Greensboro, and very violently attacked the house with rocks and brick-bats. Mr. Johnson endured it until his patience was exhausted, and stepped out to his store a few paces distant, to get a gun, when the mob fired on his mortally wounding him. He died the next day. (Walthall Pioneer)

November 8, 1879

A difficulty occurred at Vaughns Station, on Saturday night, between two colored men, Jim Peyton and Jerry Roberson, in which the former shot the latter dead with a pistol. Peyton made his escape. (Canton Mail)

On October 24th, little Louie Kemp, aged about 1 year, second son of Mr. G. R. Kemp, was at play with several other children at the lumber yard of Mr. R. H. Hoffman, near his parents residence on Union Street, when a large pile of planks toppled over and fell upon him, crushing his body and killing him almost instantly. His elder brother, aged six years, was also badly bruised. (Canton Mail)

One of the most painful accidents resulting in death that it has been our duty to record in some time, happened last Saturday, the 25th, at West Pascagoula, the victim being Fernando Gautier, aged 18 years and 4 months, son of Mr. F. Gautier, proprietor of the mills at the West Side. (Democrat Star) (Author's note - This is all there was)

On last Wednesday afternoon a serious shooting affair occurred between Mr. Raynor Whitfield and Mr. Newman Byrn, in which the former was wounded in the mouth and hip. Pistols were used in the recounter which came on Front Street between the grocery stores of Messers. Cunningham and Borroum.

Later - Since writing the above we learn that Mr. Whitfield died on Thursday morning. (Corinth Herald)

Yesterday evening Mrs. Thomas Garner gave her little child, aged about fifteen months, a fatal dose of morphine, by mistake, supposing it to be quinine. About 1 o'clock at night the little one breathed it's last.

November 15, 1879

From Eureka, Sunflower County -- Mr Robert Rayford, a young man, was chosen Assessor of Sunflower County at the recent election. After his election he said, "The people of this county have honored me with this office, and I will deserve their confidence. This is my last day for drinking." That evening he was left in charge of the grocery store of Messers, Faison & Heathman, and retired to the bedroom in the rear of the store. During the night, cries for help were heard, and the neighbors reached the spot only to find the grocery wrapt in a sheet of flame and almost consumed. When daylight broke, nothing remained but the ashes of the building and the charred remains of young Rayford.

December 13, 1879

Died at Concordia, Miss., on the 24th of November, Mrs. Indiana C. Barlow, aged about 40 years, wife of Mr. Frank Barlow, formerly of Raymond. The deceased was the youngest daughter of Saml. T. and Mary King, among the earliest settlers in Raymond. She leaves two children.

Capt. S. A. Matthews, of Summit, passed through Jackson last Wednesday, on his way to Indian Bay, Ark., where he goes to look after the affairs of his son, Eugene, recently accidentally wounded by himself with a pistol, which caused his death. Capt. Matthews will take his remains to Summit. The deceased was a brother of Sergeant Matthews, of the Penitentiary.

January 24, 1880

On Wednesday evening last, a colored man by the name of Williamson Baylor, descended into a well on Mr. J. C. Falconer's place, near Terry, Miss., for the purpose of cleaning it out. After he had been in the well for some time without making any noise, Mr. Falconer became alarmed and called him without elicting any reply. Another colored man named Stephen Jordan, volunteered to go down in the well and see what was the matter. As he never re-appeared, the truth flashed upon Mr. Falconer, that foul air was the cause, and Jordan was also a victim. He summoned assistance as was endeavoring to recover the unfortunate men.

The following is the verdict of a Coroner's jury in the case of a colored woman named Mollie Moore, who died on Sunday night, near this city: We the Jury of Inquest, to sit upon the body of Willie Moore, col., aged 32, who died near the Tinnin Monument three miles west of Jackson, Miss., are of the opinion that she came to her death from the effects of violent and cruel treatment from her husband, Isaac Moore. We the Jury believe that said Isaac Moore is guilty of murder.

Signed - Ben Jones, W. H. Robinson, Quay Hopkins, D. F. Henderson, Robt. Isler, Q. H. Hawkins.

February 14, 1880

Died at Mississippi City, on Feb. 11th, L. L. Davis. At the time of his death he held the appointment of U. S. Commissioner. For many years he was Chancery and Circuit Clerk of Harrison County.

Dr. Coles Meade Vaiden departed this life at his residence in Carroll County, on the 6th day of the present month, in the 68th year of his age.

June 12, 1880

Died in this city, June 10th, 1880, Edward Nall, infant son of Geo. W. and Lula Smith, aged 8 months.

Died in this city, June 7th, 1880, Walter Neely, son of the late Oscar Neely, of Rankin County, aged 22 years.

June 26, 1880

On last Sunday night a most cowardly murder was committed at Tougaloo, in Hinds County. Mr. J. H. Boyle, while sitting with his family in the evening, was fired upon by a concealed assassin, who discharged both barrels of a gun, and sent no less than eight balls entirely through his neck and body, and lodged at least twelve in his heart and shoulder. He lived until 6:00 o'clock Tuesday morning.

On Wednesday morning last, Miss Mary Flanery, eldest daughter of D. Flanery, Esq., 19 years of age, was found dead in her bed. Miss Flanery retired Tuesday night in her usual good health. The physician pronounced heart disease as the cause of her death.

July 10, 1880

Died near Madison Station, July 3rd, 1880, Mrs. N. J. Montgomery, wife of D. P. Montgomery, in the 30th year of her age.

Col. Wm. B. Shannon, who fell in a duel with Col. E. B. Cash, in South Carolina, on the 5th, was a brother-in-law of our townsman, Hon. Thos. A. McWillie. He was about sixty years old and leaves a wife and thirteen children.

July 17, 1880

Died in Huntsville, Ala., July 5, 1880, Charles P. Cabaniss, aged 67 years. Mr. Cabiness was a brother of the late Dr. Cabaniss, of this city.

John Nelson, Esq., an old citizen of this community, died in this city on Saturday night last, in the sixty-sixth year of his age. He was a member of the Masonic Order. Mr. Nelson leaves a large family.

The death of Sue Lemly occurred last Monday night. She was the wife of Mr Wm S. Lemly.

July 24, 1880

The Circuit Court was engaged, on Thursday, in trying the case of Henry Washington (colored), for the murder of Mr. Hill, which occurred near Mississippi Springs, about three weeks ago. The evidence elicited proved the killing to have been of the most cold blooded and unprovoked, and no mitigating circumstances were brought out, with a verdict of "guilty as charged." The Judge passed sentence as follows: "That he should be placed in the county jail, and there be kept until the 2nd day of September, 1880, to be taken thence to a place to be hung by the neck until he is dead, and may the Lord have mercy on your soul."

On Tuesday evening the body of a white man by the name of John Nelson was found in one of the frame buildings situated near the fair grounds, and owned by Col. Hamilton. The Jury of Inquest opinion was that he came to his death by his own act, by taking a dose of laudnum. The deceased had only a short time been pardoned out of the Penitentiary for the murder of his wife, in Harrison County, some years back. He was about 65 years of age and has grown children now living on the coast.

July 31, 1880

Mr. Carmel, Mississippi -- I send you a description of Sandy Strickland, who murdered Ann Pope (a negro), on the 1st, in this county. He first attempted to poison her by putting strychnine in her provisions. She would not eat it, saying it was too bitter. He afterwards must have decoyed her off about three miles, where her body was found, killed her with a wood knot, then made his escape. They had been living together as man and wife for about four years.

August 14, 1880

Died at Clarksville, Tenn., Eva May Scott, wife of Dr. W. P. Scott, of Bolivar County, Miss., aged 21 years.

Died at Clarksville, Tenn., August 10th, Georgia Yerger Scott, infant daughter of Dr. W. P. and Eva May Scott, aged 5 months and 22 days.

August 21, 1880

Last Friday Mr. Rance Magee shot and killed Cy Garner, a colored man, about six miles east of Summit. It seems that Garner was interfering in Mr. Magee's business and giving him (Magee) some jaw; that Magee told Garner repeatedly to "shut up," but he would not. Magee got his shot gun and fired upon Garner, lodging a load of buck shot in his back, which produced death almost instantly. Magee is still at large.

October 2, 1880

We learn of the death at Rosedale, in Bolivar County, on the 19th, of Dr. W. A. Scott. The deceased was a brother of Messers. Charles and George Y. Scott. (Greenville Times)

Dr. Scott was well known in this city and is a brother of our townsman, E. M. Scott.

Died at the convent in this city, this morning, Sister Mary Margaret, known to the world before she entered the Holy Sisterhood, as Miss Clara Julienne, daughter of the late Capt. Julienne, of Jackson. Sister Mary Margaret was born nearly twenty-nine years ago.

October 16, 1880

A negro woman named Mary Robinson was killed by her paramour on the plantation of Colonel W. L. Nugent, in this county, on Saturday night. Her neck was broken. The murderer, Ike McClain, claims that his mule kicked her.

Died at Hazlehurst, Miss., Oct. 10th, 1880, of diptheria, Maggie Belle, only child of Mr. E. D. and Mrs. Ella Elliott, aged one year, ten months and ten days.

December 11, 1880

Died Dec. 10, 1880, at her residence in Jackson, Mrs. Louisa Masters, aged 68 years, 1 month and 15 days.

We regret to announce the death of Hezekiah Holcombe, which took place at his residence in Rankin County, near Byram, on Nov. 28th. He died of pneumonia. Mr. Holcombe was about 75 years old and had lived in Rankin County for more than 40 years.

Our community is in deep distress at the death of our townsman, Capt. J. N. Atkinson. (Summit Times)

February 12, 1881

By a cablegram from Bitsche, Germany, to Mr. John Rohrbacher, of this city, we are informed of the death of his father, a former old citizen of Jackson. M. Rohrbacher, Sr., in feeble health and being past seventy, his death was not unexpected. He leaves a widow and two daughters, besides his son John J. Rohrbacher.

July 9, 1881

Died at his residence in Madison Station, Miss., July 3rd, Thomas N. Jones, Sr., in the 54th year of his age. His remains were taken to Canton and interred.

July 30, 1881

Died at his residence in the town of Pontotoc, on the 9th, Hon. Jno. A. McNeil, in the 72nd year of his age. Col. McNeil was one of the pioneers of Pontotoc. Eight years ago he represented Pontotoc and Lafayette counties in the State Senate. Col. McNeil was never married.

Last Tuesday night, the 26th, there rang out three distinct shots, fired by Deputy Sheriff Cornelius of Issaquena County, who came here with a Mr. Rube, of Yazoo County, to arrest four or five colored hands for violating a contract to work. The result of the shooting was the almost instant killing of Henry Cole, one of the fugitives. Cornelius was arrested and sent to jail. (Vicksburg Commercial)

We are again called upon to chronicle a death in the family of Hon. J. M. Hardin. Last week we recorded the death of Benjamin, his eldest son; today it is John, his second son. The latter's death was caused by measles and meningitis.

Columbus Dispatch -- Last Sunday night, on Mr. Nick Hairston's plantation, near Crawford, a murder was committed in which Lena Borders and Jeff Wooten were the perpetrators and Alfred Borders was the victim. The particulars are: Lena Borders and her husband Alfred were walking past the house of Jeff Wooten. Jeff came out and the woman struck her husband on the head with a stick. This was followed by a heavy blow with a stick from Jeff, which prostrated their victim, and he was taken up and thrown into a cistern.

Wooten's statement is that the woman had been after him to kill her husband. He says he had no motive in killing him. Lena Borders says she was the second wife of the deceased, that there were children by the first marriage, that these children were the source of trouble, that her husband often beat her and she wanted to get rid of him.

A white man named Patterson, a carpenter by trade, committed suicide at the residence of Mrs. Kennedy at the corner of Levee and Depot streets, yesterday morning, by an overdose of morphine. The remains were interred in the City Cemetery last evening. (Vicksburg Herald)

The difficulty between McCafferty and D. B. Archer, in Choctaw County, resulting in the death of the former, grew out of a political difference. Mr. Yewing McCafferty made a speech in which he referred to certain proceedings as not being right and fair. Afterward Capt. D. B. Archer asked Mr. McCafferty if he meant what he said, and Mr. McCafferty said he did not intend to insult anyone; and before he could explain Archer shot him down and made his escape. Capt. Archer was one of the leading lawyers of Choctaw. Friends of Mr. McCafferty have offered a reward of $2000 for the arrest of Archer.

August 27, 1881

We announce the death of Capt. Harris Barksdale, which occurred last Monday, at his father's residence in this city. Capt. Harris was the eldest son of Maj. E. Barksdale, and member of the firm of Power and Barksdale. Capt. Harris had been in feeble health for some months with consumption.

Died in this city, the 22nd, Florence Medora, youngest child of Mr. & Mrs. E. C. Carroll.

September 24, 1881

Mr. H. Hofmaster, a respected citizen of Summit, died on the 16th.

October 1, 1881

We learn of the death of Rev. Thos. H. Hines, faithful minister of the Gospel, which occurred at Weatherford, Texas, on the 15th. He has relatives and friends in this city. He leaves a wife and five children.

December 10, 1881

A. T. Harvey, who was killed by the negro desperadoes at Marion, received fourteen wounds during the late war, and leaves a wife and six small children.

February 4, 1882

The death of John H. Echols occurred in this city last Sunday night. He was a native of Huntsville, Ala., and was forty-six years of age on the first of September last. He was State Treasurer immediately after the war, and State Revenue Agent.

February 11, 1882

Died at his father's residence near Forest, Robert C. Halbert, aged 29 years, of typhoid fever.

Died at Enterprise, Miss., Jan. 28th, Mr. W. H. Wolverton.

Died Jan. 19th, 1882, near Ripley, Sallie Tigert, daughter of Elisabeth and Thos. Tigert.

Died near Ashland, Benton County, Jan. 26th, Mrs. Sarah A. Tate, widow of Caswell Tate. She was a native of Rankin County and a member of the Baptist Church.

February 18, 1882

Mrs. Flora A. Anderson, the mother of the late Judge Fulton Anderson, died last Wednesday at the residence of Col. J. D. Stewart, in this city. She was a native of Kentucky and had attained the age of 98 years, keeping all her faculties to the last. Her funeral was preached at the Presbyterian Church and her remains were interred in the City Cemetery.

March 11, 1882

Mr. Sam'l. B. Knight, a native of this city and whose family now reside here, died suddenly in New Orleans last Wednesday, of apoplexy. At the time of his death he was employed as a compositor on the *Times Democrat*.

On February 28, 1882, a negro, David Parish, and the mule he rode, were instantly killed by lightening just as they were approaching main street Coffeeville.

The death sentence by hanging was duly executed against W. R. Jones, white, and Wm. Miller, colored, at Aberdeen, March 3rd. It will be remembered that they murdered the three Walker brothers near Aberdeen in November last.

March 18, 1882

Victor W. Thompson, for many years connected with the press of this State, passed away last Friday at Savannah, Tennessee, where he was engaged in the publication of a newspaper. He was the only brother of Col. S. M. Thompson, of the *Oxford Eagle*.

April 22, 1882

Died, Mr. Jno. H. Glass, editor of the Trenton, Tenn. *Mirror*.

Died, W. E. Bass, aged 49, near Frost Bridge, 3rd inst.

Died, Mary Newman, the little daughter of Jno. G. and Mary W. Breviard, on the 9th, at Natchez.

Died, Mrs. Bettie M. Ivy, Palo Alto, on the 5th.

Died, Mr. C. W. Braswell, at West Point, on the 14th.

Mr. Jno. T. Sanderford, a citizen of Lauderdale County, was run over and killed last Monday morning at the crossing of the Alabama Central and the Mobile and Ohio, by an engine of the latter.

June 10, 1882
Died in this city, the 8th, Julia, daughter of our fellow townsman, Mr. J. Feibleman.

June 17, 1882
Died last Sunday night, Ruth, infant daughter of Mr. & Mrs. G. E. Galceran.

We announce the death of Chas. Feibleman which occurred Wednesday night, after an illness of a week or ten days. In the last issue of the *Comet* there was a notice of the death of his sister from the same terrible disease -- typhoid fever. Mr. F. was a member of Gem Fire Company, No. 2.

At it's meeting on the first Monday of June, 1882, the members of the Board of Supervisors of Lawrence County expressed their appreciation of the services of Hezekiah Weatherby, late clerk of the Circuit and Chancery Courts of this county. He was killed in the ruins of the court house on the 22nd day of April, 1882, by the terrible tornado which left a track of destruction across the county and utterly destroyed nearly every house in the town of Monticello. Many lives were lost and many wounded.

Walter S. Davis, who for quite a while was a resident in this city and at one time editor of the *Jackson Daily Times*, was killed recently at Collinsville, Ala. Two young men named Walter Davis and W. B. Clay became engaged in a difficulty, which resulted in the death of Davis. The quarrel began by Davis accusing Clay of stealing some whickey from him. (Author's report -- a lengthy report followed)

June 24, 1882
Died June 14th, 1882, Mrs. Fannie Saul, daughter of Jno. Paden, aged 21 years.

Died near Aberdeen, May 20, Augusta Viola, daughter of L. J. and Mrs. N. E. Hilburn, aged 12 months, 2 days.

Died June 2, Henry Scarber, found dead near his camp.

July 8, 1882
Died June 29th, Louisa, daughter of W. I. and M. E. Smith, of Hazlehurst.

Died June 28th, Annie Laurie, infant daughter of **Mr. & Mrs. R. H. Henry,** of Brookhaven.

June 25th, Joseph Bennett, of Brandon, died near Madison Station.

Tom Jones, of Louisville, Miss. was shot and killed by F. L. Jones, a photographer, of the same place, last Monday evening. The difficulty originated about some conversation in regard to a young lady, Tom Jones having said that F. L. Jones had made certain remarks in regard to the lady, which F. L. Jones denied. F. L. Jones drew his pistol and fired upon Tom. The shooting occurred in front of **Dr.** Woodward's store.

July 22, 1882

Died near Atlanta, Calhoun County, on the 16th ult., Mrs. Dillania Walton, wife of Thos. Walton.

Died near Houston, Miss., on the 10th, Mr. A. K. Craig, an old and respected citizen.

Died in Yazoo City, Miss., on the 7th, William R. Patterson, in the 41st year of his age.

Died in Terry, Miss., on the 14th, Capt. W. D. Terry, one of the oldest citizens.

Died in Mobile, Ala., on the 14th, Wm. Arnold, an aged citizen.

Died near Louisville, Miss., on the 1st, Mr. Cass Covington.

Died near Oakland, Miss., Mr. A. C. Sheely, of consumption.

Died near Pontotoc, Miss., on the 8th, Col. Henry Duke, in the 64th year of his age.

Died in Meridian, Miss., on the 9th, Wade R. Thomas, aged 79, after a brief illness.

Died in Mississippi City, on the 10th, Charlie Estelle, infant son of Mr. & Mrs. W. H. Sims, of Raymond.

Died in Durant, on the 16th, Mrs. Julia Clay, wife of J. W. Clay.

Died in Forest, Miss., July 14, Mrs. Hattie E., wife of Mr. Wm. H. Gardner.

Died in Rankin County, Miss., July 1, Mrs. Ida Quinn Cofer.

August 5, 1882

Died in Vicksburg, on the 28th, Mr. John Henry Walters, an old and respected citizen.

Died at Holly Springs, on the 25th, at the residence of Mr. John Burton, Willie, son of Mr. & Mrs. Lowell, of Helena, Ark.

Died in Aberdeen, Miss., on the 19th ult., Mrs. Mattie B. Moore, of paralysis of the heart.

Died in Jackson, Miss., on the 1st, Mr. Jas. S. Barfield, one of the oldest citizens of this place.

Died at Henderson Point, Harrison County, Miss., July 14th, 1882, Mrs. Lena Kelly Vickars, mother of the late Wm. Vickars, of Mobile, Ala. Her age was about 88 years.

Died at Greenwood, in Leflore County, Miss., on the 12th ult., John R. Resor, in the 74th year of his age.

Died at Water Valley, on the 24th ult., J. S. Phillips.

Died at Terrell, on the 23rd, Mrs. Mary J. H., wife of Dr. W. H. Monday, after a short but severe illness.

Died in Jackson, on the 2nd, Mr. W. B. Ross, of hemituria.

Died in Forest, on the night of the 29th, Emma R. Killian, little daughter of Mr. & Mrs. J. D. Killian.

With sorrow we announce the death of Rev. T. J. Rowan of Memphis, Tenn., on the 28th of July, of typhoid fever. His remains were brought to Crystal Springs, Miss., his birthplace and the home of his parents. His remains were deposited in the Crystal Springs cemetery.

August 19, 1882

Died near Banner, Miss., on the 7th, Virgil Lee, eldest son of Addie and H. W. McGuire.

Died near Pittsboro, on the 19th ult., Zachariah David, youngest son of Larken and Sue Pate.

Died in Attala County, Miss., on the 23rd ult., Miss Zelda Dotson, oldest daughter of G. M. and S. L. Dotson, of Kosciusko.

Died near Booneville, Miss., on the 8th, Mrs. Fallis, wife of Mr. L. A. Fallis.

Died at Meridian, on the 7th, **Mr. W. L. Payne**, a young man.

Died in Carthage, on the 9th, the **Rev. H. P. Davis**, in the **68th** year of his age.

Died in Sharkey County, Miss., on the 9th, **Thos. J. Shelby**, aged **65** years.

Died at St. Louis, Mo., on the 13th, **Lizzie**, daughter of **T. B. Johnson**, of Concordia, Miss.

Died at his home on Yazoo river, nine miles below Yazoo City, on the 30th of July, Mr. Otho S. Paul, in the 35th year of his age.

Died in West Station, July 29th, 1882, little Pearl, daughter of Mr. & Mrs. Gaines Anderson.

Died at Greenwood Springs, Miss., July 31st, D. C. Greenwood, an old citizen of Monroe County.

Died in Winston County, July 30th, Mr. J. B. Mitchell.

Mr. Bryant Harrell, an old citizen of Scott County, died last week while on a visit in Alabama.

Wilhe W. Erwin, formerly of Charleston, Miss., died at Columbus, Ky., on the 22nd July, in the 27th year of his age.

Died on Wolf River, near Pass Christian, Miss., July 30th, Mr. Edward Crosby, a native of Belfast, Maine, and for many years a citizen of Harrison County, Miss.

Died in Meridian, August 1st, Donald Augustus, youngest son of Hon. H. M. and Mrs. C. E. K. Street.

Mr. Eugene Lawson, lately publisher of the *Greenville Mississippian*, died in that city a few days ago.

Died August 2nd, 1882, Eugene L. Weeks, Noble Grand of Franklin Lodge No. 5, I. O. O. F., aged 26 years and 4 months.

At the residence of her sister, in this city, on the 12th, died suddenly, the wife of Dr. John Hunter, in the twentieth year of her age. (Mobile Register)

Estelle Gaddis died of consumption, July 30th, 1882. (Ouchitta Telegraph)

August 26, 1882

Died in Macon, Miss., July 22nd, 1882, Mrs. Dora E. Connor.

Died in McComb City, August 13, 1882, Mrs. J. Collins, in the 23rd year of her age.

Died in Wesson, Miss., on the 14th of August, Miss Eva Cransby, at the residence of her father.

Died at Haulka, Aug. 8th, 1882, John Istell.

Died at Sardis, Panola County, Miss., Aug. 2nd, 1881, Prince V. Short, son of W. H. and Victoria Short.

Died in Natchez, Miss., Aug. 18th, Mrs. Matilda Healy, wife of Peter Healy, in the 82nd year of her age.

Died at her residence in West Station, Aug. 19th, Mr. Wm. Anderson, one of the oldest citizens of Holmes County.

September 23, 1882

Died near Columbus, Miss., September 2nd, 1882, Susan Pittman, in the 25th year of her age.

Died near Summit, Miss., on the 26th of August, 1882, Otto Clifton Kenna and Bessie Lea Kenna, children of F. J. and Laura E. Kenna.

Died on Deer Creek in Washington County, on the 3rd ult., Mr. T. G. Walcott.

Died in Rolling Fork, Aug. 3rd, little Bertha, daughter of Dr. and Mrs. A. M. Waddell.

Died at McKinneyville, Miss., August 22nd, 1882, Miss Susie H. Shelton, daughter of Rev. James Shelton.

Died in Fort Adams, Miss., August 18th, Mr. Sith Kline, in the 72nd year of his age.

Died in Starkville, Miss., on the 18th ult., Robert S. Turner.

Died in Shubuta, on the 7th, George, infant son of Dr. and Mrs. R. M. Hand.

Died in Yazoo City, August 29th, Ex-Mayor J. H. Holt, a member of the bar.

Died at Strayhann, Miss., August 25th, Patt Floyd.

Died in Vicksburg, September 7th, Col. L. A. Campbell, one of the leading men in the affairs of Vicksburg.

Died in Port Gibson, August 6th, 1882, Mrs. Fannie Barnett, in the 35th year of her age.

Died September 7th, at Conway, Mississippi, Mrs. Emily Fulton, aged 45 years; and little Martha Allen, aged one year, eight months and two days. Mrs. Harriet Finklen, aged 65 years, died September 13th, 1882.

October 7, 1882
Died at Milliken's Bend, Jno. V. McPherson.

Died at the residence of his parents, on the 24th, William Y. Brown, in the 3rd year of his age.

Died at Briarfields, Claiborne County, Sept. 22nd, Robt. Ralston, in the 3rd year of his age.

Died at Sardis, the 22nd ult., little Robin, son of R. P. and Kate Jenkins.

Died at his residence on Big Black (river) in Hinds County, Sept. 19th, 1882, Mr. E. F. Campbell, in the 45th year of his age.

Died at the residence of Mr. W. A. Taylor, Jackson, Tenn., Emma Alla Johnston, formerly a citizen of this place.

Died in Canton, September 26th, 1882, Adolphus Brown, Professor of Music in the Canton Female Institute.

Died near Chattanooga, Tenn., on the Alabama Great Southern Rail Road, Mr. James McCutchen, of Washington County, Miss.

Died at the residence of her son-in-law, Mr. J. F. Sexton, Mrs. Elizabeth Hays, aged 79 years.

October 14, 1882
The death of Mr. A. S. Watts occurred at his father's house in Newton, on Wednesday night last. Sank, as he was called by his friends, was a young man.

Died at her residence in Canton, Oct. 1st, Mrs. M. V. Richards.

Died in Canton, Oct. 2nd, Daisy Euphemia, youngest child of Jas. W. and Mattie Walker, age 9 years, 9 months and 18 days.

Died at Liberty, on the 3rd, after a long illness, Miss Arminta McElwee, wife of Jas. M. McElwee, of this county. Her remains were deposited in the old family burying ground three miles north of Liberty.

Died at Nebraska Landing, La., on the 27th Sept., 1882, Geo. Xavier, aged three years and one month, son of William T. and Eliza S. Sefferied.

Died at his residence on Big Black, in this county, Sept. 19th, 1882, Mr. E. F. Cambell, in the 45th year of his age.

Died near Torrance, September 17th, of consumption, Willie, daughter of Mr. J. F. and Elizabeth Smith, aged five years.

Died at the residence of her nephew, Ed. McD. Anderson, in St. Helen's Parish, La., on the 18th of September, 1882, Mrs. Martha Melissa Courtney, daughter of David and Nancy Lea, of Amite County, aged _9 years, 7 months and 13 days.

Died at Lake city, Yazoo County, Miss., Sept. 5th, 1882, Mrs. Sallie N. Withers, formerly of Grenada, Miss., and wife of C. A. Withers, Esq., of Virginia.

Died at Mount Pleasant Landing near Port Hudson, La., the 1st of October, 1882, T. C. Borum, aged 29 years, 8 months and 20 days.

October 21, 1882

The death of Dr. A. K. Martin, brother of Gen. Wm. Martin, stamps "finis" to a life. Deprived of speech, he presided over the deaf and dumb institutions in Mississippi, Missouri and Louisiana. His demise transpired at the residence of his brother near this city yesterday morning, in the 58th year of his age.

The late James Tapley, of Jackson, died on Tuesday last in Louisville, Ky., at the residence of Mr. Wm. Tabb. He was raised here in Jackson. In 1880 he married Miss Annie E. Hyatt, of Louisville. He struggled hard against the consumptive cough, but in vain. He leaves a daughter aged one year.

October 28, 1882

Col. William Arthur died at the Neely House, in this city, on Wednesday night, aged about seventy years. Col. Arthur was for twenty-five years a wealthy and prominent citizen of Holly Springs, and subsquently of Bolivar County in this state, but about twelve years since removed to Kansas. He leaves surviving him, one daughter, the wife of Gen. J. R. Chalmers, of this state, and also a widow, his third wife, and a minor daughter in Kansas.

Died on Thursday last, after a long and painful illness, Janie, eldest daughter of Mr. and Mrs. D. Flanery.

Died in Canton, the 19th, Mrs. Jane Hawkins, mother of the late Mrs. D. H. Otto, aged 88 years.

Died in Canton on the 18th, of diptheria, Jessie, youngest child of Mr. Wm. and Mrs. Lizzie Priestley.

Died at the residence of his grandfather, John G. Wallace, three miles north of Holly Springs, Wallace Manning, infant son of Ben T. and Mary E. Harris.

Died at Yorktown, Va., on October 7th, 1882, Nathaniel Taylor, Esq.

Died at Free Run, Yazoo County, Miss., July 16, 1882, Mrs. Emma Shurley, wife of J. R. Shurley, aged 34 years.

Died at Free Run, Yazoo County, Miss., Joseph Hughes Frazier, infant son of Mr. James Frazier, aged 3 years, 9 months.

November 11, 1882
Died in Winona, the 30th, Ruth, little daughter of Mr. & Mrs. Stratton.

Died at the residence of her husband, in the southwest corner of Attala County, October 25, Mrs. Caroline Shrock, wife of the Hon. Jos. K. Shrock.

Mr. Robt. Wynn, a resident of Meridian for a number of years, died at his home in this city, on the 25th, and was buried in McLemore cemetery.

Died in Summit, October 26th, 1882, Henrietta, infant daughter of Mr. & Mrs. L. W. Howard, aged two months and ten days.

Died in this city, the 26th of October, 1882, Mrs. Martha E. Knox, aged 39 years. - Panola

Died near Pittsboro, Calhoun County, Miss., Sept. 21, 1882, Mrs. Barshaba Maxey, wife of W. F. Maxey.

Died in Natchez, Miss., Nov. 3, 1882, Edwin G., son of Alphonse and Louise Bahin, aged 3 years, 5 months.

November 18, 1882
Died in Shuqualak, on the 10th, Col. Thos. Haynes, an old citizen of Noxubee County. He was one of the first settlers of the county.

Died at her home on Lake Bolivar, the 24th of October, 1882, Mrs. Mary E. Ballore, in the 58th year of her age.

Johnnie T., son of Thos. L. and Sarah E. Sullivan, was born March 7, 1874 in Marshall County, Miss., and died after a brief illness November 5th, 1882, near Ennis (his home) in Ellis County, Texas.

THE NEW MISSISSIPPIAN
Jackson, Mississippi

December 18, 1883
Macon, Miss., Dec. 12 -- Bill Norris, colored, was executed this afternoon for wife murder last July.

Col. J. R. Powell, a wealthy planter, was shot and killed at Modoc on the Sunflower River last Saturday night. The cause was not given, but Robinson made his escape. The slayer of Powell is the eldest son of Mr. Gordon Robinson, for many years a respected citizen of Vicksburg. By strange coincidence, about one year ago Col. Powell shot and killed his overseer on his plantation near Yazoo City, whose name was also Robinson. He was no relation, however, to the man who slew him. At the time of his death Col. Powell was a resident of Washington County, though he had lived in Yazoo County a number of years. He was 69 years of age.

January 10, 1884
The remains of Mr. J. M. Buckley, who died at McKenneville in Sharkey County, reached this city last evening. Mr. Buckley was born in Lawrence County and was fifty-three years of age. He leaves a wife and five children.

February 19, 1884
The Hon. Benjamin King died yesterday at his home in Beauregard. He was sixty years of age. Up to the time of his death he was one of the leading lawyers of South Mississippi.

Capt. James M. Buckley was born in Lawrence County, Miss., November 10, 1830. On April 1, 1856 he was married in Pike County to Miss Bethany Craft, with whom he lived to the day of his death. In 1862 he was elected Chancery Clerk of Lawrence County, which position he held until 1869, when he removed to Brookhaven. In

1872 he was elected Chancery Clerk of Lincoln County and held that office until 1879, when he was made Deputy Auditor of the State.

July 29, 1884

Mr. George Fearn, one of the oldest citizens of this city, died last Saturday morning, aged 87 years. He was by birth a Virginian.

February 3, 1885

Sidney, young son of Gen. A. M. West, of Holly Springs, shot himself through the head accidentally, on the 24th, causing death instantly. This sad affair occurred at Oxford, where the deceased had established himself as a lawyer. He was carelessly handling a pistol when it accidently fired.

In Lawrence County, in August last, a young white man named James S. Lotlin, killed his own brother and escaped, leaving the country. The culprit was at last captured in Navarro County, Texas and he is now in jail at Hazlehurst.

Judge A. H. Arthur, of Vicksburg, died at his residence on the 28th. He was president of the Board of Supervisors at the time of his death.

Col. Fleet C. Mercer, an old citizen of Holmes County and one of the noted surveyors in the State, died in that county last week. He was the father of Capt. F. C. Mercer, of Yazoo City.

March 24, 1885

Mr. E. D. Clarke, recently appointed Assistant Secretary of the Interior, late of Vicksburg, died of pneumonia in Washington City yesterday.

Judge Jeffords, member of Congress from the Vicksburg-Greenville district, died unexpectedly in Vicksburg.

March 31, 1885

Hon. Jacob Thompson died in Memphis on Tuesday last, in the seventy-fifth year of his age. The deceased came from North Carolina to this State in early manhood. He was Secretery of Interior in Mr. Buchanan's Cabinet.

May 12, 1885

In Greene County, while Mr. Milton McKay was driving with several children, to church, a cowardly assassin fired from ambush, killing the father instantly but did not hit either of the children. The eight year old boy, largest of the children, was trying to turn the horse and go home when a neighbor rode up and led the buggy with the weeping children and murdered father home.

A jury of inquest was summoned at Rolling Fork in reference to the death of Mr. S. F. Shelton, the mayor, J. H. Cartright, acting coroner. The finding: "S. F. Shelton came to his death by a gun shot wound inflicted by W. K. McLaurin."

June 2, 1885
The death of Miss Sue Wilkinson occurred Saturday night, very sudden and unexpected. Miss Wilkinson had been a teacher in the College Green Public School.

July 16, 1885
Died in this city yesterday, at the residence of her mother, Miss Sallie O'Sullivan, after a lingering illness.

August 11, 1885
Mrs. Helena Muller, relict of the late Christian Muller, died last Thursday. She had been a resident of Jackson for many years.

September 15, 1885
Mr. H. C. Daniel, one of Hinds county's oldest citizens, died at his residence near this city, last Sunday night, after a lingering illness. The deceased was a civil engineer by profession. He leaves a large family of sons and daughters.

We are pained to record the death of Miss Nora Schwartz, daughter of Mr. I. Schwartz, only eighteen years of age.

September 29, 1885
An old gentleman who has been around Jackson for quite a while, Mr. Miall by name, was found dead in his room Sunday morning. He was an Englishman by birth. The Jury of Inquest opinion: "he came to his death from old age and general debility."

October 20, 1885
Died on the 16th, T. M. Henry, Jr., aged five weeks and five days.

October 27, 1885
Robt. J. Doxey, who poisoned his wife in Marshall County on the 8th of last August, and deserted five small children preparatory to fleeing with a Mrs. Johnson, was taken from the jail at Holly Springs by a mob of armed men and hung one mile north of town.

November 10, 1885
Mrs. Mary J. Moore, wife of A. V. Moore, died on Wednesday night last, after a brief illness. Her husband was in New York at the time.

December 1, 1885
Died in Jackson, on November 14th, 1885, Marie, daughter of Mrs. Mary O'Brien.

December 8, 1885
Died at an advanced age, Dec. 7th, 1885, Mrs. E. A. Shackleford, of this city. Mrs. Shackleford was probably Jackson's oldest lady resident and was mother-in-law of John Echols, deceased, at one time State Treasurer of Mississippi.

December 15, 1885
We learn of the death of John F. Vance of Hazlehurst. For forty years he has edited and published the old *Copiahian*.

NATCHEZ DAILY DEMOCRAT
Natchez, Mississippi

January 8, 1876
Died January 6, 1876 at the residence of Mrs. Edward, in Natchez, Miss., of lung disease, Andrew Thomson McChesney, of Galesburg, Ill., aged 45 years and 3 days.

January 23, 1876
Died at her residence on Pine St. in Natchez, on Jan. 17th, 1876, Mrs. Virginia Burns, in the 38th year of her age, wife of William Burns.

February 5, 1876
Sexton's report of deaths within the city of Natchez:
Jan. 21 - Marcella Brannock, c., of diptheria, aged 51 years
  22 - Alice Withers, c., spasms, aged 18 months
  24 - William Williams, c., pneumonia, aged about 25 years
  26 - Easter Ford, c., pneumonia, aged about 25 years
  27 - Infant of Emma Harris, premature birth
  29 - Matilda Wade, c., chronic uterus disease, aged 45 years
  30 - Alonzo C. Goff, heart disease, aged about 65 years
  30 - Betsy Bell, c., dropsy, aged 82 years
Feb. 2 - Fannie Johnson, c., dropsy, aged about 75 years

February 11, 1876
Died at Retirement, Adams County, Feb. 10th, Edwin R. Bennett, in the sixty-fifth year of his age.

February 12, 1876
Died at Annapolis, Md., Feb. 10th, 1876, Reverdy Johnson, in the 80th year of his age.

February 13, 1876
Died in this city, Feb. 11th, 1876, Mollie E. Peebles, in the 18th year of her age.

February 19, 1876
Sexton's report of deaths within the city of Natchez:
Feb. 4 - Chas. Wolcott, convulsions, aged 56 years
7 - Margaret Scott, c., burns, aged 4 years
9 - Marcellus Brannock, c., diptheria, aged 4 years
12 - Mary E. Peebles, typhoid fever, aged 18 years
16 - Mrs. Harriet Dowling, gastric ulcer, aged about 82 years

February 22, 1876
Died suddenly, on Ridges Plantation, Corcordia Parish, (La.) Feb. 7, 1876, Fountain Winstone Ford, Jr., aged ten years, three months and three days, the youngest son of Fountain W. Ford.

Died at his residence in this county, on Feb. 20th, 1876, Edward Dixon, in the 66th year of his age.

February 23, 1876
(Holly Springs South) Our community was startled yesterday morning by the intelligence that the body of Marcus Louis had been found in his store, stiff in death, with his head crushed and his brains scattered, by a blow from an axe, which was lying by his side. The object, it is believed, was robbery. Circumstances strongly point to one John Kennedy, an Irishman, as the perpetrator of this diabolical act. He is about twenty-five years of age, wears his hair short, no whiskers, light complexion, heavy set, blue eyes, worked on the railroad near this place a short time, but for several weeks has been doing nothing but gambling.
Later -- The testimony before the Jury of Inquest tends to show that Kennedy was the murderer, and that Miles Washington, (col.), who has been arrested, was accessory.

February 29, 1876
Died at Nina Plantation, suddenly, the result of an accident on the 24th of February, 1876, Mrs. Lizzie Adams, wife of W. A. Adams, and daughter of Wm. H. Dunbar, in the 39th year of her age. She was trimming a lamp before the fire when it broke in some way,

and the fluid ran down her clothes, and as she was standing before the fire her clothes immediately caught and in an instant she was ablaze and no available assistance near. Her husband lying sick, was unable to rise but crawled to her and in his feeble efforts to assist her, his clothes also took fire and he was also considerably burned. After lingering a few hours, she died.

March 3, 1876

Died in Natchez, February, 1876, Robert McKee, a native of County Cavan, Ireland, in the 62nd year of his age.

The news reached town yesterday of the cold-blooded murder of Frank Pressly, step-son of our fellow citizen, John M. T. Reid. All the information we could obtain was that Frank was sitting eating his supper, and was shot through the window and killed by some unknown assassin. This occurred on his farm near Nashville, in Noxubee County, where he had lived since last year. (Columbus Independent)

News comes from Honduras of the death of Hon. Colin J. McRae, a brother of the late John J. McRae, who was at one time Governor of and Congressman from Mississippi.

March 4, 1876

Sexton's report of deaths within the city of Natchez:
February 17 - Israel Barnes, c., injuries, aged 40 years
19 - Mary Henderson, c., pneumonia, aged 75 years
19 - Terry Coyle, heart disease, aged 60 years
23 - Milly Roach, c., pneumonia, aged 65 years
24 - Ross Spires, acrofula, aged 20 months
25 - Infant of Susan Smith, c., acute meningitis, aged 18 months
25 - James Ross, c., heart disease, aged 6 years
28 - James McKee, gastritis, aged 62 years
March 2 - Anna Wood, c., consumption, aged about 25 years

March 12, 1876

Died on the 5th of March, 1876, at Nina, W. A. Adams. Three months ago, the mother, by an appalling accident, was cut down in the bloom of life. The father, already enfeebled by disease and injured by the accident, succumbed to the shock, and so the two have fallen asleep together.

Departed this life at Wyolah, his residence near Church Hill, Jefferson County, Mississippi, the 7th of February, 1876, in the 63rd year of his age, Francis B. Coleman, M. D., a native of Kentucky.

March 14, 1876
Died in Franklin County, Miss., on the 11th, Elkins, only child of John and Eliza Overton Calcote, aged 9 months.

March 18, 1876
The friends and acquaintances of the late Ignatz Fraesli are invited to attend his funeral from St. Mary's Cathedral this Saturday afternoon.

April 6, 1876
Died in Natchez, Miss., on the 4th, George W. Koontz, in the sixtieth year of his age.

Christy Jones, the son-in-law of Col. Martin Keary, was killed; the cook, a colored woman, was severely wounded; and Col. Keary dangerously and perhaps fatally wounded. From all we can gather concerning this affray, it appears that Jones, who had been drinking all Saturday night and a good deal for two or three days previously, and whose brain was crazed with whiskey, went into the yard early Sunday morning with a loaded pistol, to shoot a dog, saying to Henrietta, the cook, that he intended to kill every living thing on the place. Henrietta remonstrated with Jones, which seemed to infuriate him, and rushing upon her violently, he knocked her down, dragged her out on the porch, and left her there while, as he said, he went for an ax to chop her head off. Henrietta rushed into the house to Col. Keary's apartment, aroused him and the entire household with her frightened cries. Col. Keary rose up immediately, seizing a gun rushed down stairs to the yard where he met Jones. Darting at Col. Keary like a madman, he attempted to snatch the gun from him and a scuffle for life ensued. Jones, wrenching the gun from his adversary, dealt him a severe blow with the stock, the hammer penetrating Col. Keary's skull just above the left eye. While Col. Keary was lying stunned on the ground, Mr. Pat Keary, his brother, and O'Callahan, the gardener, appeared on the scene and the former had struck Jones over the head, they pulled him off Col. Keary. The Colonel, as soon as he recovered himself, seized the barrel of the broken shotgun and belabored Jones about the head till the last particle of life was extinct.

April 8, 1876
Sexton's report of deaths within the city of Natchez:
March 17 - Ignatz Fracale, aged 56 years
    20 - Henry Hazegood, cancer in the heart, aged 60 years
    20 - Mary Burdon, c., small pox, aged 15 years
    24 - Infant of Delsey Edwards, c., tetanus, aged 7 days
    28 - Lewis L. Allen, c., consumption, aged 2_ years
    29 - Eustis Smith, gunshot wounds, aged 28 years

April   4 - George W. Koontz, aged 60 years

April 22, 1876
Sexton's report of deaths within the city of Natchez:
April 10 - Harriet Ball, c., asthma, aged about 34 years
       19 - Geo. Smith, c., uremic poisoning, aged about 30 years

April 27, 1876
Died at "Arlington" on the 25th, Miss R. R. Wilkins.

May 6, 1876
Sexton's report of deaths within the city of Natchez:
April 23 - Mrs. Mary Bruner, dropsy, aged 23 years
       26 - Miss R. R. Wilkins, convulsions
       27 - Wm. E. Wells, hydrocephalus, aged 8 weeks
       28 - Mrs. Mary St. Clair, hepatitis, aged 40 years

Kosciusko Star, 28th -- On last Saturday between Goodman and Richland, the wife of Mr. J. H. Johnson, of the firm of J. H. & R. N. Johnson, of Durant, came to her death. Mr. Johnson is a son of Mrs. Morrow, of Richland, and being desirous of visiting his mother, took the train with his wife, a babe and a little girl, for Goodman. There they were met by a buggy in which to travel to Richland. Mr. Johnson smoked a pipe as they drove along, and finishing laid it on the cushion, supposing it to be empty. Soon his wife said her clothes were on fire, jumped out of the buggy with her babe in her arms and he jumped out with the little girl. He made effort to extinguish the flames which soon leaped above the head of his wife and were uncontrollable. After a few hours of suffering death came to her relief.

May 9, 1876
The friends and acquaintances of Fred J. V. LeCand are invited to attend the funeral of his late wife, Mary Elizabeth, to proceed from the residence of W. T. Weldon, 57 Main St., this Tuesday morning.

May 11, 1876
Governor Stone has pardoned Livingston P. King, of Yazoo county, convicted of the charge of the murder of W. R. Vaughn. King was sentenced on the 25th of December, 1875. The pardon was granted on the ground of mitigating circumstances. Vaughn was son-in-law of King, and seduced another daughter of King's -- his own sister-in-law. King killed him. (Jackson Times)

May 20, 1876
Sexton's report of deaths within the city of Natchez:
May   4 - Child of Susan Payne, c., pneumonia, aged 15 months
        6 - Ann Louisville, c., aged 3 months
        6 - Mary E. LeCand, consumption, aged 35 years
       12 - Ella R. Foster, c., tuberculosis, aged 11 years
       13 - Gabriel Carter, c., consumption, aged 30 years
       13 - John Hayley, c., merasmus, aged 18 months
Interrments:
May   10 - Dr. James Metcalfe
       10 - Mrs. Sarah W. Metcalfe

May 25, 1876
Died at Cooper's Well, Hinds County, Miss., on the 22nd, Henry C. C. Bennett, aged 27 years and 9 months.

May 30, 1876
Died on May 28th, 1876, in the 52nd year of her age, Frances Gustine.

Died at "Linden" in Adams County, Miss., on May 23rd, Henry Conner, in the 48th year of his age.

June 3, 1876
Sexton's report of deaths within the city of Natchez:
May 21 - Emma James, marasmus, aged 2 months
       25 - Jas. Ross, c., gunshot wound, aged about 50 years
       28 - Isaac Higdon, c., consumption, aged about 55 years
       28 - Francis Gustine, c., consumption, aged 52 years
Interrments:
May 25 - Henry L. Connor
       28 - Sidney Heilbron

October 7, 1876
Sexton's report of deaths within the city of Natchez:
Sept. 22 - Johnson Allen, c., dropsy of the heart, aged 2 1/2 years
         26 - Mimie Jackson, c., consumption, aged 28 years
         29 - John Davis, c., congestion of the brain, aged 18 years
Oct.   1 - Stirling Brown, c., dropsy, aged 75 years
         8 - Mrs. Sarah E. Meeks, tuberculosis
         4 - Mrs. M. Neihysel, old age, aged almost 76 years
         5 - Gilbert Foster, c., abscess of the liver, aged about 60 years

February 1, 1883
Died in this city, on Jan. 30, 1883, Mrs. Gertrude Heene, in the 50th year of her age.

February 3, 1876
Sexton's report of deaths within the city of Natchez:
Jan. 24 - Hannah Green, c., apoplexy, aged 71 years
    28 - Caroline Breckenridge, c., paralysis, aged 90 years
    28 - Chas. N. Forman, valvular disease of the heart and Bright's disease, aged 56 years
    28 - Edgar Frank, scarlet fever, aged 6 years
    29 - Mrs. Julia Davis Kelly, consumption
    31 - Lottie Scott, c., consumption
    31 - Mrs. Gertrude Heene, heart disease, aged 50 years

Died of pneumonia, in Memphis, on Jan. 23, 1883, Lena Heene, daughter of the late Adam Heene, a native of Natchez, aged fifteen years.

July 4, 1883
Died in this city at the family residence, on July 2nd, 1883, Joseph D., son of Jno. B. and the late Margaret Quegles, in the 2_th year of his age.

July 7, 1883
Sexton's report of deaths within the city of Natchez:
June 21 - Spencer Zimmer, dysentery, age 3 months
    22 - Henry Welch, cholera morbus, age 72 years
    25 - R. M. Spurgeon, killed, age 51 years
    25 - Mrs. M. A. Russel, apoplexy, age 71 years
    27 - Walter Weir, c., congestion of the brain, age 3 1/2 years
    29 - Flora Saunders, c., age 35 years
    30 - Margaret White, c., consumption, age about 50 years
July 1 - Lewis Johnson, c., bilious fever, age 1 year, 4 months
    2 - Grace T. O'Brien, cholera infantum, age 8 months
    2 - Joseph D. Quegles, meningitis, age 25 years
    4 - Annie C. Dicks, congestion of the brain, age 6 years
    4 - Emily Price, typhoid fever, age 14 months
Interrments:
June 27 - Ellen Thompson, c., from the country
July 4 - Julius Straus, from Newelton, La.

July 10, 1883

Died July 2nd, 1883, at "Bryandale," Adams county, Eletha L., wife of W. Horton Ratcliff, aged (32 or 52) years.

July 12, 1883

Mr. T. O. Jennings, who was the conductor of the train and was killed, was a native of Alabama, but had been on our road for some time past.

The Jury of Inquest in the Cole killing in Warren County, rendered a verdict that the deceased came to his death at the hands of Dr. P. H. Cook, and that his son, Newett, was an accessory to the murder. This verdict was based upon the evidence of Miss Lillie Cook, daughter of the doctor. Miss Cook testified she witnessed the murder, but would not say positively whether or not her father was the murderer, but her lamintations were strong against him.

July 15, 1883

Emily A. Forman, wife of R. H. Forman, departed this life in the city of Natchez on 31st May, 1883. She was a native of Jefferson County, the daughter of the late James Madison Batchelor, and granddaughter of George R. Dent, and was born in 1839. Her father removed to Chicot County, Arkansas before his death. She was educated in Kentucky and graduated in 1858 at Shelbyville Female College. She was married on 6th December, 1860 to Richard Howell Forman. Her husband and four children survive her.

July 21, 1883

Sexton's report of deaths within the city of Natchez:

July 6 - Ben Melton, c., cholera morbus, age 2 years
7 - Child of Mrs. Murry, acute diarrhea, age 15 months
12 - Willie Morgan, congestion of lungs and bowels, age 8 years
12 - Jim Brooks, c., fracture of base of skull
14 - Thos. H. McClutche, encephalitis, age 2 1/2 years
16 - Richard Butler, c., cholera infantum, age 15 months
16 - Wm. R. Montgomery, c., cholera infantum, age 4 months

Interrments:

July 9 - Wm. C. Conner, from St. Louis, Mo.
13 - Samuel Junkins, from the country
15 - S. Hirsh, from Fayette, Miss.

July 27, 1883

Died in Minden, La., on 25th, in the 18th year of his age, Bennie, son of Benj. and Mittie Wade.

July 31, 1883
Died at the residence of Mr. C. J. Engles, in this city, on the 30th of July, Mrs. Mary Kiernan, mother of John and Thomas Kiernan, in the 77th year of her age.

August 4, 1883
Sexton's report of deaths within the city of Natchez:
July 24 - Jno. D. Miles, c., malarial fever, aged 31 years
    25 - Jas. Coleman, c., abscess, aged 55 years
    26 - Lawrence Marron, carbundle, aged 80 years
    31 - Mrs. Mary Kiernan, general debility, aged 77 years

August 9, 1883
Died in Natchez, Aug. 8th, 1883, in the 76th year of his age, Silas A. Richardson, a native of Maine and for the past 40 years a resident of Natchez.

August 14, 1883
Died in Natchez, August 12th, 1883, Mrs. Jeannette Mayer, wife of the late John Mayer, in the 65th year of her age.

August 17, 1883
Died in this city, the 16th of August, Jenny Ralston Sanderson, daughter of the late S. W. W. Sanderson and adopted daughter of Capt. Geo. Ralston, of Tensas parish, La., in the 22nd year of her age.

August 31, 1883
Died at "Springfield" in Adams County, Aug. 30, 1883, Mrs. Agnes Turner, aged 73 years.

September 2, 1883
Died near Washington, Adams County, Aug. 31, 1883, Percy, son of Jno. L. and Sarah Rowan Galtney, aged 8 years.

September 8, 1883
Sexton's report of deaths within the city of Natchez:
Aug. 16 - Miss Jennie R. Sanderson, malarial haematuria, age
        22 years
    17 - Margaret Flowers, C., malarial fever, age 50 years
    19 - Bryant Williams, c., old age, aged 70 years
    20 - Mary Faulkner, c., old age, age 85 years
    22 - Fannie Minor, c., typhoid fever, age 83 years
    22 - Elizabeth Wells, c., cancer, age 65 years
    23 - O. S. Miles, debility, age 65 years
    25 - Frank Smith, c., cholera infantum, age 3 months
    31 - Infant of Geo. Coleman, debility, age 5 days
Sept. 1 - Louisa Herman, typhoid fever, age 31 years
     1 - Frank Baker, diptheria, age 3 1/2 years

4 - Geo. Dillman, c., apoplexy, age about 43 years
Interrments:
Aug. 21 - Harvey M. Brown, from Concordia Parish, La.
    30 - Edw'd. A. Fisk, from New Orleans, La.
    31 - Mrs. Agnes Turner, from the country
Sept. 2 - Mrs. Anna Coughlin, from the country
    6 - Chas. Minor, c., from the county

September 22, 1883
Sexton's report of deaths within the city of Natchez:
Sept. 7 - Hester Green, c., debility, aged 75 years
    13 - Infant of Queen Johnson, c., hemorrhage, age 2 days
    19 - Sam Campbell, c., pernicious malaria anemia
    19 - Melinda Watson, c., hemorrhage, age 53 years
Interrment:
Sept. 8 - Daughter of Jno. M. Clayton, from Concordia Parish, La.

September 23, 1883
The Times Democrat, Brookhaven says: In a difficulty between Preston Smith and J. G. Evans, the former stabbed the latter three times near the heart with a pocket knife, causing death in a few minutes. Evans is a well-to-do farmer, and leaves a wife and eight children. Smith escaped.

September 27, 1883
The friends and acquaintances of the late Robert W. Fitzhugh are invited to attend his funeral, to proceed from Zion Chapel this morning.

October 2, 1883
Died at Highland plantation, Tensas Parish, La., Sept. 28th, 1883, Rachie Ulrich, wife of D. D. Miller.

A. J. Whittington, Sheriff of Amite County, was stabbed twice in the back, at Liberty, Saturday, and killed, by Eugene McElwee. After the murder McElwee was surrounded by a crowd, one of whom shot him. He died in ten minutes.

October 5, 1883
Died at Marathon plantation, on Lake Washington, in Washington County, Miss., of swamp fever, October 3rd, 1883, Gabriel Benoist, second son of Albert W. and Matilda W. Dunbar, in the twenty-fifth year of his age.

October 6, 1883
Sexton's report of deaths within the city of Natchez:
Sept. 26 - Robt. W. Fitzhugh, c., valvular disease of the heart, aged 47 years
    29 - Henry Davis, c., pericarditis, age about 23 years
    29 - Infant of Albert B. Hogue, c., inaultion, age 6 weeks
    30 - Infant of B. R.. and J. Faut, convulsions, age 5 weeks
Oct 1 - Dave Martin, alcholism
    2 - Phillip Miles, c., congestive fever, age 10 years
    2 - Mary Favors, congestive fever, age 11 years
    3 - Andrew Kelly, c., pneumonia, age 5 months
Interrments:
Sept. 21 - A. P. Merrill, from New Jersey, buried in the country
    30 - Mrs. Rachie Miller, from Waterproof, La.

Died in this city, Oct. 5th, 1883, suddenly, of congestion of the brain, Christine, youngest child of Chas. H. and D. K. Fraser.

October 9, 1883
Died in New Orleans, Oct. 6, 1883, of malarial fever, Kittie Warfield, wife of T. Quitman Munce, of Tensas Parish, La., aged 36 years.

October 11, 1883
Died in Natchez, October 10th, 1883, Emma, daughter of Jno. F. and Fannie C. Gunning, aged 9 years.

October 12, 1883
The friends and acquaintances of Mrs. L. David are invited to attend the funeral of her brother, Louis Pomet, to proceed from St. Mary's Cathedral, this morning.

October 13, 1883
Died in Chicago, Oct. 12, John Mandeville, son of George H. and Josephine Mandeville Rozet, aged 13 years.

October 17, 1883
The friends and acquaintances of the late J. A. Ligon are invited to attend his funeral at "Montrose" in Adams County, this morning.

Died on the 16th, in this city, Samuel Preston, son of Wm. H. H. and Lizzie Fox, aged two years.

October 20, 1883

Deaths within the city of Natchez:

Oct. 5 - Christine Fraser, congestion of the brain
    6 - Mary Crizler, c., age 5 years
    7 - Mamie Blackburn, c., organic disease of the heart, age 5 years
    7 - Joseph L. East, hepatitis, age 10 years
    9 - Jane Wesley Odem, c., inflammation of the bowels, age 4 months
    11 - Emma Gunning, typhoid fever, age 9 years
    11 - Louis Pomet, congestion of the liver, age 77 years
    11 - Geo. M. Davis, overdose of morphine, age 65 years
    14 - Letty Williams, c., heart disease, age 75 years
    16 - Samuel Preston Fox, diarhhea, age 2 years
    17 - Chas. Smith, c., catavihal pneumonia, age about 22 years
    17 - Infant of W. Kyle, c., croup, age 2 days
    17 - Bernard Maddix, c., consumption, age 15 years

Interrments:

Oct. 8 - Mrs. Katie W. Munce, from New Orleans, La.
    9 - Jas. Freeman, from Louisiana
    10 - Benoist Dunbar, from Mississippi

October 25, 1883

Died on Tuesday evening, October 23rd, 1883, Melanie Thirese, youngest daughter of Dr. and Mrs. L. E. Profilet, aged 21 months.

October 26, 1883

Died in this city, on the 25th, Catherine, wife of J. C. Schwartz.

October 30, 1883

It is gratifying to be able to state that Mr. L. B. Jackson, who was reported to have been drowned off the steamer *J. M. White*, at Lee's landing, on October 7th, is still in the land of the living and "one of the liveliest corpses imaginable."

We regret to hear of the death Sunday, of the little daughter, Julia Wickliffe, of Mr. & Mrs. Edmund S. Ogden. She died of congestive chill in the sixth year of her age, at the family residence near Cannonsburg, in this county.

November 1, 1883

Died in Natchez, Miss. on October 31st, 1883, Emmie H., wife of Mr. Fred J. Maher, and daughter of Mr. and Mrs. W. J. Lyle, aged 24 years.

November 3, 1883
Deaths within the city of Natchez:
Oct. 19 - Infant of Rebecca Williams, whooping cough, aged 3 months
- 22 - Jack Dickinson, old age
- 24 - Milanie T. Profilet, chronic inflammation of the liver, aged about 21 months
- 24 - Henrietta Williams, old age, about 75 years
- 25 - Mrs. J. C. Schwartz, chronic enlargement of the liver, aged about 52 years
- 27 - Mary Bush, fever, aged 3 months
- 27 - Deserce Alliman, chronic diarrhea, aged 10 months
- 29 - Preston Newman, heart disease, buried in the country
- 30 - Phillip Springs, c., pneumonia, aged 79 years, buried in the country
- 31 - Mrs. Emmie H. Maher, congestion of the stomach, aged 24 years

Nov. 1 - Ellin Miller, consumption

Interrments:
Oct. 20 - King H. Lanius, from Vidalia, La.

November 4, 1883
The friends and acquaintances of the late Henry Wilson are invited to attend his funeral, to proceed from Zion Church, this afternoon.

November 7, 1883
The friends and acquaintances of the late Michael Holmes are invited to attend his funeral, to proceed from St. Mary's Cathedral, this afternoon.

November 13, 1883
The following is a correct report of the killing of J. P. Matthews by E. B. Wheeler, at Hazlehurst, on the morning of the 6th, the day of the election. Matthews went early to the polls and said he intended voting or go to H___ in the attempt. After depositing his vote, with his pistol in one hand, he remarked to Wheeler that he was ready, or something of that kind, when Wheeler reached behind the door, where his gun was, and fired, striking Matthews with the whole load of buckshot ranging from his throat towards his head. He was killed outright and the body was carried to the family residence. Matthews and Wheeler had been unfriendly for some time, and owing to the great political excitement it was expected by his friends that Matthews would be killed by someone. Matthews was interred in a private vault near the residence of his father, John R. Matthews, in Hazlehurst.

Died in Natchez, Miss., on Nov. 11, 1883, Mrs. Martha Goetz, a native of Marburg, Germany, in the 65th year of her age.

November 17, 1883
Deaths within the city of Natchez:
Nov. 4 - Jno. Priester, convulsions, age 11 months
    5 - Lot Randall, pleurisy, aged about 22 years
    6 - Jno. Reed, dysentery, age about 3_ years
    7 - Mich'l. Holmes, acute dysentery, aged 59 years
    11 - Mrs. Martha Goetz, entertis, aged 65 years
    12 - Rufus Bowman, pneumonia, aged about 21 years
    12 - Infant of Jno. Norman, c., trismus nascenitum, aged 1 week
    11 - Ellen Whitlock, c., convulsions, aged about 1 year
Interrments:
Nov. 4 - Henry Wilson, from New Orleans
    9 - Child of D. Marshall, from New York

November 18, 1883
Died of apoplexy, in San Antonio, on the 5th, Helen C., wife of A. J. Walton, Esq., and daughter of the late Wm. and Helen C. Ferriday, of Natchez.

Mr. Willie Dear, brother of Mrs. R. M. Carruth, of Amite County, was found terribly mangled and dead upon the railroad track, a short distance above Boguechitto, last Saturday morning. His relatives have cause to suspect that he was murdered, from the fact that he had a considerable amount of money with him before his death, and when found his pockets were turned wrong side out and not one cent could be found.

November 20, 1883
Died at Kingsland plantation on Black River, Catahoula Parish, La., on the 7th, Sammie Hornsby, aged 6 years, 4 months and 3 days, third son of James Cook and Dora J. Crossgrove.

November 21, 1883
Died in Natchez, Nov. 20, 1883, Annie G., daughter of Dr. and Mrs. E. J. Van Court, in the fifth year of her age.

November 23, 1883
The friends and acquaintances of R. D. Permenter are invited to attend the funeral of his wife, Rachel Parker, to proceed from the residence of D. G. Parker, on Canal Street, this morning.

December 7, 1883
Died at Dead Man's Bend, Adams County, Miss., Dec. 3, 1883, James Biggs, aged 23 years, a native of Ohio.

December 8, 1883
Deaths within the city of Natchez:
Nov. 16 - Margaret Hunt, c., convulsions, aged 36 years
       17 - Lewis Fountain, senile debility, aged 90 years
       18 - Agnes Pomate, c., chronic diarrhea, aged 40 years
       19 - Mattie B. Grafton, diptheria, aged 13 years
       20 - Annie G. Van Court, fracture of the skull, aged 5 years
       21 - Shelby Hadley, c., heart disease, aged 38 years
       26 - Emaline Rankin, congestive fever, aged about 65 years
Interrments:
Nov. 22 - Rachel Permenter, Louisiana
Dec. 5 - Child of Ruth Young, c., Louisiana

December 22, 1883
Deaths within the city of Natchez:
Dec. 8 - Susan Williams, c., general debility
      8 - Frances Johnson, c., senile debility, aged about 80 years
      14 - Patrick Roggers, intermittent fever, aged 62 years
      18 - Dave Foster, c., gangrene and hematura, aged 40 years
      18 - Thomas Flynn, dysentery, aged about 35 years
      18 - Margaret Washington (nee Scott), c., convulsions
Interrments:
Dec. 6 - James Biggs, Dead Man's Bend, Miss.

THE MACON BEACON
Macon, Mississippi

March 29, 1879
A young son of Jas. Sconyers was accidentally killed at a Grange meeting in Yazoo County, by a boy named Henry Waters.

On last Saturday evening news came to town that Jo. Strain, acting Deputy Sheriff, was shot and killed by a man named W. S. Mills, whose arrest was being attempted at the time. The circumstances of the affair are:

Some days before the occurrance, a letter came to the Yazoo City Post office, addressed to W. S. Mills, and by mistake was taken out by another person names W. H. Mills, and the contents were such that the latter forwarded it to the Sheriff of Madison County. The letter contained words like, "Dear Willie, leave where you are at once as they are searching everywhere for you, and if you are caught, they will break your neck, certain." As a young man of Madison, by the name of William Willis, had only recently killed a Mr. McKay, of that county, by shooting him through the window at night and had fled that part of the State. It is thought that the young man now in jail for the killing of Strain and who filled pretty well the pen likeness, was Willis. (Author's note - this taken from a very lengthy report)

April 12, 1879
This morning the news reached us of the death of Judge James M. Smiley, which occurred at the residence of his son-in-law and law associate, H. C. Capell, Esq., near Magnolia, in this county, yesterday morning. He was prostrated with a serious dropsical affection. (Summit Sentinel)

April 19, 1879
Died at his residence on the 5th of April, Maj. T. J. Moore, aged 68 years. He died of heart disease.

June 28, 1879
Last Sunday evening Julius Fleetwood shot and killed Dock Owens, at Fern Springs in Winston County. He took Owens' pistol from him and when the latter drew another pistol, he shot him twice, the second time in the head, inflicting a fatal wound. Fleetwood was released by a Justice Court, the killing being done in self defense. Owens' father died in Jackson while representing his county in the Legislature.

August 23, 1879
Died near Macon, Willis Jones Doss, son of Col. W. W. and Bettie J. Doss, aged 10 months and 8 days.

OXFORD EAGLE
Oxford, Mississippi
(Author's note - many pages of this paper were too light to read from the microfilm)

January 25, 1883
Died at her home on the 6th, of eresipelas, Mrs. Elizabeth Alvis, in the 60th year of her age. She was born on 16th May, 1823, married in 1840 and joined the Yocona Baptist Church in 1841.

March 1, 1883
Death has taken one of the best young men of our county, Mr. Eddie Cowsar. He died at the residence of his father, Thomas Cowsar, on the 8th, in the 24th year of his age. He was last year a

student of the A & M College. He leaves a father and several brothers and sisters.

March 15, 1883

God has seen fit to remove from our midst by sudden death, on the 17th of February, 1883, Gaillard K. Hardin, Sabbath School attendant and Assistant Librarian..

April 12, 1883

Died at his home in Taylor's, on the 1st of March, of typhoid fever, Benjamin S. Taylor, at the age of 54 years. He was born on 29th of February, 1829, joined the Missionary Baptist Church. He leaves a wife, three sons and four daughters.

May 17, 1883

Samuel Moore Thompson, son of Bryant B. and Harriet B. Thompson, was born in Jefferson, Cherokee County, Alabama, March 12, 1842, one of five boys, the youngest two, Victor and Sam, became printers and editors. Victor died at his home at Savannah, Tennessee, a little over a year ago. The youngest, Sam, has just gone suddenly to a premature grave. In 1860 he became editor and proprietor of the *Holmes County Democrat* and six months later married Eliza A. Wood. He entered the Confederate Army as a private in the Lexington Guards and was transferred to the "Thompson Cavalry." In 1865 Capt. Thompson settled at Oxford and started the *Oxford Falcon* and in 1877 started this paper.

Capt. S. M. Thompson, editor of the *Oxford Eagle*, was shot and instantly killed Tuesday evening last, by C. E. Butler, town marshall. It is stated that Thompson was resisting arrest.

May 3, 1883

Jessie Denton departed this life April 15th, 1883, aged seven years and six months. Our sympathies to her bereaved father, uncle and aunt, with whom she lived since the death of her mother, who died when she was a year and a few months old.

June 28, 1883

We announce the death of Rev. Henry Pritchard, at his residence in this place, on the 26th, in the 68th year of his age. His death came from an attack of measles and flux.

June 19, 1883

Died at her home in Orwood, Miss., July 4, 1883, Mrs. Hannah Clayton, about 54 years of age.

August 16, 1883

Died near Delay, Miss., June 17th, 1883, Mrs. Metty Adams, wife of Mr. Jeff Adams.

August 30, 1883
We are pained to announce that Miss Mamie L. Paine died on the 26th, of typhoid fever, near White Haven, Tenn. She attended school at this place.

October 25, 1883
Gen. S. J. Gholson, a prominent citizen of the State, died on the 16th at his residence in Aberdeen. He had been in feeble health many months. (Author's note - a lengthy report followed)

December 6, 1883
Mrs. Lavina Word died on Tuesday evening at the residence of her son-in-law, Rev. W. B. Mitchell, in this place. She was born in Davidson County, Tenn., moved to Jackson Co., Ala. when she was just upon the threshold of womanhood. In 1819 she was married to Thomas Word. In 1836 she moved with her husband to Yalobusha County, Miss., where he died, leaving her with seven children. She moved to Lafayette County in 1851, where she remained until her death.

THE RIPLEY ADVERTISER
Ripley, Mississippi

December 11, 1880
Died Nov. 27th, 1880, Georgia Etta, infant daughter of W. R. and S. E. Stansell, aged 2 years and 2 months.

Died at Stonewall College, Ripley, Miss., December 4th, 1880, Miss Willie Frank Ayres, in the 18th year of her age. She was born in Tippah County, Miss., November 15th, 1863. She was the daughter of a brave hero who fell in battle in defense of the "lost cause."

December 18, 1880
Jno. W. Skinner, who has been a citizen for thirty three years, died Dec. 6th of ulceration of the stomach and bowels. He was buried at Pleasant Hill Church, near Ruckersville, Miss., Dec. 7th, 1880. He left a wife and eleven children, the youngest ten years old.

January 8, 1881
Mrs. Caroline Christian, widow of the late Col. R. N. Christian, breathed her last at the residence of Mr. Wash Read, her son-in-law, on Wednesday morning last, and was buried at the Ripley cemetery. She had been a member of the Methodist Church for many years. She was one of the pioneers of this county, having settled in Ripley about forty-five years ago.

February 19, 1881

Mrs. Sallie L. Wells, wife of Col. J. M. Wells, died on the 31st January, 1881, in the 73rd year of her age. She was born in Maury County, Tenn., July 4, 1808, was married January 14, 1880, and attached herself to the M. Episcopal Church in 1833.

September 17, 1881

Our community was surprised on Sunday last, upon the announcement of the death of Counseille, Sheriff of our county, which occurred very suddenly at his residence in this place. Having just recovered from a sickness, he attempted to discharge the duties of his office, but unequal to the task he was compelled to take to his bed on Thursday of last week. A short itme before his death he had been conversing with persons in his room, in a cheerful mood, and while sitting up complained of a "swimming" head. He immediately laid down again and in a few moments breathed his last. He was buried on Monday by the Knights of Honor, at the family burying ground four and a half miles east of Ripley.

October 15, 1881

Died on the 9th, with flux, at Rock Hill school house, this side of Middleton, Eugene T., son of Capt. Francis A. Wolff. He was buried Monday at the Mount Moriah graveyard.

October 22, 1881

We announce the death of the Rev. W. A. Gray, pastor of the Presbyterian Church at this place, which occurred at his residence, one mile south of Ripley, Sunday, October 23, 1881, after a brief illness. Mr. Gray was a native of South Carolina; removed to Starkville, Miss. before coming here, where he has lived upwards of forty years. Mrs. Gray was about 74 years of age.
(Author's note - The dates, though obviously incorrect, are copied as given in the paper.)

On the 11th, Robert, aged about 9 years, son of Capt. R. I. Hill of Orizaba, fell about fifty feet from a chestnut tree, breaking a thigh bone and receiving other injuries, from which he died on the 15th.

Our deceased friend, Mr. Matthew Spencer, was a christian man. His family has lost a loving husband and father, the community a respected citizen and the Sunday School a faithful member.

October 29, 1881

Jesse Embrey Stubbs was born in Tippah County, August 13th, 1858, and was killed by the explosion of the boiler of the steam mill of the Simpson Brothers, near Ripley, the 26th of September, 1881. He was laid away in the family burying ground.

November 19, 1881
Died November 12, 1881, Mrs. Issabella Catharine Wier. She has left three children.

November 26, 1881
Mrs. Cora Hensley, wife of Dr. J. S. Hensley, of Pocahontas, Tenn., died at her residence in Pocahontas on the 28th of October, 1881, of typhoid fever, aged 28 years. She was a member of the Baptist Church. She leaves her husband and two little children.

The youngest child of Mr. J. Samuel and Mrs. Jennie Harris, aged about 4 months, died at the residence of Dr. Jno. Y. Marry, in this place, on Wednesday last, and buried on Thursday.

December 17, 1881
A difficulty occurred yesterday four miles west of town, between Mr. J. A. Kinney and a colored man - George Pate, in which the latter was shot by the former and instantly killed. It was reported Mr. Kinney acted in self defense, as the negro had an axe raised to strike him when he fired the fatal shot. There were two or three persons present when the killing occurred.

January 7, 1882
On Saturday last, near Dumas in this county, Dr. J. L. Sadler was shot and instantly killed by Prof. S. P. Brown, a teacher of that neighborhood. The shooting resulted from an old feud between the parties. The only witness was a son of Brown.

January 14, 1882
A Jackson (Miss.) Special of the 11th, says Willie Power, son of Colonel J. L. Power and special correspondent of the *Memphis Appeal*, accidently shot himself through the heart this evening.

February 4, 1882
Died on January 19th, 1882, ten miles southeast of Ripley, Sallie Tigert, daughter of Elizabeth and Thomas Tigert.

Died near Ashland, Benton County, Miss., on the 26th day of January, 1882, Mrs. Sarah A. Tate, widow of the late Caswell Tate. She was born in Rankin County, Miss., December 15th, 182(1 or 4). She was a member of the Baptist Church.

April 15, 1882
We announce the death of Miss Rosalie, daughter of our townsman, W. P. Alvis, which occurred on Saturday morning last, after a lingering illness. The deceased was sixteen years of age. Her remains were deposited in the Ripley cemetery.

Prof. S. P. Brown, convicted at the last term of our Circuit Court, of the assassination of Dr. Sadler and sentenced to imprisonment, is said to be insane.

Since the above was in type we were informed that there has been a decided improvement in Brown's condition -- he now appears to be sane.

Died after a brief illness, Ellen, the little daughter of Mr. & Mrs. L. Rogan, aged three years, on Tuesday morning last. Her remains were deposited in the Ripley cemetery.

Died at his residence in Ripley, April 11, 1882, Andy Green (col.), aged 51 years, after a protracted illness. The deceased had been a resident of out town for many years; his occupation was that of drayman.

June 24, 1882

Departed this life at the residence of G. W. Wright, near Walnut Station, Tippah County, Miss., June 7, 1882, John Coffey Craig. He was born in Lancaster County, S. C., September 27, 1793 and was a soldier in the War of 1812. He had been a member of the Baptist Church for over 40 years.

July 1, 1882

Last Wednesday "Rufe" Jones (col.) was arrested near this place, as one of the murderers of Miss Serena Benton. of Prentiss Co., a short time ago.

July 22, 1882

The examination of Smith Shaw, charged with the murder of Gen. W. F. Tucker, concluded on Thursday evening last. At the conclusion, Judge Buchanan delivered his opinion, denying bail and committing the defendant to the county jail. Friday, writs of habeas corpus were issued for Houston Parish and Allen Horton, colored men accused of the crime and they were released on bail. Dick Shaw was arrested near Terrell, Texas, on Monday last week. It will appear that four white men: Mat Simmons, Frank Stafford, Smith Shaw and Dick Shaw are charged with this crime. (Chickasaw Messenger)

Mr. Frank Reed, a young man some 19 years of age, living near Falkner's Station, met with an accident last Sunday, that terminated in his death. In company with his brother, he had gone down to the creek to bathe. The place in which they were accustomed, it seems, had filled up until there was no more than 2 1/2 feet of water. Young Reed, not knowing this, dived in from the bank and his head sticking in the mud, held him fast. His brother jumped in and pulled him out, but he was speechless, and died the next day.

We announce the death of Mr. Spencer Gibbs, of Blue Mountain, who died at his home on Monday last, after an illness of several days. He was a member of the Baptist Church.

July 29, 1882
Col. Beverly Matthews died last Wednesday morning at his rooms in this city, after an illness of several weeks. Col. Matthews was the oldest living representative of the Columbus bar.

August 5, 1882
Died July 22, Thos. L. Ford, an old citizen of Kosciusko (Miss.), aged 75 years. Funeral services at the residence of his son-in-law, B. A. Sawrie. (Daily American, Nashville, Tenn.)

September 16, 1882
Mrs. O. A. Harris, mother of Mr. (C. or O.) L. Harris and Mrs. Bettie Hines, of Ripley, died of typhpoid pneumonia, on the 9th, at the residence of her son, Fee Harris, in Benton County, Miss. The deceased was in her 58th year.

The sad news was received Thursday of the death of Col. Mose McCarley, for a long time a citizen of this county.

Capt. W. N. Stansell, of this county, died on Monday last. He had been an invalid for several years from paralysis. He was buried at Ripley on Tuesday.

September 23, 1882
Mrs. N. C. Blair, mother of Col. Jas. A. Blair, died at Tupelo last week. Mrs. Blair was at one time a citizen of Ripley.

Mrs. S. B. Kimbrough, companion of B. T. Kimbrough, of this paper, relapsed last week and grew worse rapidly till the 10th, when she passed peacefully from earth to Heaven, leaving her husband and four children.

Died at the residence of her father, seven miles north of Ripley, Miss., on the 20th of Sept., 1882, Miss Mary Linebarger, aged 24 years. Her disease was congestive fever.

September 30, 1882
Jas. McBride, Esq., an old and respected citizen of the county, met with an accident that caused his death on Wednesday night last. It appears that his body was caught between the wagon and lever of a sorghum mill, breaking several ribs and crushing him so badly that he died in two or three days after the accident. Mr. McBride was 65 or 70 years old.

October 14, 1882

The friends of Mrs. S. M. Moseley, in this county, will regret to hear of her death, which occurred on Sunday night last at Baldwin, Miss. Her disease was paralysis. Her husband, Rev. W. R. H. Moseley, died about one month before she did.

February 10, 1883

Died February 6, 1883, at the residence of her son, W. P. Proudfit, Mrs. Eliza Proudfit, in the eighty-second year of her age, the mother of W. P., James, John H., Alexander and E. S. Proudfit., and Mrs. Lyde P. Darnes. (Memphis Appeal)

June 23, 1883

Died on last Monday, little Kavanaugh, son of William and Virginia Jackson.

October 6, 1883

Died on the 26th of September, 1883, four miles south of Ripley, Ethel, infant daughter of J. B. and Belle Jernigan. Little Ethel was but one year and 9 months old.

October 27, 1883

Miss Sue King, of this place, who had been in declining health about twelve months, died at the residence of her mother on Wednesday evening last, of consumption, and was buried yesterday. Miss King was a member of the Methodist Church.

November 10, 1883

Mr. G. W. Hall, of Union County, Miss., was fatally stabbed on Tuesday evening last, by a Mr. Bishop, a cropper living on Mr. Hall's place. Mr. Hall was the father of George Hall, formerly a citizen of this place. It was reported that two negroes were fighting and Mr. Hall attemped to part them, when one of the negroes struck Hall with a piece of fence rail, and Bishop, who was standing near by, rushed up and inflicted the fatal stab. He died almost instantly.

Buren Spight, the old colored citizen who had his leg broken a month or two ago by being thrown out of a wagon by a runaway team, died on Sunday last. There was some hope of his recovery had he consented to have his leg amputated when the accident first occurred, but this he refused to do; and when he finally gave his consent it was too late.

November 17, 1883

We have been shocked at the announcement of the death of Rev. E. T. Winkler, which occurred at Marion, Ala., Nov. 10th. He was born in Savannah, Ga., Nov. 13th, 1803; entered Brown University in 1839; graduated in 1843 and entered Newton Theological Seminary. In 1846 he became pastor at Albany, Ga. where he remained till call to Gillisonville, S. C. He became editor of the Southern Baptist Publication. In 1854 was called to the First Baptist Church, Charleston; was chaplain in the Confederate Army; pastor of the Citadel Square Church; and for a number of years pastor of the Siloam Baptist Church, Marion, Ala. In 1874 when the Alabama Baptist was originated, Dr. Winkler became editor in chief. He had a national reputation as a speaker and writer.

January 19, 1884

Mrs. Gaillard, wife of A. M. Gaillard, one of our citizens, died at their residence near this place, on Tuesday last, of consumption.

The wife and two children (one an infant) of Gabe Robinson, colored, died in this place on Sunday last, and all were buried in one coffin.

January 26, 1884

A bloody tragedy occurred at Dallas, in this county, on the evening of the 16th, which resulted in the death of two good citizens and the probably mortally of another. Doc Bishop had a difficulty a few weeks before, with Abe Cearly, and had shot him (but not fatally). On Wednesday Doc Bishop, James Bishop and Robert Lamar came into Dallas and met Abe Cearly at Latham's store. Doc Bishop and Abe Cearly made friends and shook hands. The two Bishops and Lamar went outside and commenced firing off their pistols, apparently in fun. Lamar shot Cearly in the leg and he and the Bishops started to leave. William and Evans Harmon intervened, enraging them and they commenced cursing the Harmon's and opened fire on them. Evans Harmon died in about two hours and William Harmon about twenty-four hours after the shooting. Evans Harmon was unarmed and his brother only had a small pistol. Alexander Harrison, who had nothing to do with the difficulty, was shot in the head and it is thought that he will die. Lamar was shot in the head but is only slightly wounded. The Bishops and Lamar have fled and it is supposed they have left the State. (Oxford Eagle)

Hon. Wm. R. Spears, Senator for Warren County, died last Saturday night, of consumption.

February 9, 1884

We learn that Mr. J. C. Craig, brother of Mrs. C. L. Harris, of this place, died at his residence near Saulsbury, Tenn., on Saturday last, of pneumonia. He leaves a wife and three children.

Little May, the oldest child of Mr. & Mrs. W. M. Burns, died of croup in this place, Thursday morning. She was about five years old.

February 16, 1884
Died of membranous croup, Mary Tipler Burns, Feb. 7, 1884, daughter of William and Lizzie Burns, aged 6 years and 2 months.

Mr. and Mrs. W. M. Burns youngest child, Will Etter, died Wednesday after a lingering illness, aged about eight months. The oldest having died last week, they now have only one of three children living.

February 23, 1884
Mr. Marion Cox, a farmer living in Benton County, Miss., left home last Saturday with a gun, saying he wanted to go hunting. On Sunday morning he was found dead laying by the grave of his father. It is thought he committed suicide.

The citizens of Danville have caused to be placed over the grave of Charles D. Carter, who was killed while trying to arrest the Daniel outlaws last summer, a monument to his memory. The inscription is as follows: Charles D. Carter, born Oct. 23, 1856, died Aug. 7, 1883." On the reverse side, "He who sleeps beneath was shot in Perry County, Arkansas, ont he 29th day of July, 1883, in the ill-fated attempt to capture the 'Three Corner' desperadoes ----". (Russellville Ark. Democrat)

March 22, 1884
Joseph A. Heath, son of J. H. and Mrs. Heath, died on the 4th of February, 1884, at his father's house. He was born in Rusk County, Texas on the 1st day of January, 1855.

Last Friday, in Alamo, Crockett Co., Tenn., John S. Clark and John Payne got into a difficulty and Clark shot Payne, killing him instantly. The quarrel is said to have grown out of the ownership of an ax.

April 5, 1884
The death of Levi Stokes Holcombe, in the 74th year of his age, occurred at his residence in the city of Pine Bluff, Arkansas, in the early part of this month. The deceased was formerly a respected citizen of Tippah County. He was a planter and dry goods merchant in Ripley. Mr. Holcombe was born in Union District, South Carolina and was married in that State to Miss Sarah A. Whitlow; came to this county in 1842; raised a family of children here, several of whom, with their mother, sleep in the cemetery in the town of Ripley. The deceased leaves to survive him, only two out of seven children.

April 19, 1884
(The Appeal, Oxford, Ms., April 15) Judge J. M. Howry, one of the founders of the University of Mississippi, a mason, died here this morning, in the 80th year of his age.

May 3, 1884
Died at his late residence, four miles east of Ripley, in Tippah County, Miss., on the 23rd of April, 1884, Mr. Samuel Gurney. His disease was apoplexy and he lived only a few hours after the stroke. He was born in the city of New York, July 23rd, 1801, and was eighty two years and nine months old when he died. (Author's note - a very lengthy report followed)

Mr. J. W. Kendrick died at his residence in Booneville, Prentiss County, Miss., April 19th, 1884. He was born in York District, South Carolina, March 28, 1813 and was in his seventy second year. In 1836 he was married to Miss Martha O. Glenn, who survives him. In 1839 he moved to Mississippi and joined the Presbyterian Church at Ripley, Tippah County. In 1870 he moved to Booneville.

May 10, 1884
Mrs. Elizabeth Embry, wife of Col. Jesse Embry, deceased, died at the old family homestead, five miles west of Ripley, May 4, 1884, at the advanced age of 74 years and 5 months. She had been an invalid for seven years.

Mrs. Wm. Tigert, daughter of H. H. Purnell, Esq., died May 7, 1884, of consumption. We are informed that Esq. Purnell has lost a duaghter every spring for four years.

May 17, 1884
The little daughter of Bruce Reynolds, colored, was fatally burned last Tuesday.

June 14, 1884
A difficulty occurred at New Albany, on Saturday last, between Mr. J. R. Reeves, editor of the *Optic,* and Mr. Lloyd Ford, which resulted in the killing of Ford and the wounding in the leg of Mr. E. Y. Reeves, father of J. R. Reeves, by accident. The parties had an altercation about the congressional contest for the democratic nomination. Both men drew their revolvers, each man shot five times. Reeves hit Ford in the bowels, inflicting the wound from which he died in about 12 hours.

June 21, 1884
Mrs. Dickson, wife of B. W. Dickson, Esq., died in this place on Wednesday last, of consumption.

July 5, 1884
Mr. Jacob M. Webb died at Somerville, Tenn., on the 23rd, in the 74th year of his age. He came from Lynchburg, Va. in 1832.

SUMMIT CONSERVATIVE TIMES
Summit, Mississippi

April 28, 1876
Last Sabbath at the little grave yard near Topisaw Church, the last tribute of respect was paid to the memory of the late Mr. John Felder.

Mr. Fayette Wells shot and instantly killed Mr. Francis M. Bardwell at Hammond, La. The difficulty was about Wells' wife. Wells is under arrest.

Died in Marion County, on the 14th, Mr. W. G. Dampeer

Died at the residence of her father, near Brandon, April 15, 1876, of pneumonia, Mrs. Emma E. Hill, daughter of Dr. I. M. and Mrs. Elizabeth Quin, and wife of Dr. _. D. Hill, about 27 years.

May 19, 1876
Died in Summit, Mrs. Mary Mogan, a resident of this place for 19 years.

October 13, 1876
Died at her residence near Summit, Sept. 22nd, Mrs. Eugenia Carrouth, widow of the late A. R. Carrouth, aged sixty.

Died on the 6th of October, of congestion of the brain, near Holmesville, at the residence of his parents, Franklin Furguson, youngest son of James and Cinthia Furguson, aged seven years, one month and twenty-four days.

October 20, 1876
Died in Summit, October 8th, 1876, Anne, youngest daughter of L. W. and R. M. Howard, aged twelve days.

October 27, 1876
Died in McComb City, Miss., on Oct. 15th, 1876, of congestion of the lungs, Mattie, only daughter of Mr. and Mrs. Greener, aged one year and three months.

Died in McComb City, Miss., Oct. 18th, 1876, Freddie Centennial, infant son of G. and A. M. Berglund, aged 7 months.

Died on the 1st of September, at the residence of D. A. Buie, Esq., in this county, Mr. Thomas C. Warnack, aged about (65 or 85) years.

December 1, 1876
Died at the residence of his father-in-law, H. S. Bonney, in Summit, Nov. 11, 1876, Jules Lavisson, aged 36 years, 9 months and 24 days.

January 5, 1877
Died at the residence of Mr. W. J. Jackson, the 31st Dec., 1876, Miss Minerva A. Flowers.

February 2, 1877
Died on January 28th, at her residence on Selver Creek, in this county, Ruth V., wife of Wm. Walker, in the 37th year of her age.

February 9, 1877
Died at the residence of his daughter, Mrs. F. E. Sample, in Summit, February 7th, Mr. John Williams, aged 8_ years.

February 16, 1877
Hon. George !.. Potter arrived at Lexington on the 5th of February, 1877, to attend the Chancery Court for Holmes County. He briefly addressed the Court and at the conclusion of his argument the Court requested him to draft the order, which he proceeded to do. It was soon noticed that he seemed to be sleeping. A member of the bar approaching him discovered he was unconscious. Medical aid was instantly called and all was done to relieve him. He never revived and died in the court house.

May 18, 1877
Died May 10th at his residence five miles east of this place, Jacob Curtis, aged 64 years, a native of this State.

June 22, 1877
Died on the 14th, Mary Lea, infant daughter of William and Mary V. Atkinson, aged 1 year, 1 month and 14 days.

Died the 16th, at his residence in Summit, Miss., Dr. John Holden, born in Amite County, Miss., Sept. 2, 1805, age 71 years, 9 months and 14 days.

June 29, 1877
Died at his residence in this county, the 21st, W. W. Felder, after a long illness of several weeks.

July 13, 1877
On last Sunday evening, Mr. L. P. Jouveaux, with two or three acquaintances from McComb City, were enjoying a boat ride on a pond at Stuart's Mill, about three miles from this place. From some cause, Mr. Jouveaux fell out in deep water. His companions were also thrown into the water, but succeeded in getting to shore.

Mr. Jouveaux sank and while near the bottom he caught a root and held to it until his was found in that position, dead.

August 10, 1877

Died on the 3rd, Maria, infant daughter of Mr. & Mrs. Fra___ Soluter, aged 1 year and 7 months.

September 21, 1877

Died on the 9th, Thaddeus, infant son of Thos. L. and Mattie Cotten, aged one year and twenty days.

Died at the residence of her parents, in this county, on the 17th, Lura Myrtle, infant daughter of R. N. and T. (C. or G.) Crawford.

November 9, 1877

Died in Summit on the 7th, Inez Estelle, daughter of Mr. & Mrs. J. M. Jones, aged two months and 25 days.

December 7, 1877

Died on the 10th of November, at the residence of her father, W. H. Westbrook, in Franklin County, Miss Sarah Jane Westbrook.

F. E. Strippelman, who mysteriously dissappeared on Tuesday last, was found dead this morning, in one of the unoccupied quarters at the camps. The Coroners jury rendered a verdict that Mr. Strippelman came to his death from the effects of an overdose of laudanum and morphine. (Author's note - a lengthy suicide letter was included with this notice.)

February 1, 1878

Died at the residence of his father, in this place, on the 14th, Morgan T. Kuykendall, in the twenty-fifth year of his age.

Died on the 24th at the residence of her mother, Mrs. Epstein, in this place, Lena, in the fourth year of her age.

February 8, 1878

Mrs. Elceba Bates died Dec. 22, 1877 in the building of Lea Female College, at Summit. She was born March 1, 1805, age 72 years, 9 months and 21 days.

Mrs. Elizabeth Everett died January 6, 1878 at the residence of Dr. Z. Lea Everett, at Summit, aged 75 years, 1 month and 14 days.

Both were born near Knoxville, Grange County, Tennessee. Their father, Zachariah Lea, moved to Mississippi in the spring of 1806. He landed at Natchez and thence moved to Amite County, Mississippi Territory. Mrs. Bates was on a visit to Summit and was taken sick. In a few days her brother and sister residing in Amite County, were sent for. Mrs. Everett and Mrs. Lucinda Richmond, a twin sister of Mrs. Bates, both came to attend their sister. On the Sunday following, Mrs. Everett was taken sick and was conveyed to the residence of her son, Dr. Z. L. Everett.

Their grandmother, Mrs. Margaret Jane Clay, was the wife of James Clay, a cousin of the Kentucky statesman. This lady was tied to the stake in Virginia, and would have been whipped had not the fine been paid by a stranger. She was baptised in the James River.

March 1, 1878

Died in Perry County, Miss., on January 29th, at the residence of her father-in-law, Dr. E. Frost, of consumption, Mrs. Louisa A. Frost, aged 22 years and 6 months.

Died in McComb City, on the 16th day of February, 1878, Adolph, aged 5 years and 6 months; died on the 26th, Julius, aged 8 months, sons of Mr. & Mrs. A. Heidenrich.

April 5, 1878

Died on the 28th of March, at the residence of her father, Mr. James A. Jenkins, of Amite County, Miss Nannie Jenkins, disease congestion of the stomach.

Died in San Antonio, Texas, on March 28, Benjamin Palmer Hamilton, infant son of Col. W. B. and Annie H. Hamilton.

Died at the residence of her son, Mr. G. C. Rainer, in St. Helen's Parish, La., on the 9th, of pneumonia, Mrs. Elizabeth Strickland, in the 73rd year of her age.

May 3, 1878

Died at his residence April 25th, in Amite County, Miss., James E. Lea, aged about 59 years.

June 21, 1878

Mr. James Everett Lea, parted three weeks ago in good health, on a journey north. He died after an illness of ten days. James E. was the fourth son of Zachariah and Sabrina Clay Lea. The other children were: Alfred Mead, Iverson Green, Nancy, Margaret A., Elceba, Elizabeth, Lucinda Clay, Hampton M. and Wilford Z. James was born July 28, 1819 in Amite County. He lived all his life on the old homestead and died on the same hill where he was born. His remains repose in the family burial ground, where rest his father, mother, grandmother Clay, brothers and sisters. (Author's note -- a very lengthy report followed)

July 19, 1878

Died at Anderson Texas, July 9th, 1878, Rosa Kemp, daughter of Peter Kemp, of Greensburg, La., and wife of Mr. J. P. Stree Thompson.

August 9, 1878

Died July 29th, 1878, at Jackson, La., Thomas Mosby Simmons, a native of Kentucky, and a residence of New Orleans for 32 years, aged 52 years.

Died August 4th, Miss Julia M. Simmons, daughter of T. M. Simmons, aged 18 years, 1 month and 18 days.

August 16, 1878

Died at his residence in Franklin County, Miss., on the 11th, Mr. Moses Hunt, after a lingering illness.

August 23, 1878

Died at the residence of Mrs. Annie Austin, Carrollton, La., June 25th, 1878, Mrs. Mary L. Jones, aged 65 years.

Died in Lincoln County, Aug. 15th, 1878, Orrie Belle, daughter of Dr. C. P. and Mrs. Margaret Conerly, aged 1 year and 22 days.

Died August 21st, after a short illness, Young M. Griffin, eldest son of Young F. and P. J. Griffin, aged 19 years, 5 months and 21 days.

Died at the residence of his brother-in-law, Mr. R. B. Sudduth, on the 14th, Mr. John Crosley, aged about 20 years.

Died on August 20th, 1878, Carrie Jeanette, daughter of J. P. and Mrs. Nellie Evans, aged 1 year, 11 months and 8 days.

August 30, 1878

Died in Summit, August 28th, 1878, Augusta Matilda, infant daughter of Capt. A. A. and Fannie A. Boyd, aged 10 months and 13 days.

Died on August 20th, 1878, near Holmesville, Miss., Miss Maggie Rebecca, youngest daughter of W. E. and R. L. Brent, aged 7 years, 6 months and 11 days.

Died at the same place, August 21st, Alexander Ware, third son of Young F. and P. J. Griffin, aged 13 years, 11 months and 21 days.

Died at the same place, August 22nd, Young F. Griffin, aged 65 years.

Died at the same place, August 24, 1878, Mary Elizabeth, only daughter of Mrs. P. J. and the late Young F. Griffin, aged 9 years, 1 month and 17 days. (Author's note - a lengthy report of the Griffin family who died of yellow fever is given in the March 28, 1879 issue of this paper.)

September 20, 1878
Died in Osyka, Miss., September 12th, 1878, Margaretha, aged 10 years and 7 months, daughter of Philip and Barbara Sippel.

October 11, 1878
Died on Clear Creek, Pike County, October 5th, 1878, Catharine, infant daughter of John and L. Boggs, aged 2 years, 1 month and 5 days.

November 15, 1878
Died at Liberty, November 11th, of congestion of the lungs and liver, E. J. Wicker, in the 69th year of his age.

November 29, 1878
Died at his residence in Amite County, Miss., on November 21, 1878, Mr. J. E. Westbrook, of pneumonia.

December 6, 1878
On Monday night last a number of gentlemen arrested Jack Pittiford, a negro of desperate character, in Franklin County, for an attempt to commit an outrage on a young married lady of high respectability. He was conveyed to the county site by R. M. Newman, S. K. Magee, E. H. Montgomery, G. Flowers, James Allford, W. D. Moore and James Bicker. On their arrival the negro seized Mr. Newman's gun, firing almost in the face of Mr. Newman, who dodged, the load passing over his head. Mr. Newman drew his pistol, wounding the desparado, who fired the second barrel of the gun wounding Mr. Moore, though not seriously. He attempted to make his escape, but was fired at by S. K. Magee and G. Flowers, from the effects of which he died in a few minutes.

March 7, 1879
Died at Myrtle Place, Miss. on February 24, 1879, Jacob Tristem, son of T. S. and Mrs. M. L. J. Thomas, aged 15 months.

Died at the residence of her son-in-law, Mr. J. M. Lewis, Tangipahoe, La., January 9th last, Mrs. J. A. Pound, aged 78 years.

March 14, 1879
Died at his residence in this city, on the 8th, Mr. P. C. Crossman, in the 69th year of his age.

Died at the residence of his parents, in this city, March 10th, 1879, D. Warren Hurst, youngest son of Mr. & Mrs. D. W. Hurst, aged 13 years and 2 months.

April 4, 1879

Died in Macon, 20th ult., Mrs. Virginia Sargent.

Died at Carrollton, 22nd ult., Dr. W. M. Stansbury.

Died at Columbus, 25th ult., Mr. Hal Worthington.

Died in Rankin County, 19th ult., George Edward Stacey.

Died in Yazoo City, 20th ult, William Byrns, aged 35 years.

Died near Oakland, 13th ult., Wm. Lamar Burdeshaw, infant.

Died in Attala County, 6th ult., Mrs. Lydia Buford, aged about 89 years.

Died at Pope Station, Miss., 18th ult., Col. Joseph Waters, aged 65 years.

Died at Austin, 22nd ult, W. R. Neblett, aged 26 years, 2 months and 20 days.

Died in Jackson, 18th ult, Turner Patterson, an old and faithful servant of Geo. S. Yerger.

Died in Natchez, 7th ult., Jane Simmons, aged 5 years; 11th ult. three children of Patrick Murphy; 12th ult., Chas. A. Pipes; 13th ult. Jos. Welsh, drowned, aged 17 years; 17th ult., Peggy Downs, aged 60 years; and Tillman Taylor, an infant.

April 11, 1879

Died at Holly Springs, 7th ult., T. L. Brady, aged 10 years and 6 months.

Died at Pratt's mill, DeSoto County, 27th ult., M. Miller, aged 57 years.

Died near Batesville, 31st ult., Miss Mattie Simpson.

Died near Corinth, 25th ult., Mrs. O. C. Key.

Died in Pontotoc County, 29th ult., Mrs. John P. Miears.

Died at Holly Springs, Miss., 29th ult., Mrs. Virginia A. Tyler.

Died in Claiborne County, 13th ult., W. T. Lewin.

Died near Carrollton, 2nd inst., W. H. Bates, aged 68 years.

Died in Brandon last week, Samuel C. Myers.

Died in Starkville, 28th ult., (B. or H.) W. Brown.

Died at Yazoo City, 12th ult., Andrew, son of Mr. & Mrs. J. D. Callihan.

April 25, 1879

Died in Lauderdale County, 10th, Johnson P. Dansby.

Died in Madison County, 14th, Mrs. Jane P. Divine.

Died in Madison County, 4th, J. M. Wiles.

Died in Choctaw County, 14th, Julia Pinnix.

Died in Noxubee County, 5th, T. J. Moore.

Died in Panola County, Mrs. Sallie Beanland.

Died in Tupelo, on the 11th, S. M. Robertson, Sheriff of Lee County.

Died in Warren County, 15th, Mr. Brunni.

Died in Holmes County, 14th, Mrs. P. Brantly.

Died in Sumner County, 14th, Col. Chas. M. Holland, aged 86 years. (Author's note -- Sumner Co. was changed to Webster Co.)

Died in Benton County, 22nd ult., Mrs. N. B. Hix.

May 2, 1879

Died in Yazoo City, 24th ult, Mrs. Mary Grace, wife of Sheriff H. L. Taylor; 22nd ult., H. D. Meade.

Died in Yazoo County, 19th ult., R. C. Dickson.

Died near Iuka, 23rd ult., W. J. Hart.

Died in Wesson, 19th ult., John W. Greenlee.

Died in Coffeeville, 21st, Louis Taylor.

Died in Coffeeville, 25th ult., Homer Moring.

Died near Pine Bluff, March 31st, S. L. Caraway.

Died in Enterprise, 12th ult., Wesly Drane.

Died in McComb City, 10th ult., Charles H., only son of Mr. & Mrs. W. D. Mitchell.

May 9, 1879

Died at Ocean Springs, April 26th, at the residence of his son, Mr. Robt. B. Downer, Capt. J. C. Downer, aged 80 years.

Died at Port Gibson, 27th ult., Judge Volney Stamps.

Died in Lexington, 5th, Mrs. Caroline Williams.

Died in Wilkinson County, 16th ult., W. M. McGraw.

Died in Greenville, 13th ult., John B. Simmerman.

Died in Crystal Springs, 30th ult., Mrs. Mollie Lewis.

Died in Baldwin, 27th ult., W. D. Burge.

Died in Raymond, 5th inst., J. M. Hawkins.

Died in Copiah County, 23rd ult., B. C. Foster.

Died in Crystal Springs, 24th ult., Mrs. A. Mims.

Died in Lexington, 25th ult., Hosea Barger.

Died in Coahoma County, 26th ult., Robt. Glover.

Died near Thomastown, 21st ult., J. T. Donald.

Died in Columbus, 26th ult., J. A. McReynolds.

Died in Amite County, 5th inst., J. S. Bilis.

May 16, 1879

Died in New Orleans, 1st, Mrs. Cecelia Henderson.

Died in Port Gibson, 9th, Mr. Thos. A. Briscoe.

Died in Vicksburg, Dr. J. R. Barnett.

Died in Coahoma County, Mrs. Hammet.

Died in Marshall County, 16th ult., Mrs. H. R. H. Hawkins.

Died in Marshall County, 20th ult., Mrs. Lizzie M. Hastings.

Died in Holmes County, 28th ult., Moses B. Rogers.

Died in Durant, G. S. Muirhead.

Died near Hazlehurst, 1st, ___ Roberts.

Died in Holly Springs, 4th, Col. G. B. Myers.

Died in New York, Nathan Gross, of Columbus.

Died in Jackson, 29th ult., Virginus Daniel, infant.

Died in Tallahatchie County, 1st & 2nd, Mr. and Mrs. Bryant Peterson, of pneumonia.

Died in Charleston, 5th, Robert D. Diddick.

Died near Cherry Creek, 16th ult., Mrs. Jane Howell, aged 42 years.

May 30, 1879
Died in Port Gibson, 21st, W. McN. Russell, aged 55 years.

Died in Port Gibson, 23rd, Robt. M. Hastings, aged about 36 years.

Died in Vicksburg, Dr. Emanuel.

Died in Chickasaw County, 15th, W. H. Johnson.

Died in Oxford, E. G. Wood.

Died in Copiah County, 18th, Joseph Price.

Died in Austin, 5th, Ada Fletcher, aged about 14 years.

Died in Pontotoc County, Mrs. Ella Worsham.

June 6, 1879
Died in Tupelo, 26th ult., Mrs. Wm. Gray.

Died in Jackson, 9th ult., Mrs. Henry C. Havens.

Died in Booneville, Mr. John M. Walker.

Died near Pontotoc, 24th, Mrs. Nellie D. Penson, aged 33 years.

Died in Chickasaw County, 27th, Mr. A. L. McJunkin.

June 13, 1879

Died near Chester, 26th ult., Mrs. Elizabeth Cork, aged about 92 years.

Died in Oxford, Beverly Chew, of Yazoo County.

Died lin Monroe County, 10th ult., Mrs. M. M. Rowland, aged 79 years.

Died in Shannon, 29th ult., Mrs. Lou Weightman

Died in New York City, W. M. Bell, Jr., of Starkville.

Died in Starkville, some days since, Cowan Erwin.

Died in Hernando, Mr. Walter Glynn, of epilepsy.

June 20, 1879

Died in Woodville, 23rd ult., Mrs. Mattie James, aged 34 years.

Died in Tate County, Mrs. Julia A. Broadaway, aged 28 years.

Died near Corinth, on the 5th, Mrs. Priscilla Duncan, aged 21 years.

Died in Corinth, the 8th, Mrs. A. W. Patterson.

Died in Corinth, 8th inst., Terry Young, aged 2 years.

Died near Hazlehurst, 7th inst., Wm. P. Pool.

Died in Simpson County, 24th ult., Wm. C. Brown.

Died in Meridian, Mrs. W. V. Rainey.

Died in Yazoo County, Miss Katie Clark, aged 16 years.

Died in Wilkinson County, James Tyler, aged 88 years.

Died in Algiers, La., 24th ult., Mrs. Olivia D. Watson, aged 32 years.

June 27, 1879

Died at Castillian Springs, some days since, Rev. Mr. Montgomery.

Died near Natchez, 22nd, Mrs. M. J. Denison.

Died in Shubuta, 19th inst., Mrs. Ada Turner.

Died in McComb City, 18th, Willie Harper, infant son of John and Eliza Harper.

Died in Durant, W. R. Hamilton.

Died near Columbus, Mr. Cullen Battle, in the 94th year of his age.

Died in Vicksburg, some days since, Mrs. Margaret Hartman.

Died in Columbus, W. F. Crawsford.

Died near Winona, 11th inst., Lelia Davis Purnell.

Died near Huntsville, 7th inst., Henry Bramlett, aged 78 years.

July 4, 1879

Died in Jackson, Judge A. Johnston.

Died in Columbus, 22nd ult., Ross Tabb.

Died in Mayhew, 22nd ult., A. W. Richardson.

Died in Carrollton, 13th ult., F. F. Vickers.

Died in Carrollton, 22nd ult., A. J. Tidwell.

Died in Winona, 21st, H. T. Lott, aged 25 years.

Died in Kosciusko, 15th ult., Isaiah Frazier.

Died in this city, 1st inst., at the residence of her father, Mr. G. T. Bunch, Miss Alice V., aged 13 years, 11 months and 21 days.

August 1, 1879

Died near Eggs Point, 24th inst., Fulton A. Stewart, son of Col. J. D. Stewart, of Hinds County.

Died in Raymond, Joseph Gray.

Died in Canton, 17th ult., Mary Clare.

Died in Handsboro, 17th ult., Mrs. Catharine Buwe, aged 84 years.

Died in Monroe County, 13th ult., Maud B., infant daughter of H. M. and A. H. Franklin.

Died in Meadville, 22nd ult., John E. Smith, aged about 56 years.

Died in Mayorsville, 12th ult., John Howard, infant son of J. W. and Lizzie Howard.

Died in Handsboro, 11th ult., Annie M. Crawfoot, aged about 54 years.

August 8, 1879

Died in Carrollton, some days since, and infant daughter of D. D. Shaw.

Died near Kosciusko, 28th ult., David Cook.

Died in Martinsville, 30th ult., T. Garrison.

Died in Simpson County, 20th ult., Mrs. Penny Mangum.

Died in Woodville, 20th ult., Johnnie A. McNeely.

Died in Lexington, 29th ult., Dr. F. M. Phillips.

Died in Vicksburg, Jerald, son of Joseph Herman.

Died near Kossuth, 28th ult., B. B. Kerr, aged 57 years.

Died near Covington, La., 29th ult., Rev. W. G. Stovall, aged 49 years.

August 15, 1879

Died in Winona, 22nd ult., Mrs. Sallie A. Erwin, aged about 40 years.

Died in Madison County, Mary F. Hickman, aged about 43 years.

Died in Simpson County, the 4th, Johnny, infant son of F. P. and Mrs. Allie Berry.

Died near Pine Valley, 2nd, Jimmie, infant son of J. M. and Mrs. M. A. Tate.

Died in Holly Springs, 3rd, Mrs. Jennie McD. Dancy.

Died in Amite County, H. G. Street, an aged resident.

Died in Lauderdale County, 2nd, William Frederick, aged 22 years.

Died in Chicago, 1st, Hon. Henry Musgrove, of the State.

Died in Corinth, 6th, a daughter of Mr. & Mrs. Vanderford.

August 22, 1879

Died in Copiah County, 31st ult., Robert Saunders; 8th inst., Chas. L. Haley.

Died in Kemper County, Mrs. Matilda Sanders.

Died in Oxford, some days since, Miss Hattie Leland.

Died in Jackson, 9th, T. J. Funchess.

Died in Monroe County, 2nd inst., Mrs. B. U. Wood.

Died in Holly Springs, 11th inst., Herman Snider.

Died in Amite County, 10th, Dr. A. E. Eppi_on.

Died in Bay St. Louis, 11th, Hubbard Saunders.

Died in Biloxi, 6th, Mrs. Theresa Cousins.

Died in Harrison County, 13th ult., J. B. Evans.

Died in Meridian, 14th inst., Mrs. Sol. Levy.

Died near Cato, 10th inst., Irvin Donnell.

Died in Jackson, 12th, Mrs. Sarah Adkinson.

Died in Meadville, 8th, Rowan Wentworth.

Died in Alcorn County, 9th inst., Miss Elder Paralee Vanderford.

March 19, 1880

Died in Chickasaw County, Mrs. M. L. Dearing.

Died in Yalobusha County, Mr. G. M. Hardy.

Died in Wilkinson County, Mr. R. A. J. Sessions.

Died in Yazoo County, Mr. J. L. Mitchell.

March 26, 1880

Died in Winona, Arthur Green.

Died in Mushulaville, Mrs. Anna Westerfield.

Died in Macon, Mrs. Dantzler; Mrs. Doracott.

Died in Cooksville, Col. J. L. Hibbler.

Died in Bayou De Glaise, P. V. Van Norman.

Died in Pascagoula, Mary Wolf Howell.

Died in McNairy County, Tenn., Mrs. Strickland.

Died in Corinth, J. F. Potts.

Died in Hardeman County, Tenn., John J. Buffaloe.

Died in Franklin County during March:
C. C. Keen, aged 30 years.
Mrs. Tempa Cain, aged 50 years.
Thos. Butler, aged 35 years.
J. R. Wactor, aged 53 years.
Mrs. Martha Wilkinson, aged 30 years.
Miss Wilkinson, aged 10 years.

April 9, 1880

Died in Hinds County, Wm. Edmondson.

Died in Port Gibson, Dr. A. H. Peck.

Died at Cold Springs, Mrs. Laura Maud McCaleb Guilotte.

Died near Vaiden, S. R. Sproles

Died near Byram, Mrs. Ione Funches.

Died near Oxford, Mrs. Lillie D. Cassey.

Died in Clinton, H. L. Poindexter.

Died near Crystal Springs, J. E. Alford.

Died in Oktibbeha County, Henry Sikes.

Died in Martinsville, R. E. Barry.

Died near Three Rivers, John Robinson.

Died in Chickasaw County, Kenneth Clark.

Died in Monticello, J. E. Farmer.

Died in Georgetown, James L. Forsyth.

April 16, 1880
Died at the residence of Mr. J. J. White, near McComb City, Miss Maggie Andrews.

Died near Houston, Mrs. Cora Davis.

Died in Meridian, Frederick Smith.

Died in Meridian, H. H. McQueen.

Died in Harrisville, Norman McLeod.

Died near Tupelo, James Rufus.

April 23, 1880
Died at J. J. White's mill near McComb City, April 15th, Eddie Thomas, son of G. W. and Mrs. Fannie B. Wyatt, aged 4 years and 6 months.

VICKSBURG DAILY HERALD
Vicksburg, Mississippi

September 1, 1876
Died at the residence of her father, in Delhi, Louisiana, on the 29th, Mary Brame, wife of Joseph M. Brounley, of Madison Parish, La.

July 28, 1877
The friends and acquaintances of the late A. R. Murphy are requested to attend his funeral, to proceed from his residence on Cherry St., Saturday afternoon.

July 29, 1877
Died on the morning of July 28, 1877, from injuries received by a fall, Mary E. Swafford, aged sixteen months.

The friends and scquaintances of the late Peter Libel was requested to attend his funeral, to proceed from the Vicksburg House, Levee St., Sunday evening,

July 31, 1877

Departed this life July 23, 1877, at the residence of Mr. Joseph Noland, at Omega, Miss Laura A. Mills, of Vicksburg, aged 17 years, 11 months and 23 days.

August 5, 1877

The friends and acquaintances of Mr. and Mrs. Wm. and Rozina Voellinger are requested to attend the funeral of their little son, Chas. Eddie Voellinger, from their residence on Main St., between Monroe and Cherry, this Sunday morning.

August 7, 1877

The friends of C. W. Dwight are requested to attend the funeral of his late wife, this morning, from his residence corner Jackson and Third North streets.

The friends and acquaintances of C. A. Manlove and Mrs. R. A. Folkes are invited to attend the funeral of their late sister, Elizabeth B. Dwight, at above place and hour.

The friends and acquaintances of Jas. N. and Maggie V. Reynolds are invited to attend the funeral of their late daughter, Addie, to proceed from their residence on Great Street, between South and Harrison, today.

August 11, 1877

The friends and acquaintances of Thomas and Virginia Young are invited to attend the funeral of their infant daughter, Victoria A., to proceed from their residence on Harrison Street, this morning.

August 14, 1877

Sexton's report of deaths - City of Vicksburg:
Aug. 6 - Addie Reynolds, 1 year, 9 months, dysentery & congestive chill
6 - Wm. Carr, 50 years, thrown from a window at the Hill City Infirmary
7 - Child (colored) of Susan Chases
7 - George Broom, colored, 21 years, consumption
7 - Louisa Ross, colored, 17 years, 10 months, congestive chill
7 - Mrs. E. B. Dwight, 61 years, 10 months, congestive fever
8 - Mrs. Annie Purcell, 30 years, intermittent fever
8 - Ben Haynes, colored, 80 years, chronic diarrhea
8 - Wm. Smith, colored, 88 years, dropsy

10 - Victoria A. Young, colored, 9 months, 22 days, teething
10 - Charles E. Dorwart, 9 months, 24 days, teething
10 - Lucy Williams, colored, throwing herself into a sink or privy vault, being insane

August 16, 1877

The friends and acquaintances of R. D. and S. E. Rowe are requested to attend the funeral of their infant daughter, Roberta, to proceed from the residence of John A. Peale, on Harrison Street, this evening.

August 19, 1877

Died August 10, 1877, Victoria A., only daughter of Thomas and Virginia Young, aged nine months and twenty-three days.

August 28, 1877

Died at Bolton, Miss., August 24, 1877, Mrs. Fannie E. Y. Alexander, wife of A. Alexander and daughter of the late Major Calin Buckner, U.S.A., War of 1812. Born in Lynchburg, Va., she resided formerly in Vicksburg.

August 29, 1877

A most distressing accident occurred near Mackville, Saturday, the particulars as follows: Thomas Shelby, Jo. Thomas and H. E. Shannon, while riding along the public road on their way to attend a political convention at Mackville, were annoyed by a dog barking at the horses which they were riding. Young Shelby pulled his pistol and fired at the dog without effect. Thomas then drew his pistol and fired, but through some unaccountable cause, the ball took effect in Shelby's spine, producing almost instant death. Shelby's death is greatly deplored, and by none more than Mr. Thomas.

September 4, 1877

Died September 2nd, at her late residence on Grove Street, Mrs. Margaret Mygatt, in the 63rd year of her age.

The friends and acquaintances of the late Hon. Alston Mygatt are informed that his remains will arrive from Jackson this morning, for interrment along with the remains of his late wife.

Sexton's report of deaths - City of Vicksburg:
Aug. 27 - John J. Tierney, 2 years, 6 months, 15 days, diptheria
29 - Maggie Harvey, colored, 18 years, bilious remittent fever
31 - C. W. Brooks, 45 years, consumption
29 - Wm. H. Bowman, colored, about 20 years, gun shot wound inflicted by Hezekiah

Bowman with Isiah Bowman as accessory
31 - Ellen Wethers, colored, 1 year, 3 months, diarrhea
31 - Willie Bryson, colored, 1 year, 4 months, teething
31 - T. A. Thomas, 26 years, congestion, died at his residence in Delt_, La.
Sept. 1 - Mrs. Ann Davidson, 62 years, 4 months, 22 days, brain fever
2 - Jestana Thompson, colored, 7 years, 7 months, 7 days, typho-malarial fever
2 - Jacob F. Bellinger, 54 years, typho-malarial fever

September 5, 1877

The friends and acquaintances of Jerry and Louisa O'Brien are invited to attend the funeral of their late daughter, Julia, to proceed from their residence corner Second North and Clay streets, this morning.

September 6, 1877

Died August 30, in Palestine, Texas, Miss Florida Meade Jones, in the 24th year of her age.

September 7, 1877

The friends and acquaintances of Mr. Joseph Hirsch are invited to attend the funeral of his late brother, N. Hirsch, of Port Gibson, Miss., to proceed from the steamer R. E. Lee, this morning.

Died at his residence on Bayou Vidal, August 30th, Gipson C. Bettis, in the 54th year of his age.

September 30, 1877

Died Sept. 16, Richard Percy Arendale, at his grandfather's residence, R. B. Powell, at Goodrich's Landing, La., aged six years and one month.

October 3, 1877

The community will be shocked to learn of the death last evening of Edward S. Hawkes. He had been confined to his house only two days subject to a violent cough, and complained of severe pains in the region of the heart and stomach. Dr. E. H. Gregory attended him, calling on him yesterday. Last evening while Mrs. Hawkes was at dinner, she heard her name called by her husband. She hurried to him, only to find him almost unconscious and in great suffering. On examination in the evening Dr. Gregory pronounced the cause of death to be neuralgia of the heart.

Mr. Hawkes was married to Miss Lillie Sharp, daughter of the late Fidelio C. Sharp, Esq., on the 25th of April last, in Chicago, Ill.; lately moved into the residence on the north-east corner of Twenty-first and Pine streets. Mr. Hawkes was born in Vicksburg, where his mother still resides. (St. Louis Globe-Democrat)

October 4, 1877
The friends and acquaintances of Charles F. Taffe are invited to attend the funeral of his late wife, Mrs. K. J. Taffe, to proceed from his residence, corner of Locust and Madison streets, Springfield, this morning.

October 16, 1877
Died at her residence in this city, on the 13th, Mrs. Catharine Foley.

October 17, 1877
Died on the 14th, at the residence of his brother, Mr. A. R. Churm, on Diamond Island, Miss., William Augustus, youngest son of Thomas O. and Mary B. Davis, formerly of Hinds County.

October 21, 1877
The friends and acquaintances of Martin Keary are requested to attend the funeral of Mrs. Conroy, consort of the late James Conroy, to proceed from his residence on Clay street, this afternoon.

October 31, 1877
The friends and acquaintances of Joseph P. and Sallie M. Royall are requested to attend the funeral of their only son, Joseph Royall, Jr., to proceed from their residence near the corner of Clay and Farmer streets, this morning.

Died in Tensas Parish, La., October 27th, 1877, J. T. Pigford, formerly of Lauderdale County, Miss., aged 25 years, 1 month and 2 days.

November 2, 1877
Died of congestion, at Spring Vale, near Church Hill, Jefferson County, Oct. 22nd, Mrs. Julia A. West, wife of Capt. G. J. West. She was about 30 years old and left a husband and six young children.

November 6, 1877
The friends and acquaintances of Edwin W. Folkes are requested to attend the funeral of his late wife, Emily M. Folkes, to proceed from his residence, corner of Jackson and Farmer streets, this afternoon.

Sexton's Report of Deaths - City of Vicksburg:
Oct. 30 - Joseph Royall, Jr., 2 years, pneumonia with menengitis
31 - Jake Dinkelspell, (35 or 85) years, consumption, residence Louisville
31 - Lewis Banks, (col.) cirrhosis of liver

Nov. 2 - William Weber, bilious congestive fever
4 - Martha Walker, (col.), 33 years, pneumonia
4 - J. C. Pritchett, 60 years, congestion of the brain

November 9, 1877
The friends and acquaintances of William Hennessey are requested to attend the funeral of his late brother, Dennis Hennessey, to proceed from his late residence on Mulberry Street, this morning.

November 13, 1877
Died on the 11th, at her residence near Baldwin's Ferry, Hinds County, Mrs. Minerva S. Hubbard, after an illness of 14 days with dysentery. Mrs. Hubbard was in her 67th year.

Sexton's report of Deaths - City of Vicksburg:
Nov. 5 - Nick Oliver, colored, 30 years, dropsy
5 - Peter Gilmore, 27 years, dysentery
5 - Mrs. M. E. Folkes, 41 years, 7 months, 5 days, dysentery
8 - Patrick Scanlon, 65 years
8 - Dennis Hennessey, 32 years, consumption
10 - Ann Green, colored, 21 years, disease of the heart
11 - Edward Cavanaugh, 18 years, admitted in articuto mortis into the Hill City Infirmary

November 14, 1877
The friends and acquaintances of the late John Porterfield are invited to attend his funeral to proceed from his late residence on Mulberry Street, this afternoon.

November 20, 1877
Our brother, Wm. Webb, died on the 3rd day of November, 1877. He was born in Sarralbe Lotheringen.

November 21, 1877
Sexton's Report of Deaths - City of Vicksburg:
Nov. 12 - William Maxwell, 47 years, pneumonia, died in Hill City Infirmary
12 - Celia Keeliar, colored, 8 years, whooping cough
12 - Julia Ford, colored, 30 years, small pox
12 - John Porterfield, 58 years, probably heart disease
13 - Nicey Williams, colored, old age and general debility
13 - Jane Payne, colored, 43 years, dropsy
14 - John Peterson, 28 years, swamp fever, died in Hill City Infirmary
14 - Mary L. Brown, colored, 1 year, 1 month, 10 days

14 - Mary E. Betties, colored, 7 years, 6 months, effects of a burn
15 - M. Burns, 38 years, swamp fever, died in Hill City Infirmary
15 - Wm. H. Benson, colored, 6 years, croup
15 - Toliver A. Hubbard, colored, 1 year, 1 month, 15 days, congestion of the brain & stomach
17 - Michael Hannon, 40 years, overdose of chloral administered by himself
17 - Mary E. Royall, 11 years, 11 months, 25 days, effects of a burn, Tate Co., Ms.
18 - Andrew Jackson, colored, 56 years, consumption
18 - Mike O'Herrin, from wounds inflicted by sharp instrument in the hands of John Bracken
19 - Frank Shultz, colored, 32 years, pneumonia, in Hill City Infirmary
19 - E. N. Peterson, 35 years, artieuto mortis, Hill City Infirmary

November 27, 1877

Died in Memphis, November 22, 1877, Joseph Leroy, aged 61 years, of Bright's disease.

Sexton's Report of Deaths - City of Vicksburg:
Nov. 20 - George Syms, colored, 37 years, gastro enteritis
20 - Mary Chapman, 60 years, spasms
23 - Robert Emmerson, 52 years, congestive chill
23 - Ellen Hall, colored, 8 years, diptheria
25 - Albert Ford, colored, 6 years, small pox

November 28, 1877

Died at Rolling Fork, Sharkey County, November 19th, 1877, Willie, son of Judge and Ella Wright Powell, aged 2 years and 6 months.

December 2, 1877

The friends and acquaintances of Mr. and Mrs. Leopold Clausman are invited to attend the funeral of their infant daughter, Carrie Louisa, to proceed from their residence on Cherry Street, this afternoon.

Died at the residence of her parents, in Senatobia, Mississippi, Nov. 17, 1877, Mary Ella, daughter of A. A. and Priscilla Royal, in the eleventh year of her age. Death was caused by an explosion while she was filling lamps with coal oil. (Author's note - a lengthy report followed)

December 4, 1877
Sexton's Report of Deaths - City of Vicksburg:
Nov. 30 - Wm. B. Alexander, 28 years, rheumatism of the heart
Dec. 1 - Mary Mathews, colored, 27 years, childbirth
      1 - Carrie L. Clausman, 10 months, 29 days, pneumonia

December 11, 1877
The friends and acquaintances of the late John A. Forqueran are invited to attend his funeral to proceed from St. Paul's Catholic Church, this morning.

December 13, 1877
The friends and acquaintances of the late Dr. W. T. Balfour, Sr., are invited to attend his funeral this morning, to proceed from his residence, corner of Crawford and Cherry streets.

December 14, 1877
The friends and acquaintances of the late Dr. Charles Nystrand are invited to attend his funeral this afternoon, to proceed from his residence on Crawford Street, between Mulberry and Levee.

The friends and acquaintances of the late Joseph M. Bonelli are invited to attend his funeral, to proceed from his late residence on Washington Street.

January 1, 1878
Died December 25, 1877, of pneumonia, at Calao, Sunflower River, Washington County, Mr. G. P. Walne, in the 4_th year of his age.

January 2, 1878
Died at Yazoo City, Miss., December 30, 1877, Jennie, wife of Capt. Charles A. Boccaletti.

January 4, 1878
The friends and acquaintances of Mrs. Nora White are invited to attend the funeral of her daughter, Mary Ann, to proceed from St. Paul's Catholic Church, this evening.

January 10, 1878
Died on January 9th, 1878, of diptheria, Edwin Grammer, only son of the late Wm. B. Grammer.

January 15, 1878
Sexton's Report of Deaths - City of Vicksburg:
Jan. 9 - Edward Williams, colored, 57 years, pneumonia
     9 - Robert E. Grammer, 8 years, 9 months, diptheria
    11 - Susie Polk, inflammation of the bowels & stomach
    11 - Maggie Howard, 20 years, congestion of the brain

January 16, 1878
Died January 15, 1878, of diptheria, Clarence, youngest child of G. A. Grammer and M. Ella Grammer, aged 2 years, 11 months.

F. M. Miller died at his residence at Johnsonville, in Sunflower County, Miss., on the 10th January. Francis Marion Miller was born in North Carolina in 1839. He went to Sunflower County in 1859. During the war he served four years, after which he embarked in business in Johnsonville.

January 17, 1878
Died January 13, 1878, Eleanor Durkee, wife of Henry Green, aged 77 years, a native of Baltimore, Md.

January 25, 1878
The friends and acquaintances of Mr. George Booth are invited to attend the funeral of his late wife, Terese, to proceed from his residence on Cherry Street, this morning.

January 29, 1878
The friends and acquaintances of Mrs. A. N. Meehan are invited to attend the funeral of her late daughter, Mrs. Ellen E. Saxton, to proceed from her residence on Main Street, between Cherry and Monroe, this morning.

Sexton's Report of Deaths - City of Vicksburg:
Jan. 21 - Judge Benjamin Springer, 82 years, cancer
22 - Phil Schaffer, colored, 24 years, articilo mortis
22 - J. B. Jones, colored, 20 years, pneumonia
23 - Mrs. Nancy Bellinger, 52 years, dropsy
24 - Ella Thomas, colored, 16 years, consumption
24 - Mrs. T. Booth, 36 years, pneumonia
25 - Henry Reimer, 47 years, pneumonia
25 - Herman Wira, 4 years, effects of drinking lye
26 - Dave Parker, colored, 6 days
28 - Mrs. Ellen E. Saxton, 27 years, 9 months, consumption

February 5, 1878
Sexton's Report of Deaths - City of Vicksburg:
Feb. 2 - Willie Johnson, (col.), 9 days, croup
3 - George Douglas, (col.), 20 years, pneumonia

February 6, 1878
The friends and acquaintances of N. G. Bryson are invited to attend his funeral to proceed from Christ Church this morning.

February 8, 1878
Died at her late residence in Vicksburg, on the 7th January, 1878, in the 72nd year of her age, Mrs. Eliza Potter Brown, nee Throckmorton, relict of the late Robert T. Brown, and a native of Adams County, Miss.

February 12, 1878
Sexton's Report of Deaths - City of vicksburg:
Feb. 4 - N. G. Bryson, 64 years, engargement (copied as found) of the lungs
    5 - Francis Wall, (col.), cancer
    6 - Jesse Hildebrand, 44 years, pneumonia
    7 - James White, (col.), 51 years, pneumonia
    7 - Henry Phillips, (col.), 12 years, bilious fever
    8 - Jacob Proctor, (col.), 38 years, consumption
    10 - George Jones, (col.), 28 years, variola
    11 - Lizzie Sanders, (col.), croup

February 13, 1878
The friends and acquaintances of Mr. & Mrs. E. D. Bickley are invited to attend the funeral of their infant daughter, Viola, from their residence today.

February 14, 1878
The friends and acquaintances of John Bingley are invited to attend his funeral to proceed from the A. M. E. Church today.

February 16, 1878
Died at Monroe, La., on the 14th, in the 2_th year of her age, Katie W., eldest daughter of Dr. R. H. Winter, of Jackson, Miss.

February 19, 1878
Died at his residence in Warren County, February 18th, Maj. Lewellyn Price, in the 75th year of his age.

February 24, 1878
Died at the residence of his mother, in this city, on February 23rd, Wm. Grimes, aged 23 years.

Died at Jackson, Miss., Dec. 8, 1878, James A. Claver. He was born in Saulsbury, North Carolina, Oct. 21st, 182_, married Miss Harriet C. Ulmar at Westport, Ky., July 3rd, 1849, who with four children survive him, two having died in childhood. For many years he was a resident of Vicksburg.

March 5, 1878
Died in Fredericksburg, Va., of pneumonia, on March 1st, Mrs. Robt. W. Hart, mother of Mrs. James W. Gray and sister of Mrs. A. M. Paxton and Mrs. S. M. Crump, of this city.

March 9, 1878

Died at his residence in Hinds County, on the 6th, Col. John Ervin, aged 86 years. The deceased was the father-in-law of Capt. E. B. Willis, of Warren (county).

March 12, 1878

Died at Brookside, Claiborne County, Miss., March 5th, of congestion of the brain, John Guion, third son of Col. Wm. H. McCardle, of this city, in the 31st year of his age.

Sexton's Report of Deaths - City of Vicksburg:
Mar. 9 - Mrs. F. C. Devenney, 2_ years, disease of the lungs, Sunflower County
9 - Sophia S. Gibson, colored, six weeks, spasms
10 - Willie Penelton, colored, 8 years, scrofula
11 - Charles Thompson, 82 years, congestion of the brain

March 16, 1878

Died of pneumonia, in this city, March 15th, 1878, William King, son of King and Anna Dorwart, aged 5 years, 5 months and 20 days.

March 26, 1878

Died at Lavonia, Wilson County, Texas, of heart disease, November, 1877, at the age of 26 years, Welton L. Arnold. He was the eighth son of the late Jackson Arnold, of Lowndes County, and a brother of Hon. Judge Jas. M. Arnold, of Columbus, Felix B. Arnold, of Sharon, Rev. Z. T. Arnold, of Crawfordsville, and John C. Arnold of Johnsonville.

Sexton's Report of Deaths - City of Vicksburg:
March 20 - Moses Solomon, 4 years, croup
20 - Fanny Stonewall, colored, 53 years, womb disease
20 - Rosa Jones, colored, 1 year, measles
22 - Ward Preston, colored, 23 years, consumption
24 - Caroline Johnson, colored, 60 years, cancer

March 28, 1878

Died at his late residence on Grove Street, Dr. M. Gilman, in the 5_th year of his age.

March 29, 1878

The friends and acquaintances of Mr. Jerry Healey are invited to attend the funeral of his late wife, Mrs. Julia Healey, to proceed from the Catholic Church, this afternoon.

April 4, 1878
The friends and acquaintances of Mr. W. J. Miller are invited to attend the funeral of his late wife, Marion C. Miller, to proceed from the residence of Mrs. D. S. Arnold, corner of Harrison and Martha streets, this morning.

April 5, 1878
The friends and acquaintances of John Ryan are invited to attend the funeral of his son, John Ryan, Jr., to proceed from his residence on Mulberry Street, this morning.

April 7, 1878
The friends and acquaintances of the late John J. Rigley are requested to attend his funeral to proceed from his residence at the Marine Hospital, this afternoon.

April 25, 1878
Died at Mrs. Sexton's, on the 8th of April, 1878, little Leonora, infant daughter of D. A. and Theresa Alverson, aged eight months.

April 28, 1878
Died at Santa Rosa, California, April 26th, 1878, Judge A. L. Dabney, formerly of Raymond, Hinds County, Miss.

Miss Biddy McTagart died at the residence of Mr. Ed Wilson, in this city, April 21st, after a painful illness of a few days.

May 3, 1878
The friends and acquaintances of H. H. and Jennie A. Moore are invited to attend the funeral of their infant daughter, Jennie James, this morning.

May 10, 1878
The friends and acquaintances of the late James R. Johnson are invited to attend his funeral to proceed from his residence on the railroad, near east end of Harrison Street, this morning.

May 14, 1878
The friends and acquaintances of John R. Edwards are invited to attend the funeral of his late wife, Sarah C. Edwards, this morning.

Sexton's Report of Deaths - City of Vicksburg:
May 7 - John Brereton, 11 hours
    7 - Thomas Johnson, (col.), 15 months, dysentery
    8 - James R. Johnson, 34 years, injuries received on railroad
    9 - Susan Williams, (col.), 63 years, heart disease

11 - Jim Brown, (col.), 50 years, pneumonia et hepatitis
11 - Annie Harwood, (col.), 40 years, apoplexy
12 - Louisa Craig, (col.) 65 years, delirious fever
12 - Mahala Platt, (col.), 21 years, typhoid fever

May 17, 1878

Mr. Edwin Cocke, 19 years of age, died from pulmonary consumption, at the residence of Mr. G. L. Boney, Duckport, La., May the 9th.

May 21, 1878

The friends and acquaintances of Mr. John D. Allen are invited to attend his funeral this morning.

May 29, 1878

The friends and acquaintances of C. A. Manlove and Mrs. R. A. Folkes are invited to attend the funeral of the late Armistead Burwell, to proceed from Christ Church this morning.

May 31, 1878

Died at residence, South Street, May 30th, Mary Mayrant, infant daughter of Alfred M. and Lena R. Lea, aged 4 months.

June 8, 1878

The friends and acquaintances of Mr. T. F. Conway are invited to attend the funeral of his late brother, M. J. Conway, to proceed from his residence on Clay Steet, between Mulberry and Levee, this morning.

June 11, 1878

Died at Diamond Landing, Warren County, Miss., June 8th, after a brief illness, Ettie Lee, infant daughter of Frank and Sallie Henderson.

June 12, 1878

Died June 11th, Mrs. Helen S. Routh, wife of the late Octo Routh, Esq., and daugthter of Gen. Wm. E. Starke.

June 16, 1878

The freinds and acquaintances of the late Raleigh Folkes, Sr. are invited to attend his funeral, to proceed from his late residence "Magnolia Hall," this morning.

June 21, 1878

The friends and acquaintances of Carmino Bunizio are invited to attend the funeral of his late wife, Mary Bunizio, this morning.

June 26, 1878
The friends and acquaintances of John Dougherty are invited to attend the funeral of his late wife, Margaret Dougherty, this morning.

January 1, 1879
Died at Vicksburg, of yellow fever, August 24, 1878, Robert Read Eggleston, who was born October 11, 1855; also John Fox Eggleston, of the same disease, on the 20th of August, 1878, who was born August 6, 18_8.

Died December 21st, George H. Record, a native of this city, aged 36 years, 3 months, 10 days. His friends and those of his father, G. L. Record, are invited to attend his funeral to proceed from the residence of his father, corner Walnut and Veto streets, this morning.

January 9, 1879
The friends and acquaintances of the late W. G. Bender, are invited to attend his funeral, to proceed from his late residence, corner Grove and Walnut streets, this morning.

The friends and acquaintances of Mr. J. W. Coffing are invited to attend the funeral of his late wife, Maggie Coffing, to proceed from his residence on Jackson Road, near Farmer Street, this afternoon.

January 10, 1879
The friends and acquaintances of Dr. B. H. Cook, are invited to attend his funeral this evening, from his residence corner of Second North and Clay streets.

January 16, 1879
Sexton's Report of Deaths - City of Vicksburg:
Jan. 6 - S. W. Cowan, 50 or 60 years
    7 - Henry Brown, 7 weeks, pneumonia, interred in Jewish Cemetery
    8 - W. G. Bender, 67 years, softening of the brain
    8 - Wm. Randolph, (col.), articulo mortis
    8 - John Dodge, (col.), 30 years, pneumonia
    8 - Mrs. Maggie Coffing, 30 years, pneumonia
    9 - Charles Bright, 22 years, pneumonia
    9 - James Linscott, 2_ years, death by pistol shot, pistol in hands of Wm. Busselman
    9 - B. H. Cook, 49 years, apoplexy
    10 - Harriett McClennon, 3 weeks, croup
    12 - Irene Manuel, (col.), 25 years, consumption
    12 - Francis C. Coffing, 4 months, maramus

January 18, 1879
Died at the Washington Hotel, the 17th, of uremia, Col. G. W. Nichols, aged 67 years, a native of Maryland and a resident of Madison Parish, La. for the last twelve years.

January 29, 1879
The friends and acquaintances of Mrs. S. A. Vandenburg are invited to attend the funeral of her late daughter, Laura Annie, to proceed from her residence on Jackson Road, this morning.

Sexton's Report of Deaths - City of Vicksburg:
Jan. 13 - Eliza Frazier, colored, 90 years, rheumatism
13 - Bill Burream, colored, 28 years, pneumonia
14 - John Swinton, 40 years, pneumonia
14 - Antony Porter, colored, 30 years, pneumonia
14 - John F. Sullivan, 2 years
14 - Ellen Peterson, colored, 2 years, pneumonia
15 - Jeff Rivers, colored, old age
15 - Melley McClain, colored, 25 years, pneumonia
16 - Wm. Colridge, colored, 21 years, pneumonia
16 - Douglas Minee, colored, 60 years, pneumonia
16 - Carter Blunt, colored, 50 years, pneumonia
16 - John Night, colored, 45 years, pneumonia
17 - George W. Nicols, 67 years, Madison Parish, La.
18 - N. N. Lanier, 38 years, pneumonia
18 - R. A. Bell, 85 years, suicide
18 - Lewis Seppard, colored, 25 years, pneumonia
20 - Thomas Fernon, 22 years, pneumonia
20 - James Wofford, colored, 65 years, general debility
- _. M. Redfield, colored, 6 months, croup
20 - John Ferrell, 56 years

January 24, 1879
Died January 23rd, 1879, at the residence of Mrs. Julia Porterfield, Joseph B. Lyons, in the 40th year of his age, of pneumonia.

The friends and acquaintances of Mr. and Mrs. James Geary are invited to attend the funeral of Mrs. Mary Geary, wife of the late Jas. W. Geary, Jr.

The friends and acquaintances of Mrs. Caroline L. Hazelett and her late husband are invited to attend his funeral, from their residence on the corner of Clay and Monroe streets, this afternoon.

January 26, 1879
John R. Hicks, born November 18th, 1839, died October 7th, 1878. In February 1863, bridal bells which rang for John R. Hicks sent forth a double chime for his friend and kinsman, Dr. P. F. Whitehead,

and by most awful coincidence, has been supplemented by a double death.

Died at Vicksburg, Miss., September 6th, 1878, of yellow fever, Robert A. Hundermark, aged 45 years. Robert Hundermark was born in Breman, Germany, April 15, 1833, whence he came to America in 1849.

Died at Vicksburg, Miss., September 5th, 1878, of yellow fever, Alice V. Hundermark, aged 14 years. Allie V. Hundermark was born February 18, 1864.

Mrs. Monette, the daughter of Thomas J. and Minerva Gibson, and the wife of Dr. Wm. E. Monette, whom she married February 10th, 1839, fell asleep in Jesus October 16, 1878, aged 44 years, in this county. Annie, 18 years of age, daughter of Dr. W. E. and Mrs. Sallie Monette, had on October 17th, followed her mother to the grave. Death came again, and on October 18th, Gibson, a bright youth of 12 years, joined mother and sister. Again he comes, and the father, Dr. Wm. E. Monette, son of Dr. Monette, grandson of Judge Gibson, peacefully passed away November 7th, 1878, aged 41 years.

February 2, 1879

Terrance Laughlin died October 3rd, 1878, aged 10 years, 11 months.

February 4, 1879

Died in Vicksburg, Miss., September 18th, 1878, of yellow fever, Miss Annie L. Bitterman, aged 21 years.

Sexton's Report of Deaths - City of Vicksburg:
Jan. 27 - Caroline James, colored, 23 years, pneumonia
    28 - Albert Jones, colored, 13 days, spasms
    28 - F. Wallace, colored, 40 years, typhoid pneumonia
    28 - Tandred Bonino, 44 years, typhoid pneumonia
    28 - Mary Thomas, colored, 50 years, paralysis
    28 - Loudie Marsett, colored, 67 years, heart disease
    29 - Leodora Smith, colored, 5 months
    30 - A. Johnson, colored, 35 years, pneumonia
Feb. 2 - Charles Owens, colored, 46 years, consumption

February 5, 1879

Died, Agnes, infant daughter of J. J. and E. J. Fitzpatrick, February 4, 1879, aged 4 weeks.

February 11, 1879

Sexton's Report of Deaths - City of Vicksburg:
Feb. 2 - Thomas McCue, 56 years, pneumonia
    4 - Francis Ely, colored, 30 years

5 - Agnes Fitzpatrick, 4 weeks
5 - John McRedmond, 38 years, neuralgia
6 - R. W. Hughes, 30 years, pneumonia, died in Isaquena County, interred at Vicksburg
7 - Charlie Hill, colored, 45 years, inflammation of the brain
7 - John Kirrwan, 40 years, intermittent fever
8 - Alfred Porter, colored, 40 years, pneumonia
9 - John R. Tryford, 25 years, malarial fever
9 - Jesse B. Porterfield, 2 months, 15 days, debility, died in Delta, La., interred in Vicksburg

February 14, 1879

Died in this city, February 12th, 1879, Miss Maggie E. Moore, sister of Captain L. C. Moore.

February 16, 1879

Died in this city, September 28th, 1878, Oscar N. Stith, aged 32 years.

February 18, 1879

Died in this city, February 17th, 1879, Sarah, wife of Rev. L. W. Seeley, D. D. of Kentucky. The funeral will proceed from the residence of her son-in-law, T. M. Folkes, this afternoon.

Mrs. Ann R. Ferguson, relict of the late John Ferguson, departed this life October 8th, 1878, at her residence in Warren County, Miss., aged 75 years. Born in North Carolina in 1803, she removed with her family to Mississippi when a girl of sixteen. (Author's note - a lengthy report followed)

The Vestry of the Parish of the Holy Trinity: Our Junior Warden, Mr. William A. Faircloth, and two of our members, Dr. P. F. Whitehead and Major D. W. Flowerree have passed from life into death.

February 22, 1879

The friends and acquaintances of Owen Royce and Mrs. Ann E. Strother are invited to attend the funeral of Mrs. Laura A. Royce, to proceed from her late residence on Clay Street, this Saturday morning.

Died at the residence of his father, on Cherry Street, February 21st, 1879, of pneumonia, Joseph Antonia Genella, age 29 years and 7 days. Mr. Genella has been confined to his bed some months past, stricken by the fever and taken some three months since with pneumonia, from which he died. He was born in San Francisco, California, and came to this city when about 2 years old.

February 23, 1879

Died at his residence in Lake Providence, La., February 15th, 1879, of typhoid pneumonia, Aljerome Burell, aged 44 years and 5 months.

The friends and acquaintances of the late Mr. E. H. Porter are invited to attend his funeral, to proceed from the residence of Mrs. M. D. Tappan, on Walnut Street, this afternoon.

Died in Vicksburg on the 14th of September, 1878, Miss Ella McCabe; also on the 20th of September, Miss Annie McCabe, both of yellow fever.

February 25, 1879
Sexton's Report of Deaths - City of Vicksburg:
Feb. 17 - Janney Clark, colored, 36 years, pneumonia
   17 - Mrs. Sarah Sealey, 56 years, asthma
   18 - Dr. George Jackson, 35 years
   21 - Mrs. Laura A. Royce, 24 years & 26 days, died of a fall
   21 - Antony Phillips, colored, 40 years, hemorrhage of the stomach
   21 - Joseph A. Genella, 28 years, pneumonia
   22 - Edward H. Porter, 53 years, apoplexy
   23 - Michael Sheehan, 58 years, consumption

March 2, 1879

Died in Warren County and interred in Vicksburg cemetery, on February 21st, 1879, of congestive chill, Mrs. Kasemer Schnurr, in the 45th year of her age.

The friends and acquaintances of Maurice Burgin are invited to attend the funeral of his late wife, Lena Burgin, to proceed from his residence on Mulberry Street, this afternoon.

March 4, 1879

Died on Triumph plantation, Bolivar County, Miss., February 13th, 1879, Thomas C., infant son of John G. and Emma B. Yeiser, aged 3 months and 20 days.

Died on Triumph plantation, Bolivar County, Mississippi, February 22nd, 1879, Emma Ballou Yeiser, wife of John G. Yeiser, aged 34 years.

March 16, 1879

Died February 21st, 1879, Laura, wife of Owen Royce and daughter of Mrs. Ann E. Strother, aged 24.

March 19, 1879

Died in Vicksburg, Miss., March 18th, 1879, H. B. Bruser, aged 41 years, born in (Milie or Milis), Warnedorf, county Munster, Germany, September 15th, 1837.

March 23, 1879

Joseph L. Doll was born of German parentage, in Cinicnnati, Ohio, March 14th, 1842, and departed this life in Vicksburg, Miss., September 2nd, 1878, of yellow fever.

In the *Vicksburg Herald* of May 16th, 1866 we find this: "Married on the 15th of May, Mr. Joseph F. Doll to Miss Rosina Hartman, both of this city." On the 6th of the same month of May, 1876, she winged her way to mansions of the blest, leaving to his care two girls and a boy.

April 2, 1879

The friends and acquaintances of Mr. & Mrs. B. McNamara are invited to attend the funeral of their infant son, Joseph Benedict, to proceed from St. Paul's Catholic Church this morning.

April 12, 1879

Died at Denver, Colorado, April 10th, Henry Kuner, son of Max Kuner, of this city.

Died at St. Louis, Missouri, April 11th, Mrs. Lizzie Schmidt, wife of H. A. Schmidt, formerly of Vicksburg.

April 15, 1879

The friends and acquaintances of Mr. Edward Crofton, are invited to attend the funeral of his late wife, Mrs. Emma Crofton, to proceed from his residence on Mulberry Street, this afternoon.

April 17, 1879

The friends and acquaintances of Capt. J. H. Gunning are invited to attend the funeral of his late wife, Ellen V., to proceed from his residence, corner Walnut and Veto streets, today.

April 20, 1879

Tribute -- Dr. Peter F. Whitehead was born in Winchester, Kentucky, on the 9th of June, 1838. He commenced the study of medicine under Dr. H. Taylor in 1857, and finished his medical education at Jefferson Medical College in Philadelphia, Pa., graduating in the class of 1859-60. He was physician for Blockley Hospital, Philadelphia, one year. He then settled in Independence, Mo. where he practised his profession. In the late civil war he enlisted as private in Erwin's Company, at Independence, Mo., shortly afterwards commissioned as Surgeon in the Missouri State Guard. He was later a surgeon with the Third Louisiana regiment, and Chief Surgeon of General Loring's Division, in which position he surrendered at Greensboro, N. C., April 1865. He married Miss Irene Cowan, of Vicksburg, Miss. in 1865 and settled in Vicksburg. (Author's note - this is part of a lengthy report)

April 23, 1879
Sexton's Report of Deaths - City of Vicksburg:
April 15 - Mrs. Emma Crofton, effects of a burn
16 - Mrs. Ellen V. Gunning, 38 years, 4 months, 26 days, nervous prostration
18 - Freddie Wallace, colored, 9 months, pneumonia
18 - Alexander Brunini, 46 years, 4 months, 13 days, apoplexy
19 - Clarissa Clay, colored, 50 years, dropsy
19 - John L. Dent, 20 years, 4 months, 14 days, effects of pistol shot wound, pistol in hands of John H. Brereton, Vicksburg
21 - P. H. Kilgarian, 36 years, gangrene
21 - Dr. L. Reinach, 48 years, consumption

April 25, 1879
The friends and acquaintances of the late Mrs. Della Bannon are invited to attend her funeral to proceed from her late residence on Walnut Street this morning.

April 27, 1879
Died in Vicksburg, Miss., on April 26th, 1879, Miss Mary E. Meade.

April 29, 1879
Col. Richard M. Hobson, citizen of this city, died at his home on the McGehee place near Jackson, Thursday morning, of pneumonia. (Jackson Comet)

Died in New Orleans, Louisiana, April 21, 1879, Herman Henry Lauel, aged 60 years, 6 months and 21 days, a native of Salsberg, Germany, husband of Sarah Ann Maples, of Vicksburg, Miss.

May 2, 1879
John L. Dent met his death on the 20th, in Vicksburg. The aim of an assassin has stilled a noble heart.

May 7, 1879
Died on May 6th, 1879, Annie E., youngest daughter of A. M. and Mary L. Paxton.

The friends and acquaintances of the late Mrs. Mary A. Hammett, relict of the late Henry Hammett, are invited to attend the funeral this morning.

May 9, 1879
Died at her residence, corner Clay and Walnut streets, May 8th, Mrs. Annie C. Flowerree, in the 31st year of her age.

May 13, 1879
Sexton's Report of Deaths - City of Vicksburg:
May 7 - Mrs. Mary A. Hammett, 53 years, inflammation of the brain
- 6 - Miss Annie E. Paxton, 25 years, 6 months, 26 days, nervous prostration
- 7 - Edna O. Stith, 4 months, 26 days, cholera infantum
- 7 - Dr. T. E. Randolph, excessive dose of hydrate of chloral, self administered
- 8 - Mrs. Annie C. Flowerree, 31 years, 1 month, 12 days, cause unknown
- 9 - Mrs. M. J. Downing, 60 years, 2 months, 1 day, Bright's disease
- 10 - Dr. J. R. Barnett, 46 years, 10 months, 28 days, dysentery

May 17, 1879
We record the death of T. J. Lackey, son of J. J. Lackey, Esq., near Crystal Springs, the 11th. About four months ago he was attacked by a rabid dog and had to fight for his life, sustaining a very severe wound on his hand by the dog mangling it with his teeth. The wound healed and time passed without any dangerous symptoms until the 8th, when he was taken with a chill and felt uneasiness in the arm that had been bitten. The first proof hydrophobia had set in came the following day. He was taken to his father's residence and died three days after the first symptoms.

May 20, 1879
Sexton's Report of Deaths - City of Vicksburg:
May 15 - William Ellis, 70 years, eutonasia(?)
- 15 - Neville H. Thorn, 10 years, anasarca
- 16 - Minor Green, colored, 80 years, bowel affection
- 16 - Jackson Ealy, colored, 60 years, dropsy
- 17 - Seeley Evans, colored, 20 years, accidentally killed by cars at Bolton's Dept

May 21, 1879
The friends and acquaintances of the late Dr. Morris Emanuel are invited to attend his funeral today.

May 27, 1879
The friends and acquaintances of the late Herman Busselman are invited to attend his funeral this afternoon.

May 29, 1879

Three weeks ago Robert M. Hastings was attacked with flux and steadily became weaker until he passed away on Friday. (Port Gibson Reveille)

Died at Hoboken, Warren County, May 28th, of pneumonia, Bertha Belle, the only daughter of Captain J. M. & Mrs. Vick Batchelor, age 10 months and 7 days.

May 31, 1879

The friends and acquaintances of (H. or R.) T. North, are invited to attend the funeral of his late wife, Susan M. North, to proceed from his residence corner of Randolph and Locust streets, Saturday evening.

June 17, 1879

Sexton's Report of Deaths - City of Vicksburg:
June 10 - Roxy Johnson, colored, 1 year, 5 months
12 - John Heasny, 34 years, malarial fever
12 - Mike Flaharty, 23 years, plotisis pulmon
13 - Frank Williams, colored, 5 months
13 - Phillip Puneky, 18 years, remittent fever
14 - W. T. Fisher, 40 years
14 - Venus Linton, colored, 90 years, old age
14 - W. J. Archer, colored, 2 years, 3 months
15 - Child of Lilly Merrill, colored, 3 weeks

June 18, 1879

Died in Algiers, La. at the residence of Rev. Louis A. Reed, on the 24th ult., of consumption, Mrs. Olivia D. Watson, daughter of the late Wm. W. Rowan and relict of Louis D. Watson, of Sharkey County, Miss., in the 32nd year of her age. She was a native of Wilkinson County.

June 20, 1879

The friends and acquaintances of the late Mrs. Eliza Young McKinney are invited to attend her funeral, to proceed from her residence on Cherry Street near East Avenue, this morning.

June 21, 1879

The friends and acquaintances of the late Mrs. Margaret Hartman are invited to attend her funeral to proceed from her residence, corner Main and Walnut streets, this morning.

June 25, 1879

$100 Reward -- for body of J. Galvan, supposed to have been lost overboard from steamer *Robert Mitchell* on night of 2_th, between Goodrich's and Barnard Landing - height 5' 5", hair little mixed gray.

INDEX

AARON, Samuel 42 47 Sara 42
ABERNATHY, Sam 142
ABLE, Samuel 117
ABNER, John 11
ADAIR, Mrs. F. A. 71
ADAIRE, M. D. 64
ADAMS, Eliza M. 37 Jeff 183 John G. 144 Joseph 3 Lizzie 168 Metty 183 Robert 145 W. A. 168 169
ADKINS, Mike 85
ADKINSON, Sarah 206
AH WAYS, 113
AICKMAN, John B. 99
ALBERSON, Mrs. 7 Wm. 7
ALCORN, George 14 Robt. J. 14
ALEXANDER, A. 210 Esther 104 Fannie E. Y. 210 J. B. 75 J. V. 14 Jacob 104 Joe 22 23 25 Joseph B. 25 Maj. 107 V. F. P. 108 Wm. B. 215
ALFORD, J. E. 207 T. M. 84 Troy M. 91
ALLEN, 97 Alice 90 Andrew 35 C. E. 90 D. R. 128 Darthnia 143 Ed. 51 Elizabeth 24 Gordon 143 Guy 144 Jas. H. 24 John D. 220 John M. 60 Johnson 172 Lewis L. 170 Liza 143 Martha 161 Miss 144 Mrs. 135 Nancy 143 Shade 138
ALLFORD, James 198
ALLIMAN, Deserce 179
ALLRED, Martha 73
ALSWORTH, B. Chase 47 Henderson 55 J. N. 44 John Lynn 52 Minerva J. 44
ALVERSON, D. A. 219 Leonora 219 Theresa 219
ALVIS. Elizabeth 182 Rosalie 186 W. P. 186
AMBERG, Rachel 111
ANDERSON, Ed. McD. 162 Flora 144 Flora A. 155 Flora F. 120 Fulton 155 Gaines 159 J. M. 57 James Monroe Sr. 52 Lomax 118 Mariah 143 Ned 45 Pearl 159 Ruby 118 S. C. 62 Wm. 160 Wm. E. 120
ANDREWS, F. G. 69 Louisa 69 Maggie 208 Warren 69 William G. 116
ANGEVINE, Misses 142
APPEL, C. 82 Charles C. 82
APPLEWHITE, E. R. 31
ARCHER, Anna P. 101 Bettie 101 D. B. 154 Dr. 112 Helen 130 James 125 John G. 130 Josie 26 Robt. H. 99 S. 101 130 W. H. 99 W. J. 229
ARENDALE, Richard Percy 211
ARMSTEAD, Henry 145
ARMSTRONG, A. A. 142
ARNOLD, Felix B. 218 Jackson 218 Jas. A. 218 John 146 John C. 218 Mrs. D. S. 219 Welton L. 218 Wm. 157 Z. T. 218
ARTHUR, A. H. 165 William 162
ASHCRAFT, J. E. 10 J. W. 10
ASKEW, A. O. 77 Dr. 74 J. O. 77 Susan 77
ATKINSON, J. N. 152 Mary Lea 194 Mary V. 194 William 194
ATTERBURY, J. T. 130 Newton West 130
AUSTIN, Annie 197
AVERITT, James L. 45
AVERY, Annie Moore 49 Effie 48 67 J. H. 43 Sue 43 T. N. 48 Thos. N. 49 67 Wm. 16
AYERS, Lizzie 142 Willie Frank 184

BACCHER, A. 90 C. E. 90 Daisie C. 90
BACKNER, W. E. 128
BADWICK, Joe 109
BAHIN, Alphonse 163 Edwin G. 163 Louise 163
BAHR, E. 51 Earhest 136
BAILES, W. J. 80
BAILEY, Agnes Jane 85 Elijah F. 73 Helen 111 James 35 Martha

Allred 73 W. W. 8 Will H. 44 William U. 44
BAKER, E. G. 134 138 Frank 175 Grafton 121 127 Ira 2 5 Leonard 2 5 Martha Gordon 138 Mrs. Grafton 121 Nancy 2 5 Percy 127 Sallie F. 134 138 Sarah J. DePriest 2 Susie 128
BALDWIN, Will 49
BALDWYN, T. M. 16
BALFOUR, W. T. Sr. 215
BALL, Harriet 171
BALLARD, James 33 John 109 John S. 110 Mrs. 109 Mrs. J. S. 108 Mrs. K. A. 108
BALLORE, Mary E. 164
BALM, Burden 108
BANKS, George 91 John 143 Lewis 212
BANNLON, John 108
BANNON, Della 227
BARBOUR, James F. 72 Mrs. Pollock 4
BARCHURST, John 110
BARDWELL, Francis M. 193
BARFIELD, Jas. S. 158
BARGER, Hosea 201
BARKER, Henry 81 84 M. A. 12 S. N. 12 Smith 144
BARKSDALE, E. 154 Ethel 98 Harris 154 James 146 Marcisse Lucille 98 Nannie P. 70 W. F. 70 William 98 William R. 70 Wm. R. 103
BARLOW, Frank 149 Indiana C. 149
BARNES, Augusta 82 83 D. P. 82 Edna Maude 82 Israel 169 Mrs. Lyde P. 189 O. P. 83 Prentiss 83
BARNET, Philip 107
BARNETT, A. W. 31 Callie 18 Fannie 161 J. R. 201 228 J. T. 12 James 57 Nancy 12
BARNHARD, Jack 93
BARNHURST, Mrs. J. S. 110
BARR, Albert 62 Forest 111 Mary Ann 112
BARRY, R. E. 207 W. S. 13 W. T. 145
BARTON, Emma 3
BARWICK, E. M. 132 E. V. 132

BASHAW, George W. 3 Mary 3
BASKINS, James S. 50
BASS, J. A. 138 J. H. 65 J. Pinkney 138 James 135 John W. 136 Mrs. S. J. 65 Paul 42 W. E. 155
BATCHELOR, Bertha Belle 229 J. M. 229 James Madison 174 Vick 229
BATEMAN, child 142
BATES, 119 Elceba 195 Joe 41 Mrs. 196 W. H. 199
BATHKE, Mrs. H. 109
BATHKEE, C. 107
BATLEY, J. N. 38
BATTLE, Cullen 204
BAUCHAMP, Willie 142
BAUGH, A. B. 122 Augusta 122 Hallie 122 John G. H. 74
BAUGHN, James W. 54
BAYLISS, Charles 67 M. 67 T. A. 67
BAYLOR, Williamson 149
BEADLES, WOOD & Co., 62
BEALL, Wm. 16
BEANLAND, Sallie 200
BEARD, Mrs. 135
BEASLEY, John 135 136 Mary 136
BEAUCHAMP, Will N. 88
BECK, J. G. 99 Mary A. 99 Mrs. 108
BEGGETT, Mr. 135
BELEW, Mrs. W. A. 142
BELFIELD, Eliza 107
BELL, Betsy 167 Emma 78 James 60 Joan 78 Joe 129 Mrs. N. 78 R. A. 222 Scott 117 T. W. 78 Tom 59 W. M. Jr. 203 Willis 36
BELLINGER, Jacob F. 211 Nancy 216
BENDER, W. G. 221
BENION, Ram 135
BENNETT, Edwin R. 168 Henry C. C. 172 Jake 128 Joseph 157
BENOIST, Gabriel 176
BENSON, Mrs. J. M. 30 Wm. H. 214
BENTON, Alice M. 28 Eula 51 135 M. 136 Serena 187 W. H. 28
BERGLUND, A. M. 193 Freddie Centennial 193 G. 193
BERGMAN, John 126
BERRY, Allie 205 Annie 110 F. P. 205 Jacob 143 Johnny 205 Walter S. 112

BESSONETT, Jno. W. 34
BETTIES, Mary E. 214
BETTIS, Gipson C. 211
BICKER, James 198
BICKLEY, E. D. 217 Viola 217
BIER, Jake 112
BIGELOW, 109 Chas. 109
BIGGS, James 180 181
BILBO, Wm. P. 50
BILBREW, James 39
BILBRO, James 40
BILES, Calista 79
BILL, H. D. 8
BILLINGSLEA, Otho 49
BILLS, J. S. 201
BILLUPS, T. C. 138
BINGLEY, John 217
BIRCH, Mrs. 3
BIRD, Geo. 108 J. M. 140 L. G. 136 Maria 126
BIRDSONG, L. F. 140 Walter L. 140
BISHOP, Doc 190 James 190 Mr. 189
BITTERMAN, Annie L. 223
BLACK, Elmirah 76 Moses B. 103 S. L. 76
BLACKBURN, Elvira 110 Jennie 127 Mamie 178 Mr. 135 William 135
BLACKWOOD, E. C. 8
BLAILOCK, Flora 63 Robert 63
BLAIR, Jas. A. 188 Mrs. N. C. 188
BLANK, Mrs. 142
BLANKS, Vannoy 34
BLANTON, M. R. 131 O. M. 131
BLUNT, Carter 222
BOATLER, P. H. 69
BOBO, C. G. 95 T. G. 95
BOCCALETTI, Charles A. 215 Jennie 215
BODKY, Louisa 111
BOGGS, Catharine 198 John 198 L. 198
BOLDING, Robt. 113
BOLES, Mattie 50
BOLLS, Mary L. 78 P. R. 78
BOLTON, T. J. 45
BOND, George Stovall 93 J. N. 93
BONELLI, Joseph M. 215
BONEY, G. L. 220
BONHAM, Ike 125
BONINO, Tandred 223

BONNER, Charles 142 Sam 142 Samuel W. 145
BONNEY, H. S. 194
BOOKER, Bella 58 C. 127
BOON, Mary E. 79 W. J. 79
BOONE, B. B. 19
BOOTH, George 216 Mrs. T. 216 Terese 216
BORDEAUX, Elbert 85 Eulah 85 Sarah 85
BORDERS, Alfred 163 Lena 163
BOREN, J. S. 25 Marcus 25 W. L. 19
BORROUM, Mr. 148
BORUM, R. 68 Sallie H. 68 T. C. 162
BOSTWICK, G. M. 17 Robert F. 88
BOSWICK, Chas. 109
BOSWORTH, Augusta S. 45 H. C. 38
BOTT, Elizabeth F. 98
BOURN, A. L. M. 65
BOWEN, General 106 Grant A. 129 J. A. 145 Martha A. 145 R. A. 145
BOWLES, Roderick 35
BOWMAN, Augustus 144 Hezekiah 210 211 Isiah 211 John 27 Rufus 180 Wm. H. 210
BOXLEY, Lucius 144
BOYD, A. A. 197 Augusta Matilda 197 Ben 143 Fannie A. 197
BOYLE, J. H. 150
BR_FORD, Mrs. A. J. 56
BRACEY, J. H. 39
BRACKEN, John 214
BRADFORD, B. M. 73 Martha 73 Millie 144
BRADY, Lee 132 Regulus 95 T. L. 199
BRAGG, Braxton 91
BRAME, Capt. 140 H. M. 20
BRAMLETT, Henry 204
BRANNOCK, Marcella 167 Marcellus 168
BRANNON, Mr. 143
BRANTLY, Mrs. P. 200
BRASWELL, C. W. 155
BRAZIER, Geo. 111
BRECK, Mary M. 49
BRECKENRIDGE, Caroline 173
BRENNAN, 3

233

BRENT, Laura A. 80 Maggie Rebecca 197 R. L. 197 W. E. 197 W. J. 80
BRERETON, Jack 114 145 John 219 John H. 227
BREVIARD, Jno. G. 155 Mary Newton 155 Mary W. 155
BREWER, David 136 Ella Eudora 136 W. B. 34
BRIDGES, Lymas 27
BRIGGS, Emily V. 74
BRIGHT, Charles 221
BRIM, Edward 144
BRINKLEY, E. T. 142 143 J. A. 67 Mary McMillan 67
BRISCOE, John J. 51 Thos. A. 201
BRISTER, Jno. T. 16 Sam 16
BRISTON, John Sr. 16 S. 51
BRITTON, J. D. 129
BROADAWAY, Julia A. 203
BROADWATER, Ezra 65
BROADWAY, Charlie 59 61
BROCK, A. H. 66 Moses 76 Mr. 134
BROGDEN, Allen 144
BROOKE, Walter 44
BROOKS, C. W. 210 D. E. 107 Fannie 107 Frank 34 Jim 174 Mary F. 76 Rebecca 127 Terrell 66
BROOM, George 209
BROUNLEY, Joseph M. 208 Mary Brame 208
BROWN, 27 28 A. F. 142 Adolphus 49 161 Agnes M. 47 B. W. 200 Eliza Potter 217 Fineese 93 Geo. 109 Gert__ Yarbrough 55 Governor 117 H. W. 200 Harvey M. 176 Henry 221 Ida 113 J. D. 93 J. M. 11 73 James Landon 55 Jim 220 Josephine 40 M. B. 128 Mary 99 Mary L. 213 Mary M. 133 Minnie 26 Narcissa Elvira 40 R. M. 98 Robert T. 217 S. B. 26 S. P. 12 186 187 Sam 113 Stirling 172 T. D. 40 T. L. 97 W. N. 93 William Y. 161 Wm. 108 Wm. C. 203
BROWNRIGG, Sallie 3
BRUCE, Thompson 77
BRUNER, Mary 171
BRUNINI, Alexander

BRUNNI, Mr. 200
BRUSER, H. B. 226
BRYAN, J. E. 120
BRYSON, N. G. 216 217 Willie 211
BUCHANAN, Judge 187 Keziah 126
BUCK, John B. 85 Mrs. 132
BUCKLEY, J. M. 164 James M. 32 129 164
BUCKNER, Calin 210 Davis 119 Jas. H. 109 Judge 101 Mrs. Davis 118 Mrs. S. F. 122 Phil 115 Preston E. 35
BUFFALOE, John J. 207
BUFORD, Lydia 199
BUIE, D. A. 193
BUNCH, Alice V. 204 G. T. 204
BUNIZIO, Carmino 220 Mary 220
BURDESHAW, Wm. Lamar 199
BURDETT, Richard 132
BURDINE, Robt. B. 1 Sallie Irene Dalton 1
BURDON, Mary 170
BURELL, Aljerome 225
BURGE, W. D. 201
BURGIN, Lena 225 Maurice 225
BURNES, Pat 111
BURNS, Lizzie 191 M. 214 Mary Tipler 191 May 190 Virginia 167 W. M. 190 191 Will Etter 191 William 167 191
BURREAM, Bill 222
BURT, C. H. 103
BURTIS, Melissa 136
BURTON, John 158
BURWELL, Armistead 220
BUSH, Isaac 70 Mary 179
BUSSELMAN, Herman 228 Wm. 221
BUTLER, 29 30 C. C. 79 C. E. 183 Celia T. 2 Lena 127 Lizzie 143 Mary Jones 56 Richard 174 Thos. 207 Walter B. 109
BUTTERFIELD, D. A. 98
BUWE, Catharine 204
BYERS, Mrs. 145
BYRD, J. M. 20 J. P. 7
BYRN, Newman 148
BYRNE, John 113 Major 124
BYRNS, William 199

CABANISS, Charles P. 151 Dr. 151
CADER, Dick 36 R. E. 36

CAFFALL, Willie 108
CAGE, A. H. 39
CAHN, Barney 131
CAIN, Tempa 207
CALCOTE, Eliza Overton 170 Elkins 170 John 170
CALDWELL, C. C. 95 S. A. 95
CALFALL, Edward 108
CALHOUN, Henry 20
CALLENDAR, Ella 83 Hiram 83 Jacob 83
CALLIHAN, Andrew 200 J. D. 200
CALVIN, James 144
CAMBELL, E. F. 162
CAMERON, D. A. 33 J. C. Sr. 22 John T. 53 William 32
CAMMACK, Will 93
CAMPBELL, E. F. 161 L. A. 161 Lucy 41 Maggie 41 R. B. 41 R. G. 142 Sam 176 W. R. 105 W. S. 97
CANCEY, Mrs. 135
CANFIELD, C. 92 May 92
CANNON, David 66 Dr. 120 Mary W. 79 Mrs. 120
CAPELL, H. C. 182
CARAWAY, S. L. 200
CARBALLO, 82
CARLISLE, J. J. 34 Mrs. E. J. 34
CARLSON, Christina 144
CARLTON, K. C. 69
CARNEY, Jas. 107
CARPENTER, Newt 25
CARR, R. W. 141 Wm. 209
CARROLL, E. C. 154 Florence Medora 154
CARROUTH, A. R. 193 Eugenia 193
CARRUTH, Mrs. R. M. 180
CARSON, Albert 97
CARTER, Charles D. 191 Charles Dudley 19 Charlie D. 19 Foote 51 Gabriel 172 H. F. 136 Henry 143 J. C. 21 37 Judge H. S. 19 Mary Aurea 93 Mrs. 21 135 Mrs. H. F. 135 Paralee 72 Phillis 113 S. Y. 72 T. W. 93
CARTHY, Clara 126
CARTMELL, Milton James 66
CARTRIGHT, J. H. 166
CASEY, Ben. 143
CASH, E. B. 150

CASSELL, Albert G. 53
CASSEY, Lillie D. 207
CASSIDY, Hiram 86
CASSING, Joseph 116
CASTELLO, Willie 143
CASTER, Elizabeth 78
CATCHINGS, J. B. 34 47 Jos. B. 137 Martha 137 Mattie 137
CATLIN, Mr. 119
CATTONHEAD, Mrs. 131
CAUSEY, Bettie 51 Mrs. 51
CAVANAUGH, Edward 213
CAVER, W. L. 16 Wm. M. 16
CEARLY, Abe 190
CHALMERS, J. R. 162
CHAMPION, Mr. 125 Mrs. A. M. 125
CHAPMAN, Mary 214 Mary M. 76 P. E. 102 W. C. 76
CHASES, Susan 209
CHEATHAM, Dick 111
CHELSA, J. A. 107
CHENOWETH, Charles 142 John 142
CHESHIRE, Bill 43
CHEW, Beverly 203 Eli 144
CHILCOTE, J. W. 118
CHILDS, Emma 113
CHISM, Angie 94 J. G. 94 James 142 Mrs. S. B. 94
CHOTARD, J. C. 98 Mary A. 98
CHRISTIAN, Caroline 184 R. N. 184
CHURM, A. R. 212
CLAIBORNE, Geo. W. 111 J. F. H. 24 131 Robert 26
CLARE, Mary 204
CLARK, Brothers 45 Charles 104 105 Eliza J. 110 Geo. R. 113 Janney 225 John S. 191 Kate 142 Katie 203 Kenneth 208
CLARKE, Charles 3 E. D. 165 Louisa 112
CLAUDING, Anna 135
CLAUSMAN, Carrie L. 215 Carrie Louisa 214 Leopold 214
CLAUSSING, Annie 51
CLAVER, James A. 217
CLAY, Clarissa 227 J. W. 157 James 196 Julia 157 Margaret Jane 196 W. B. 156

CLAYTON, A. M. 6 Bettie Childers 80 Hannah 183 I. B. 37 Isaac B. 14 Jno. M. 176 Mrs. 6
CLEARY, Robert 124
CLEATON, William A. 122
CLEMENT, M. J. 84 Oliver Cromwell 84 T. D. 84 Thomas Eddie 84 Walter Dorsey 84
CLINDINING, J. M. 95
CLOSSING, Annie 136
COBB, E. S. 54 Ella 74 J. H. 74 Jennie 74 Katie Semmes 46 Katie Winter 46 Stewart 46 Stuart 46
COCHRAN, A. 69 Eugene 145 J. H. 69 74 L. J. 69 Rachel 144 William Hamilton 69
COCKE, Edwin 220
COCKRELL, Leon 61
COFER, Ida Quinn 157
COFFALL, Louis 108
COFFIN, Mrs. Sam 145
COFFING, Francis C. 221 J. W. 221 Maggie 221
COFFMAN, Kate 142 Mrs. Chas. 142
COHN, Marx 35
COLE, 174 Henry 153 J. B. 102 John 65 M. L. 18
COLEMAN, Asa 43 Eva 49 Francis B. 169 Geo. 175 Gus 46 Jas. 175 John 125 Mrs. M. A. 49
COLLIER, J. N. 100 Levin Henry 117 Payton Knox 100 S. C. 100
COLLINS, Mrs. J. 160 Wm. 143
COLLUM, Susan 91
COLRIDGE, Wm. 222
COLTHARP, A. J. 34 Jane 34
COLTHER, Benjamin 65 Martha 65
COMMACK, Mary J. 86
COMPTON, Dr. 145 Mrs. 145
COMSTOCK, Elisha J. 99 L. J. 99
CONERLY, C. P. 197 Margaret 197 Orrie Belle 197
CONLY, Langdon 142 M. 142
CONNELL, Jas. 109
CONNER, Henry 172 Wm. C. 174
CONNINGTON, Barton 144
CONNOR, Dora E. 160 Henry L. 172
CONROY, James 212 Mrs. 212

CONWAY, Catlett 50 Eugene 50 John 50 Lena May 50 51 M. J. 220 T. F. 220
COOK, B. H. 221 Charles P. 133 David 205 Ellen 17 Emily A. 133 Hewett 18 J. P. 17 James Thomas 17 Lillie 174 Lilly 18 Mary A. 112 Mary Belle 133 Newett 174 P. H. 18 174 Wm. 123
COOLEY, H. W. 59
COONEY, James 100
COOPER, Elizabeth 95 F. T. 93 Fleet T. 10 46 J. J. 95 James R. 95 M. E. 65 Rev. 32 Robt. 109
CORBIN, Jordan 85
CORINTHIA, Sister 144
CORK, Elizabeth 203
CORNELIUS, Deputy Sheriff 153
COTHRON, John Williams 69
COTRELL, John 113
COTTEN, Mattie 195 Napsy L. 62 Thaddeus 195 Thos. L. 195
COUGHLER, Gus 109
COUGHLIN, Anna 176 Annie 137
COUNSEILLE, 185
COURTNEY, Jane E. 105 Jno. 105 Martha Melissa 162
COUSINS, Theresa 206
COVINGTON, Cass 157
COWAN, Drusilla 53 E. D. 53 Henry 144 Irene 227 S. W. 221
COWSAR, Eddie 182 Thomas 182
COX, Marion 191 Mollie 143 Mrs. A. 107 Mrs. S. A. 9
COYLE, Terry 169
CRADDOCK, Mattie A. 75 W. Y. 75
CRAF, Bethany 32
CRAFT, Bethany 164 Mrs. Dow 144
CRAIG, A. K. 157 Francis Jerome 132 J. C. 190 John Coffey 187 Louisa 220
CRANSBY, Eva 160
CRAWFOOT, Annie M. 205
CRAWFORD, Celia A. 136 J. L. 135 Jane 77 Jennie 136 John 135 John N. 136 Lura Myrtle 195 N. R. 77 R. N. 195 T. C. 195 T. G. 195

CRAWSFORD, W. F. 204
CRIEL, Ophelia 68
CRISLER, John W. 32 Mary 178
CROCKET, Sam 113
CROCKETT, Elenora 126 Sam 142
CROFTON, Edward 226 Emma 226 227
CROMWELL, Geo. 142 Joe 142
CROSBY, Edward 159
CROSLEY, John 197
CROSS, Marshall 115
CROSSGROVE, Dora J. 180 James Cook 180 Sammie Hornsby 180
CROSSMAN, P. C. 198
CROW, Fielding 16 Mary 16
CROWDER, D. C. 142
CRUM, O. C. 90
CRUME, E. W. 89
CRUMP, A. S. 3 B. S. 142 E. H. 144 E. S. 3 Joseph 3 Mrs. S. M. 217 Wm. 142
CUMING, Charles 29
CUMMING, Charles 22
CUMMINGS, W. C. 13
CUNNINGHAM, Mr. 148
CURTIS, Brothers 28 Jacob 194

DABNEY, A. L. 219
DADLY, Chas. 128
DAILY, Mr. 144
DALEY, John 94
DALTON, Sallie Irene 1
DAMPEER, W. G. 193
DANCY, Jennie McD. 205
DANEY, John W. 55
DANIEL, H. C. 166 Mrs. Richard 142 Richard 142 Vriginus 202
DANIELS, Bud 19 Jack 19 M. F. 38
DANSBY, Johnson P. 200
DANTZLER, Mrs. 207
DAVENPORT, Robert 104
DAVID, Mrs. L. 177
DAVIDSON, Ann 211 Jas. 109 Lizzie 8 Mrs. 142
DAVIS, A. K. 57 A. V. 87 Anna 77 Annie Laurie 77 Augustus 115 Bedia 31 Clarissa 142 Clifton 31 Cora 208 Elijah 84 English 126 Geo. M. 178 Geo. W. 49 H. P. 159 Henry 177 I. H. 77 J. R. 35 Jasper 31 Jefferson 123 Jim Buck 63 John 172 John Gabriel 49 L. L. 150 Laura B. 49 Mary B. 212 R. M. 87 Reuben 3 S. 91 Thomas O. 212 Walter 156 Walter E. 104 Walter S. 156 William Augustus 212 William J. 99
DAWKINS, Mrs. Chas. 6
DAY, James W. 7 Robert 54
DEADNER, 6
DEAN, F. F. 81
DEAR, Willie 180
DEARING, Mrs. M. L. 206
DECELL, F. H. 27 Fanny 27 T. H. 27
DEER, Wm. 28
DEES, John 85 Mary 85 Wirt LeRoy 85
DEJOURNETT, Sallie 142
DEMMEY, Laura 143
DENISON, Mrs. M. J. 203
DENT, George R. 174 John 114 John L. 227 John M. 145
DENTON, Jessie 183
DEPRIEST, Sarah J. 2
DEUPREE, Fanny 73
DEVENNEY, Mrs. F. C. 218
DIAL, Ada Virginia 56
DICKERSON, Isaac 93
DICKINSON, Jack 179
DICKS, Annie C. 173
DICKSON, B. W. 192 Mrs. 192 R. C. 200
DIDDICK, Robert D. 202
DIDLAKE, Jno. M. 80 Martha 80
DIGGS, Bennie 109 Fanny 110
DILLER, Mr. 144
DILLMAN, Geo. 176
DILLON, Mrs. 31
DINES, Jordan 128
DINKELSPELL, Jake 212
DINKINS, Ann Mary 57 F. Hudson 57 Hammie 53 James 43 James A. 53 M. L.. 57 Margaret 43
DIVINE, Jane P. 40 200 Samuel 40
DIXON, Edward 168 Henry 146 Henry M. 146
DODGE, Elliott 108 John 221
DOLL, Joseph F. 226 Joseph L. 226
DONAHOE, James 12
DONAHUE, James 145
DONALD, J. T. 201

DONALDSON, Berkley 11 J. B. 11 John B. 11 Robert 16
DONNELL, Irvin 206
DORACOTT, Mrs. 207
DORMAN, George 108
DORSTER, James M. 23
DORWARD, King 218
DORWART, Anna 218 Charles E. 210 William King 218
DOSS, Bettie J. 182 W. W. 182 Willis Jones 182
DOTSON, G. M. 158 S. L. 158 Zelda 158
DOTY, Caroline 14 P. L. 14
DOUGHERTY, John 221 Margaret 221 Mrs. J. R. 142
DOUGLAS, George 216
DOWLING, Harriet 168
DOWNER, J. C. 201 J. H. 74 Robt. B. 201
DOWNING, M. J. 228
DOWNS, E. L. 142 Peggy 199
DOXEY, Robt. J. 166
DOYLE, John 39
DRANE, E. B. 148 Emmett 42 Judge Wesley 42 W. 148 Wesly 200
DRESSLER, Thos. 145
DRUMMOND, T. W. 92
DRUMMONS, Lize 92
DRYFUS, 20
DUBOIS, Peter M. 14
DUDLEY, Mrs. 94 Pulaski 78 Susan 78 William 89
DUDSON, Sheriff 28
DUFFY, John A. 61 M. 110 Mr. 86
DUKE, Henry 157
DUNBAR, Albert W. 176 Benoist 178 H. E. 88 Matilda W. 176 Wm. H. 168
DUNCAN, Mrs. 135 Priscilla 203
DUNN, Harriet Theobold 130 Mr. 143 Patrick 120 S. R. 130 Sam'l. R. Jr. 130
DUPAS, Sam 20
DUPREE, J. I. 73
DURHAM, Annie 75 W. H. 75
DURRET, Frank 147
DUVALL, Emma 107
DWIGHT, C. W. 209 E. B. 209 Elizabeth B. 209
DYRRICK, Mr. & Mrs. 142

EADS, John D. 74 Martha E. 74 Walter J. 74
EALY, Jackson 228
EAST, Joseph L. 178
EASTERLING, J. 136
EATON, S. T. 35
EBLERS, Mrs. Wm. 108
EBLES, Willie 108
ECHOLS, John 167 John H. 154
EDE, Alice Maude Mary 117 Eliza 117 Joshua 117
EDINGBURG, Rosa 112
EDMONDSON, Chany 113 Charles 106 Wm. 207
EDMUNDSON, child 144 Henry 144 Mrs. Paton 144 Paton 144
EDWARD, Mrs. 167
EDWARDS, Delsey 170 Elias 63 John R. 219 Samuel 96 Sarah C. 219 Willis 144
EGGLESTON, John Fox 221 Lizzie 64 Robert Read 221
EHLERS, Wm. 109
ELDER, Pe__ 25
ELDERS, Thos. 25
ELDRIDGE, J. W. 96
ELLET, H. O. 54
ELLETT, Henry 129
ELLINGTON, G. B. 9
ELLIOTT, E. D. 86 152 Ella 152 G. W. 112 Henry 144 Maggie Bell 86 Maggie Belle 152 Mrs. G. W. 111
ELLIS, Bud 105 Caleb 51 135 136 Jesse J. 5 John 144 Julia S. 5 Perry 113 William 228 Wm. E. 15 Wood Sadler 5
ELY, Francis 223
EMANUEL, Dr. 202 Morris 228
EMBRY, Elizabeth 192 Jesse 192
EMMERSON, Robert 214
ENGLES, C. J. 175
EPPI_ON, A. E. 206
EPPS, Henry 143 Scott 143
EPSTEIN, Lena 195 Mrs. 195
ERVIN, John 218 W. Luther 99
ERWIN, Cowan 203 Pope 81 Sallie A. 205 Wilhe W. 159
ESKRIDGE, Fox 142 W. C. 142
ESTILL, J. C. 100 James C. 100 Nellie Virginia 100 R. C. 100

EVANS, Carrie Jeanette 197 Emma E. 122 J. B. 206 J.G. 176 J. P. 197 Louis de N. 122 Nellie 197 Richard 13 Sarah J. 33 Seeley 228
EVERETT, Elizabeth 195 Mrs. 196 T. C. 61 Z. L. 196 Z. Lea 195
EVERITTE, J. E. 113
EWING, Adam 55 John T. 55 Mary 46 Samuel 46 Wm. 58
EYRNE, E. J. 107

FAIRCLOTH, William A. 224
FAIRMAN, L. Q. 91 Mrs. V. V. 91
FAISON & HEATHMAN, 149
FAISON & SMITH, 125
FALCONER, Howard 143 145 J. C. 149 Kinloch 143 Thomas A. 142
FALER, M. 134
FALLIS, L. A. 158 Mrs. 14 158 N. L. 14
FANCHER, H. H. 76 J. W. 76 Mrs. R. E. 76 P. H. 76
FANT, Glenn 143 Seldon 144
FARLEY, G. P. 147
FARMER, J. E. 208 R. A. 114
FARR, C. K. 92 Mary Elizabeth 92 N. E. 92
FATHEREE, Elizabeth 85
FAULCONER, Nicholas 79 W. H. 79
FAULKNER, Mary 175
FAUT, B. R. 177 J. 177
FAVORS, Mary 177
FEAM, George 165
FEATHERSTON, Elizabeth A. 145 Georgia 144 Lizzie Georgia 145 Mrs. W. S. 143 W. S. 145 Winfield S. Jr. 142
FEIBLEMAN, Chas. 156 J. 156 Julia 156
FELDER, John 193 W. W. 194
FELLOWES, Eliza B. 47 J. G. 47
FELTUS, Ed. 64 H. J. 114 P. G. 64
FENNELL, F. M. 143 J. W. 143 John 143
FERGUSON, Ann R. 224 Austin 88 Ed. V. 103 John 224 Moses 85 Willette 103
FERNON, Thomas 222
FERRELL, John 222

FERRIDAY, Helen C. 180 Wm. 180
FERRIS, Catharine 17 Sue D. 17 W. D. 121 William 17
FIELD, Harry 142 Mrs. 142
FINCH, Mrs. 135
FINKLEN, Harriet 161
FINLAY, James Archer 125 John P. 125
FINLEY, A. B. & Co. 118 Helen 109 Mary 145 W. P. 69
FINNEGAN, Pat 106
FISHER, W. T. 229
FISK, Edw'd. A. 176
FITCHETT, J. V. 39 47
FITTS, H. E. 1 Katie May 1
FITZHUGH, Robert W. 176 Robt. W. 177
FITZPATRICK, Agnes 223 224 E. J. 223 J. J. 223
FLAHARTY, Mike 229
FLANERY, D. 150 163 Janie 163 Mary 150
FLEETWOOD, Julius 115 182
FLEISCHER, A. 111 Adolphe 110
FLEMING, Moses 65
FLETCHER, Ada 202 Monroe 112 Mrs. 108
FLINN, Pat 21
FLOURNOY, Mrs. L. M. 111
FLOWERREE, Annie C. 228 D. W. 224
FLOWERS, G. 198 Margaret 175 Minerva A. 194
FLOYD, Patt 160
FLYNN, Pat 128 Thomas 181
FOLEY, B. F. 113 Catharine 212
FOLKES, Edwin W. 212 Emily M. 212 Mrs. M. E. 213 Mrs. R. A. 209 220 Raleigh Sr. 220 T. M. 224
FOOTE, Wm. 128
FORD & PEAK, 118
FORD, Albert 214 Easter 167 Fountain W. 168 Fountain Winstone Jr. 168 J. J. 83 Jabez 83 Jobe 88 Julia 213 Lloyd 192 Sallie 51 135 Thos. L. 188 W. G. 36
FOREMAN, Dr. 39 Mrs. 39 Mrs. John 143

FORMAN, Chas. N. 173 Emily A. 174 R. H. 174 Richard Howell 174
FORQUERAN, John A. 215
FORRESTER, Gus 109
FORSYTH, James L. 208
FORT, James 142 Lucy 144 R. W. 142
FORTENBERRY, 83
FORTNER, John W. 90
FOSTER, A. B. 96 B. C. 201 Dave 181 Ella R. 172 Gilbert 172 Joseph P. 124 Kansas 40
FOUNTAIN, Lewis 181
FOWLER, Jim 143
FOWLES, Mrs. 135
FOX, Dr. 99 J. 99 Josephine 107 Lizzie 177 Mat 106 Robert 6 7 Samuel Preston 177 178 Wm. H. 177
FRACALE, Ignatz 170
FRAESIL, Ignatz 170
FRANK, Edgar 173
FRANKLIN, A. H. 205 H. M. 205 Maud B. 205
FRASER, Chas. H. 177 Christine 177 178 D. K. 177
FRAZIER, Eliza 222 Isaiah 204 James 70 163 Joseph Hughes 70 163
FREDERICK, William 206
FREEMAN, Isaac 106 Jas. 178 Margaret 113
FREENY, Ella 63 James R. 63
FRENCH, Margaret 110 Mrs. 142 W. J. 111 Wm. 24
FREUNDT, Henry 109
FROST, E. 196 Louisa A. 196
FULKS, E. 80 R. C. 80 Sallie 80
FULLILOVE, Chas. 61
FULTON, Emily 161
FULTZ, H. H. 18
FUNCHES, Ione 207
FUNCHESS, T. J. 206
FUQUA, Robert 55
FURGUSON, Cinthia 193 Franklin 193 James 193

GADDIS, Estelle 159 George 137 Madge 57 Pauline 57 W. E. 57
GAGE, J. B. 64

GAILLARD, A. M. 190 Mrs. 190
GAINS, Charity 144
GAITLEY, Mrs. 143
GALCERAN, G. E. 156 Ruth 156
GALESPIE, Dr. 142
GALLAGHER, Frank 109
GALTNEY, Adaline 77 Jno. L. 175 Percy 175 Sarah Rowan 175
GALVAN, J. 229
GANTER, Frank 142
GARDNER, Hattie E. 157 Wm. H. 157
GAREY, B. F. 46 J. A. 46
GARNER, Cy 152 Thomas 149
GARRETT, Mrs. S. D. 39
GARRISON, T. 205 William B. 10
GAUTIER, F. 148 Fernando 148
GEALER, Peter 145
GEARY, James 222 Jas. W. Jr. 222 Mary 222
GEINELLE, Addaline 113
GENELLA, Joseph A. 225 Joseph Antonia 224
GEORGE, Frank 51
GERDINE, A. S. 112 Dr. 106 Sallie West 106
GEREN, T. D. 67
GERMAN, Jno. 144
GHEELAN, Mrs. Peter 145
GHERY, Mrs. M. 143
GHOLSON, Mary 143 Mr. 143 S. J. 184 Samuel J. 3 5 Samuel Jamison 127
GIBBS, Spencer 188
GIBSON, J. T. 135 Jane N. 86 Judge 223 Minerva 223 Mrs. Wm. 50 Sophia S. 218 Thomas J. 223 Turner 135
GIDERY, Mrs. 53
GILBERT, Roswell B. 133 Thos. 144
GILDART, Mary E. 118 W. K. 118
GILLESPIE, W. P. Sr. 4
GILLEWATER, J. D. 35
GILLIUM, brothers 15
GILMAN, J. J. 51 M. 218
GILMORE, Peter 213 William 114
GILWOOD, Dennis 145
GINSBURGER, Julia 124 Marx 124 Samuel 124
GINSEY, Chas. 142

GIRAULT, Emma E. 88 J. M. 88 Minnie 88
GLASS, Jno. H. 155
GLASSEY, Margaret 143
GLENN, Martha O. 192
GLICK, Monroe B. 48
GLIDDEN, H. A. 105
GLOVER, Robt. 201
GLYNN, Walter 203
GODDARD, William 125
GOETZ, Martha 180
GOFF, Alonzo C. 167
GOLDSTEIN, Leon 104
GOODGER, D. A. 25 Georgia 25
GOODRICH, A. W. 142
GORDON, C. M. 75 Herbert Inge 75 Ida I. 75 Mary 75
GOSSETT, J. 111
GOULD, James 51 Rebecca 52 Reuben H. 52
GRACE, Wm. 94
GRAFTON, Mattie B. 181
GRAHAM, A. T. 54 Minnie J. 54
GRAMMER, Clarence 216 Edwin 215 G. A. 216 M. Ella 216 Robert E. 215 Wm. B. 215
GRANBERRY, A. R. 81 Catherine 81
GRANLING, A. D. 90
GRANT, A. H. 63 Alice 111
GRANTHAL, W. A. 114
GRANTHAM, Ben 86
GRAVES, Ed 21 Edmund 141 Eli 21
GRAY, Coley B. 127 Daniel 144 Elijah 107 James W. 217 'Joseph 204 Mrs. Wm. 202 Nellie 107 W. A. 185
GREATHOUSE, Anderson 111
GREAVES, S. A. D. 43
GREEN, Anderson 139 Andy 187 Angeline 127 Ann 213 Arthur 207 D. C. 109 Eleanor Durkee 216 Hannah 173 Henry 216 Hester 176 Minor 228 Ned 59 Stephen 109 T. 51 Theophilus 136 W. F. 86 William P. 118
GREENER, Mattie 193 Mr. & Mrs. 193
GREENFIELD, Mrs. 113
GREENLEE, John W. 200
GREENWOOD, D. C. 159
GREER, Eliza 71
GREGG, Mrs. 4
GREGORY, E. H. 211 Gus 111 Thompson 3
GRIFFIN, Alexander Ware 197 Chas. 111 Lorenzo 111 Mary Elizabeth 197 P. J. 197 Young F. 197 Young M. 197
GRIFFIS, Francis 68 James 68
GRIMES, Wm. 217
GRISHAM, B. W. 23
GROOME, Jolie 139 Rice 139 T. E. 139
GROSS, Nathan 202
GUILOTTE, Laura Maud McCaleb 207
GUNNING, Ellen V. 226 227 Emma 177 178 Fannie C. 177 J. H. 226 Jno. F. 177
GURNEY, Samuel 192
GUSTINE, Frances 172 Francis 172
GUTHERIES, Mrs. 145
GUY, Griffin 108
GWINNER, Henry 48 Peter 48

HABICHI, Mrs. 109
HACKETT, Annie Storts 70 J. A. 70
HADLEY, Shelby 181
HAGOOD, S. A. 14
HAIRSTON, Nick 153
HALBERT, J. J. 67 Robert C. 154
HALDER, Fritz 129
HALEY, Chas. L. 206 Mrs. 144
HALIDER, Fritz 54
HALL, Arthur 8 Ellen 214 F. K. 142 G. W. 189 George 189 H. E. 8 Willie 80
HALLOS, Amelia 79
HALSEY, Ann 98
HAMBLEN, Cartha 44 Dan 44
HAMBURGER, Abe 111
HAMILTON, Annie H. 196 Benjamin Palmer 196 Col. 151 J. C. 20 W. B. 196 W. R. 204
HAMMET, J. R. 100 Mrs. 201
HAMMETT, Henry 227 Mary A. 227 228
HAMPTON, Anna Fitzsimmons 105 Christopher F. 105 General 116
HAND, R. M. 160

HANDY, A. H. 52 Alexander Hamilton 52 Horace 49 Joe 51 Mrs. John 51 Samuel 49 Susan W. 52
HANLAN, Lou 110
HANLY, Lee 48
HANNON, Michael 214
HANSON, Col. 43
HARBICHT, Theo. 108
HARDAWAY, E. M. 8 Walter 8
HARDIN, Benjamin 153 Gaillard K. 183 J. M. 153 John 153
HARDY, G. M. 206 R. T. 98
HARGON, Jno. R. 45
HARMON, Evans 138 190 William 190 Wm. 138
HARPER, A. S. 70 Eliza 204 John 204 Martha 70 Willie 204
HARREL, Geo. 34
HARRELL, Bryant 159
HARRINGTON, D. 34 Mrs. 143 Wm. 13
HARRIS, Ben T. 163 C. L. 188 Capitola 107 Charles 143 Chas. 144 Dave 108 Emma 167 Fannie Mayes 136 Fee 188 George 20 George C. 42 Green 61 Henry 108 143 Henry Monroe 90 J. Samuel 186 James 94 Jennie 186 Mary 2 Mary E. 163 Millie Evelyn 47 Mrs. C. L. 190 Mrs. O. A. 188 Mrs. V. C. 30 O. L. 188 R. G. 90 R. N. 93 Rosa 61 Sarah E. 2 Selina M. 90 W. P. 136 Wallace Manning 163 Wiley 2 Willie 109 Yerger 93
HARRISON, Alexander 190 G. W. 74 Jas. T. 13 Maggie 65 Sterling 65 William H. 103
HART, Chas. 31 Mrs. Robt. W. 217 W. J. 200
HARTJE, Allen 57 Mr. & Mrs. 57
HARTMAN, Marcella 112 Margaret 204 229 Rosina 226
HARTWELL, Mrs. 133
HARVEY, A. T. 154 Annie 48 Capt. 96 George 48 James B. 102 Lyons 55 Maggie 210 Moses 77 Senator 55
HARWOOD, Annie 220
HASBERG, Mrs. B. 108

HASTINGS, John 143 Lizzie M. 201 Mrs. R. 143 Robert M. 229 Robt. M. 202
HATHAM, James M. 61
HATHORN, Carl 146 Scott 146 Susie R. 146
HAUGHTON, Lafayette 3 Sallie Brownrigg 3
HAVENS, Mrs. Henry C. 202
HAWKE, 36
HAWKES, Edward S. 211 Mrs. 211
HAWKINS, Charlie 60 61 Dr. 142 Ella 61 Emma 108 J. M. 201 Jane 163 John 144 Malissa 12 Martha 61 Mary Jane 61 Mrs. H. R. H. 201 Q. H. 150 Riley 15 Wm. G. 12
HAYCRAFT, W. A. 107
HAYES, Jackson 109
HAYLEY, John 172
HAYNES, Ben 209 Jno. L. 13 Leonard 13 Thos. 164
HAYS, Elizabeth 161
HAZEGOOD, Henry 170
HAZELETT, Caroline L. 222 Mr. 125
HEAD, Oliver J. 124
HEAGAN, J. W. 19
HEALEY, Jerry 218 Julia 218
HEALY, Matilda 160 Peter 160
HEARD, Nathan A. 115
HEASNY, John 229
HEATH, J. H. 191 Joseph A. 191 Mrs. 191
HEBDON, Thomas 145
HEENE, Adam 173 Gertrude 173 Lena 173
HEIDENRICH, A. 196 Adolph 196 Julius 196
HEILBRON, Sidney 172
HEISEN, C. C. 2
HEMBY, Louisa 68 N. W. 68 S. B. 68
HEMPHILL, E. M. 61 W. L. 72
HENDERSON, A. C. 144 Ann Eliza Webb 78 Beulah Eunice McCoy 78 Cecelia 201 D. F. 150 Elisha Williams 78 Eliza Emmie 78 Ettie Lee 220 Frank 220 M. L. 75 Mary 169 Nettie 14 Sallie 220 Thomas 143
HENDRICK, J. A. 63 M. E. 63
HENDRICKS, John F. 53

HENLY, Charles 146
HENNEN, Duncan N. 116 Elenora 116
HENNESSEY, Dennis 213 William 213
HENNINGTON, Mr. 136
HENRY, Annie Laura 35 36 157 Ida 35 Ida J. 36 James 144 Jim 117 R. H. 22 35 36 129 157 T. M. Jr. 166 Wm. 94
HENSLEY, Cora 186 J. S. 186
HENSOD, Mrs. Alex. 35
HENSON, Alex. 87
HERMAN, Jerald 205 Joseph 205 Lena 112 Louisa 175
HERR, infant 144 Joseph 144 Mrs. J. C. 144
HERRING, Bettie 74 M. D. 74
HESLEP, T. B. 72
HESLIP, A. B. 114
HESS, A. J. 144
HEWLETT, Graves 71 Lillie 71 Miss 77
HEXTER, Clara Estella 104 Lee 104
HIBBLER, J. L. 207
HIBLER, Robert 127
HICKMAN, Mary F. 205
HICKS, J. W. 52 James 40 John R. 222 Robert 52
HIGDON, Isaac 172
HIGGINBOTHAM, J. J. 73
HIGGINS, P. H. 36
HILBURN, Augusta Viola 68 156 L. J. 68 156 N. E. 68 156
HILDEBRAND, Jesse 217
HILL, Albert P. 57 Alberta 57 Charlie 224 Dr. _. D. 193 Emma E. 193 Isaac 33 J. W. 113 Jane 144 Margaret A. 57 Mr. 151 R. I. 185 Richard 33 Robert 185 Tobe 42 Will 62
HINCHIE, Jennie 48
HINDS, King 112 Merrett 122
HINES, Bettie 188 Thos. H. 154
HINTON, Thomas P. 148
HIRSCH, Clemmence 119 Henrietta 119 Jacob 119 124 Joseph 211 N. 211 S. 174
HIX, Mrs. N. B. 200
HOBDON, P. 143
HOBSON, Richard M. 227

HODGES, Jim 37 Martha 37 Rebecca 69
HOFFMAN, R. H. 148
HOFMASTER, H. 154
HOGAN, Wm. 142
HOGE, H. J. 60 Mary E. E. 60
HOGUE, Albert B. 177
HOHENWURT, Alex. 143
HOLCOMBE, Hezekiah 152 Levi Stokes 191
HOLDEN, John 194
HOLDING, Robt. 113
HOLLAND, Chas. M. 200 John 16 Mrs. 30 W. J. L. 145
HOLLIDAY, F. M. 82 Francis M. 82 M. T. 82 T. L. 54
HOLLINGSWORTH, 1 Dorcas 5 L. D. 5 Thadeus E. 1 Wm. 5
HOLLIS, 106 D. U. 37
HOLLOMAN, Mrs. T. B. 54
HOLLOWAY, George 51 134 I. G. 2 Mrs. Ira G. 2
HOLMAN, D. A. 146
HOLMES, Albert 128 J. T. 42 Mich'l. 180 Michael 179
HOLT, Ben 140 David 119 J. H. 160 Jno. T. 90
HON, Long 109
HOOD, Mrs. J. B. 116
HOOKER, C. E. 87 Wm. R. 87 Zadock 87
HOPKINS, Quay 150
HORN, Adam 140
HORNE, Geo. H. 84 Geo. W. 85 Joseph A. 133 Mrs. A. P. 85
HORTON, Allen 187
HOSEA, Benjamin 72 Joseph W. 5
HOUSTON, Boynton 108 Green 6 Jonas 107
HOWARD, 21 Anne 193 Henrietta 163 J. W. 205 John 205 L. W. 163 193 Lizzie 205 Maggie 215 Nettie 45 R. M. 193 Rufus 144
HOWCOTT, Mrs. E. W. 147
HOWELL, E. 70 Hattie 137 Jane 202 John Anderson 70 John D. 47 Lewis 74 Mary Wolf 207 W. J. 70
HOWLE, William 64
HOWRY, J. M. 191
HOYLE, Ellen E. 15 P. R. 15

HUBBARD, Minerva S. 213 Toliver A. 214
HUBER, Mrs. 51 136
HUDSON, Jno. S. 101
HUFFINGTON, Marion 142 Mary 142 Sallie 142
HUGHES, Gassamore 43 George 35 87 R. W. 224
HUMPHREYS, B. G. 123 G. B. 123
HUNDERMARK, Alice V. 223 Allie V. 223 Robert A. 223
HUNT, James R. L. 143 Joe 51 Joseph 136 Margaret 181 Moses 197 Thos. H. 131
HUNTER, Charlie 59 John 159
HUNTLEY, Chas. 107
HURLBUTT, L. 66
HURST, D. W. 198 D. Warren 198
HUSK, Jake 109
HUTCHINSON, Mrs. 143
HYATT, Annie E. 162
HYLAND, Henry 83

INGE, Mary J. 75
INGRAHAM, Lotta 143
INGRAM, Dina 143 Mrs. 142
IREYS, H. T. 128
IRISH, H. Mary 116 Henry T. 116
IRVING, Chas. 107
ISLER, Robt. 150
ISOM, Smart 7
ISTELL, John 160
IVEY, Winfield 131 132
IVIE, W. S. 7 W. T. 7
IVY, Bettie M. 155

JACK, Sister 71 W. H. 71
JACKSON, Andrew 4 214 D. C. 98 Dr. 106 Eudora 77 George 225 Hattie 98 John 77 John F. 77 Kavanaugh 189 L. B. 178 Mimie 172 Steve 128 Virginia 189 W. J. 194 William 189
JACOBS, John 93
JAMES, B. F. 127 Ben 126 Caroline 223 Chas. 46 Emma 172 Jesse 129 John 54 128 129 Mattie 203 Mrs. 112 Mrs. F. 77 Nora 46
JAMISON, David 4 David W. 2 John T. 2
JARVERS, Mary 110

JEFFERDS, Judge 94
JEFFORDS, Judge 165 Judge E. 58
JENKINS, J. F. 76 James A. 196 Kate 161 Nannie 196 R. P. 161 Robin 161 S. G. 121
JENNINGS, T. O. 174
JERNIGAN, Belle 189 Ethel 189 J. B. 189
JEWELL, Mr. 115
JOBES, C. S. 4
JOHNSON, 128 A. 223 Alex 112 Brutus 99 Calvin 26 Caroline 218 Charles 129 Dan 112 E. F. H. 148 Eugene 113 F. C. 93 Fannie 167 Frances 181 Fred 113 George 143 H. J. 22 H. P. 18 Hal 142 144 Isaac 58 J. H. 171 James Crowley 93 James R. 219 John 126 Judge 59 Lewis 173 Lizzie 108 159 Lou F. 93 M. W. 112 Mrs. 166 N. B. 101 Queen 176 R. N. 171 Reverdy 168 Roxy 229 Sarah Margaret 29 T. B. 159 Thomas 219 Thos. 113 W. H. 202 Willie 216
JOHNSTON, Emma Alla 161 Judge A. 204 Mr. 143 O. L. 69 P. W. 58 Peter W. 58
JOHNSTONE, Mrs. M. L. 42
JONES, 34 Albert 223 Barbery 74 Ben 150 Christy 88 170 D. 134 Dr. 136 Ella 109 Em. 143 F. L. 13 157 Fannie 56 Florida Meade 211 George 217 Hattie 107 Henry 113 140 Inez Estelle 195 J. B. 216 J. C. 141 Johnnie 51 Joseph Blake 42 Lafayette 138 Luther 51 136 M. Henryetta 141 M. J. 114 Margaret 57 Mary 109 Mary L. 197 Milton 107 Mrs. J. M. 195 Mrs. Luther 51 136 Oscar 138 Parker 85 Rosa 218 Rufe 187 Thomas N. Sr. 153 Thos. N. Sr. 45 Tom 13 157 W. R. 155 Wood 51
JORDAN, 105 Benj. 20 Craig 119 Parker 119 Stephen 149
JOSELYN, Robert 31
JOSLYN, Robert 53
JOUVEAUX, L. P. 194

JULIENNE, Capt. 152 Clara 152
JUNKINS, Samuel 174
JUSTICE, Emma A. 3 G. W. 3 4

KANATEER, Mrs. John 124
KANATZER, John 102
KAVANAH, H. H. 23
KAVANAUGH, H. H. 29 55 130 138
KEAN, James M. 143
KEARY, Martin 88 170 212
KEARY, Pat 170
KEATING, Mrs. 135 R. 136
KEELIAR, Celia 213
KEEN, C. C. 207
KEENAN, T. J. R. 31
KEENE, Nancy 112
KEETING, Wm. T. 51
KEFAUVER, W. M. D. 121
KEIRN, Anthony 19 W. L. 19
KEITHLEY, Bryant M. 86 Charles Edgar 86 Luis E. 86
KELLY, Andrew 177 Fanny 111 James 48 Julia Davis 173
KELTER, Calvin 110 Milton 112
KEMP, E. F. 62 G. R. 41 148 Louie 148 Louis George 41 Peter 196 Rosa 196
KENDALL, W. J. 49 56
KENDRICK, J. W. 17 24 192 Lavenia 17
KENNA, Bessie Lea 160 F. J. 160 Laura E. 160 Otto Clifton 160
KENNEDY & HANWAY, 100
KENNEDY, John 168 Mrs. 153
KENOYER, Lewis 39
KENT, John H. 67 Smith H. 67
KERNAN, Mike 126
KERNER, Bishop 90
KERR, B. B. 205
KEY, Mrs. O. C. 199
KEYES, Wm. 59
KIELHER, Minnie 112
KIERNAN, John 175 Mary 175 Thomas 175
KILGARLAN, P. H. 227
KILLIAN, Emma R. 158 J. D. 158
KIMBALL, George 143 Mrs. Geo. 143 Sam 143
KIMBROUGH, B. T. 188 John 145 Mrs. S. B. 188

KING, Ben 22 Benj. 32 Benjamin 95 164 Jim 137 Livingston P. 171 Mary 149 Robert 144 Saml. T. 149 Sue 189
KINNEY, J. A. 186
KINSTLER, Jas. 110
KIRBY, Dr. 113 Mrs. Peter 142
KIRKLAND, Mrs. L. A. 97
KIRRWAN, John 224
KLASTLER, Amelia 111
KLINE, Sith 100
KLOG, Jim 137
KNABLE, Mrs. Martin 143
KNAPP, Mrs. Stephen 142 Stephen 143
KNIGHT, Fayette 19 Sam'l. B. 155
KNOWLES, Hugh A. 2 Katherine K. 2 Lewis Gifford 2
KNOX, Martha E. 163
KOONTZ, George W. 170 171
KRAUS, Jacob 144
KRESS, Eliza 111
KRETSEHMAR, W. P. 110
KUABLE, Martin 144
KUFFER, A. M. 5
KUNER, Henry 226 Max 226
KUYKENDALL, Morgan T. 195
KYLE, Mark 107 Thos. 109 Thos. J. 15 W. 178 Wm. 15

LACKEY, J. J. 228 T. J. 228
LACOCK, Minnie 142
LAKE, Annie 142 Gus 142 Miss 142 Mr. & Mrs. Geo. 142
LALLANDE, Felicite 57 J. G. 57
LAMAR, Robert 190
LAMBUTH, John R. 43 Wm. R. 43
LAMKIN, Mrs. 113
LAMPKINS, Dr. 134
LAMPLEY, L. J. 148
LANCASTER, Melvina 79 R. A. 79 T. 73
LANDAU, 119 Julius 125
LANE, 27 28 Dennis 144 Lizzie 143 Mrs. 144
LANGLEY, L. M. 112
LANIER, J. T. 10 Mr. 11 N. N. 222
LANLUS, King H. 179
LARD, L. H. 132 P. J. 132 Purser 132

LARNER, Robt. 138
LAROUCHE, John 143
LATHAM, Florence 38 Harvey 38 Lucy 38 Moses 127
LATIMER, Adaline Augusta 41 Angie 41 Clara 67 Robert 41
LAUEL, Herman Henry 227
LAUGHLIN, Terrance 223
LAUGHRIDGE, J. A. 96
LAURENS, Henry 109
LAVISSON, Jules 194
LAWSON, Eugene 159 Eugene W. 122 Frank 113 J. B. M. 120
LAY, W. H. 71
LEA, Alfred M. 220 Alfred Mead 196 Alsey 144 David 162 Elceba 196 Elizabeth 196 Hampton M. 196 Iverson Green 196 James E. 196 James Everett 196 Lena R. 220 Lucinda Clay 196 Margaret A. 196 Mary Mayrant 220 Nancy 162 196 Rebecca 143 Sabrina Clay 196 Wilford Z. 196 Zachariah 195 196
LEACHMAN, Robt. 73
LEAK, Mrs. 142
LEATHERS, Mrs. T. P. 26
LEATHERWOOD, Clark 71 W. B. 71
LEAVELL, N. B. 92
LEAVENWORTH, Bros. 130 J. H. 130 Noah Huny 129
LECAND, Fred J. V. 171 Mary E. 172 Mary Elizabeth 171
LEE, Adedese Farrar 117 Geo. 139 George 23 John M. 117 Mary 76 Mrs. C. A. 37 Myron E. 86 Sow 107
LEFFINGWELL, 82
LEGGITT, Alexander 66
LEIDY, Eugene Jr. 143
LEIGH, Macon 18
LEITCH, Fannie W. 39
LELAND, Hattie 206
LEMLER, Henry 112
LEMLY, Sue 151 Wm. S. 151
LENNARD, James 40
LEROY, Joseph 214
LESSEUR, Lula 144
LESTER, Freeman 14 37
LEVY, Mrs. Sol. 206
LEWIN, W. T. 199
LEWIS, D. H. 146 Dickson H. 7 Dr. 143 G. M. 77 Hattie 77 J. M. 198 Leatha 1 Lilla Sykes 4 Marrin 77 Mollie 201 Mrs. C. L. 42 Thomas A. 4
LEWY, B. M. 124 Ernestine 124
LIBEL, Peter 209
LIDDELL, Dr. 99 W. W. 147
LIGON, J. A. 177
LINDSEY, Mr. 37
LINEBARGER, Mary 188
LINFIELD, W. E. M. 35 133
LINK, N. D. 37
LINSCOTT, James 221
LINTON, Venus 229
LOCHMAN, Julius 110
LOCKHART, J. T. 10
LOFTIN, Nathan 135 Z. 51
LOFTON, Jos. E. 140 Moses 140
LOGAN, Tyler 76
LOMAX, A. A. 69 Alex. A. 77 Lewis 69 Louis Alfred 77
LONG, Hon 109 Frank 22 Lillie 64 Richard 64
LONGINO, S. A. 79
LORENTIA, Sister 144
LOTLIN, James S. 165
LOTT, H. T. 204
LOUIS, Marcus 168
LOUISVILLE, Ann 172
LOVE, C. C. 2 D. A. 116 D. L. 10 11 98 W. Allen 116
LOVING, W. C. 88 135
LOWE, D. B. 86 Mary A. 67 W. M. 15
LOWELL, Mr. & Mrs. 158 Willie 158
LOWENBERG, S. 135
LOWENSTEIN, 119
LOWRY, W. L. 146
LUCKETT, Brad 53 Johnnie 44 Mrs. Clinton Hanson 43 O. A. 53 O. A. Jr. 43 44
LUCKEY, Joel 144
LUGENBUHL, Charlie 82 E. C. 82 May 82 R. A. 82
LUMPKIN, J. M. 143
LYLE, W. J. 178
LYNCH, Minerva 143 Virginia 142
LYONS, Joseph B. 222 Willie 42
LYTLE, Helena 72
LYTTLE, Sylvester 128

MABRY, 106
MACK, Ned 24
MACKEY, Samuel 65
MACKIN, Wm. 142
MADDIX, Bernard 178
MADDUX, T. Clay 146
MAGEE, Mrs. C. E. 28 Rance 152 S. K. 198 Sam 28
MAGRUDER, Bettie 52 L. W. 48 W. H. 52
MAHER, Emmie H. 178 179 Fred J. 178
MALCI, Jake 144
MALER, Lizzie 144
MANDEL, N. 139
MANGER, Cesar 112
MANGUM, Penny 205
MANIFOLD, John 104 111
MANLOVE, C. A. 209 220
MANN, William B. 63
MANNING, Dr. 143 Mrs. 102 103 Sheriff 103
MANUEL, Irene 221
MAPLES, Joe 44 Sarah Ann 227
MARAINSKI, Blanche 112
MARETT, W. J. 142
MARGARETTE, Sister 144
MARKS, Caroline 110
MARRON, Lawrence 175
MARRY, Jno. Y. 186
MARSALIS, Ephram 28 F. E. 28
MARSETT, Loudie 223
MARSHALL, D. 180 Raphael 109 Wm. 106
MARTIN, A. J. 84 A. K. 162 Amelia 145 C. A. 84 Dave 177 John R. 12 Joseph 64 Josephine 145 Laura Augustus 84 Lucy 80 Nettie 46 Polly 144 W. T. 46 Wm. 162 Wm. R. 8
MASON, Armistead Thompson 6 Hattie E. 79 J. S. 147 J. S. Jr. 147 J. W. 6 M. B. 6
MASSENGILL, Kate 134 M. J. 134 Mrs. S. F. 141
MASSEY, Louisa 108
MASTERS, Louisa 152
MATHENY, F. A. 81 Lillie May 81 W. T. 81
MATHEWS, Lillian 10 Mary 215 Wm. 59

MATHIS, J. W. 83
MATTHEWS, Beverly 13 188 Eugene 149 G. E. 95 J. P. 20 28 95 179 John R. 179 Prince 89 Print 89 127 S. A. 149 Sergeant 149
MAUGHAN, Amelia 143
MAUGHON, child 144
MAULDIN, C. 5
MAULEY, W. J. 110
MAXEY, Barshaba 163 W. F. 163
MAXWELL, A. M. 31 Lizzie 31 William 213
MAY, Dick 10 Dr. 142 J. L. 61 James W. 70 Mrs. 142 Robert Nelson 70 Sue 70
MAYBERRY, 8
MAYER, Jeanette 175 John 175 Sigmund 101
MAYERS, Mrs. 34 P. K. 34
MAYES, Daniel 136
MAYHEW, Robt. 142
MAYNARD, Camille 96 D. B. 96 Maggie 96
MAYNOR, A. H. 52 Henry Clifton 52 L. A. 52
MAYSON, Charles 41 Dr. 126 Gertrude 41 Jno. R. 43 John Robert 41 Lena 44 Robert C. 43 W. L. 44
McALLISTER, C. K. 112 D. 40 Mrs. A. W. 112
McALPINE, Mr. 147
McBRIDE, Jas. 188
McCABE, Annie 225 Ella 225
McCAFFERTY, Joe 130 Yewing 154
McCALL, J. S. 112
McCANN, James 109
McCARDLE, John Guion 218 Wm. H. 218
McCARLEY, Mose 14 188
McCARTY, 130 Ada Virginia 56
McCATCHERN, John C. 57
McCATHERN, Maggie 57
McCHESNEY, Andrew Thomson 167
McCHRISTIAN, Perry 60
McCLAIN, Ike 152 Melley 222
McCLENNON, Harriett 221
McCLURE, Alice W. 94 J. W. 94
McCLUTCHE, Thos. H. 174
McCOY, Beulah Eunice 78

McCROSKY, H. A. 142
McCUE, Thomas 223
McCULLOUGH, Richard 107
McCUTCHEN, James 161 Jno. 118
McDANIEL, Noah 66 Selena 66 Thos. R. 66
McDANNIEL, Ned 131
McDERMOTT, Mrs. 144
McDONALD, E. J. 6 J. M. 6 James 37
McELMORE, 83
McELWEE, Arminta 162 Eugene 176 Jas. M. 162
McFARLAND, James 41
McGARY, Jane 143
McGAUGHEY, S. D. 43
McGAVOCK, Dr. 118 119
McGEE, Lila 128
McGILL, Charles L. 75 Mrs. S. 75
McGOWAN, Bill 140 Ida 144 Jeff 144 Mrs. Jeff 143
McGOWEN, Harry 130 T. H. 130
McGRAW, W. M. 201
McGUIRE, Addie 158 H. W. 158 Mrs. Crown 143 Pat 143 Virgil Lee 158
McHUGH, James 144
McINIS, D. S. 30 Jones Neil 30 T. J. 30
McINNIS, Mary Ann 55 R. N. 55
McINTOSH, Alex. 84
McJUNKIN, A. L. 202
McKAY, Albert 140 James M. 103 Milton 165 Mr. 182
McKEE, James 169 Robert 169
McKENNA, Jack 22 28 29 138
McKENZY, Ed 107
McKEON, Pat 112
McKEUGH, H. J. 144
McKIE, M. J. 57
McKINNEY, 59 Eliza Young 229 Mac 92 Mrs. 145 W. O. 144 Wm. 61
McKISSACK, Haywood 144
McLAIN, Robert 142
McLAUREN, Wm. K. 9
McLAURIN & McLAURIN, 58
McLAURIN, A. J. 59 W. K. 58 59 140 166
McLEAN, J. N. Sr. 26 Jas. 110 Lula 142 Mrs. 142 Mrs. Ph. 113 Thos. 109

McLEMORE, J. W. 134 Leon 134
McLEOD, Norman 208
McMACKIN, Lucinda 147 T. C. 147
McMECKLIN, John 103
McMILLAN, Mary 67 N. J. 75 S. A. 75
McMILLEN, Mr. & Mrs. 142
McMORRIS, Thos. 112
McMULLEN, Chas. 81
McMURRY, J. J. 100
McNAMARA, B. 226 Joseph Benedict 226
McNEELY, Johnnie A. 205
McNEIL, E. B. 21 J. W. 141 Jessie Kitredge 21 Jno. A. 153 John 22 23
McNULTY, W. M. 19 Wm. M. 31
McPHERSON, Jno. V. 161
McQUEEN, H. H. 208
McRAE, Collin J. 169 John J. 169
McREDMOND, John 224
McREYNOLDS, J. A. 201
McSWINE, Alice 142
McTAGART, Biddy 219
McWHORTER, Gillie 1
McWILLIAMS, Alonzo 137 Cora 145 R. A. 145
McWILLIE, Thos. A. 150
MEADE, H. D. 200 Mary E. 227
MEANY, Ed 96
MEDLEY, George B. 102
MEEHAN, Mrs. A. N. 216
MEEK, A. B. 24 S. M. 24
MEEKS, Sarah E. 172
MEISNER, C. F. 111
MELCHOR, Henry 102
MELTON, Ben 174 Eugene 62
MELVIN, Rebecca 113
MENNIFIELD, Caleb 114
MERCER, F. C. 165 Fleet C. 165
MERIWETHER, W. P. 72
MERRILL, A. P. 177 Lilly 229 N. 99
METCALFE, F. A. 123 James 172 Sarah W. 172
MIALL, Mr. 166
MICHORICSBURG, Wm. 36
MICKLE, Mary 136
MICOW, Jane Mariah 65 John 65
MIDDLETON, E. 141 Elizabeth 141 Fannie 141 Georgia A. 141 J. B.

141 John B. 141 Lewis A. 98 Louis A. 11
MIEARS, Mrs. John P. 199
MIGGINS, Thos. 110
MIKEL, Mary 30
MIKELL, Mary 51
MILES, Jno. D. 175 O. S. 175 Phillip 177
MILLAN, Sister 72
MILLER, Alfred 79 D, D. 176 E. D. 143 Ellin 179 Francis Marion 216 G. W. 89 Geo. W. 31 Joseph H. 86 Lillie 31 Lilly 89 Luke 21 141 M. 199 Marion C. 219 Mr. 144 Mrs. James 144 Rachie 177 Richard 21 W. J. 219 William 34 Wm. 155
MILLS, Laura A. 209 W. H. 181 W. S. 181
MILSTEAD, Alexander 147
MILTON, Albert Byron 79 J. L. 142
MIMMS, Florence 147 G. W. Sr. 71 Sam 147 Susan Dudley 71
MIMS, Mrs. A. 201
MINEE, Douglas 222
MINOR, Chas. 176 Fannie 175
MITCHEL, Georgiana 136 Mrs. 112
MITCHELL, Arcola 37 Charles H. 201 E. C. 16 Georgia 51 Georgianna B. 135 J. B. 159 J. L. 206 Mary 16 W. B. 184 W. D. 201 Walter Trawick 37 Wm. L. 37
MIUZLES, Jas. 109
MOBLE, H. 138 Minnie Christine 138 Mrs. A. J. 138
MOGAN, Mary 193
MONAHAN, Jas. 40 Maggie 40
MONDAY, Mary J. H. 158 W. H. 158
MONETTE, Annie 223 Dr. 223 Gibson 223 Mrs. 223 Sallie 223 Wm. E. 223
MONK, Henry 112
MONOHAN, Elizabeth 50
MONSINGO, Kinchen 75
MONTGOMERY, Charles 104 D. C. 104 D. P. 42 150 E. H. 198 Ella 38 Eugene 104 H. H. 38 Jennie Magruder 42 Kate 106 M. A. 106 Mr. 203 Mrs. J. A. 65 Mrs. Wm. 112 N. J. 150 S. W. 106 W. P. 102 Wm. 112 Wm. R. 174
MOODY, Ham 134 Mr. 135
MOONEY, Mr. 144
MOORE, A. F. 142 A. V. 166 Bettie G. 45 Chas. P. 45 David 142 Frank 136 H. H. 219 Harry 125 Isaac 150 Jas. C. 118 Jennie A. 219 Jennie James 219 John 118 L. C. 224 Maggie E. 224 Mary J. 166 Mattie B. 158 Mollie 149 Mr. 46 142 Mrs. 46 136 Randall 144 T. J. 182 200 W. D. 198 Willie 150
MORAY, Alex 110
MORGAN, C. E. 107 George 19 L. E. 111 Mrs. 106 Rebecca 107 Willie 174 Wm. 81 Wm. M. 99
MORIARTY, John 17 26
MORING, Homer 200
MORRIS, Bertha 111 D. 112 Dave 110 J. S. 38 Kate 38 M. 110 Mrs. D. 107 Mrs. M. 107 Mrs. S. M. 70 Samuel 70
MORRISON, John 72
MORROW, Joe 142 Mrs. 171 J. A. 99
MORTON, Henry 143 Sam. 101
MORZINSKI, M. J. 112
MOSBY, John B. 102 L. H. 106 Wm. 55
MOSELEY, 125 Harriet 145 Joseph 81 Mrs. S. M. 189 W. R. H. 189
MOSELY, Joe 84
MOSS, Harry 129 Henry 22 James M. 79
MOWBRY, Mrs. Thos. 107
MOYSE, Harriet 100 Leon 100
MUIRHEAD, G. S. 202
MULLER, Christian 166 Helena 166 Henry 44
MUMFORD, John P. 52 Wm. T. 52
MUNCE, Katie W. 178 T. Quitman 177
MUNN, Mattie Means 77 W. S. 77
MURDOCK, John 33 Wm. 33
MURNEY, Andrew 83 J. W. 83
MURPHREE, Sam 147
MURPHY, A. R. 208 Annie 25 J. L. 25 James 25 Jeremiah 54

Joseph Bernard 54 Lillie 25 Patrick 199 Tommie 25 Willie 25
MURRAH, Jno. 139 Myra 139
MURRAY, Elizabeth 8 Patrick 100 T. J. 8 79
MURRY, Mrs. 174
MUSGROVE, H. 146 Henry 206
MYERS, Andrew H. 120 Emanuel 32 G. B. 202 J. S. 120 Jerry 99 Mrs. B. A. 144 Samuel C. 200 Wm. 113
MYGATT, Alston 210 Margaret 210

NABERS, B. D. 142
NALL, B. 68 John M. 68
NASH, Mr. 136
NATIONS, Mazilla 31 Wm. 31
NEBLETT, W. R. 199
NEELY, Mr. 28 Oscar 150 Walter 150 Wm. M. 27
NEIHYSEL, Mrs. M. 172
NEIL, W. L. 11
NEILSON, Julia 94
NELMS, Tede 145
NELSON, A. M. 19 Fannie 136 G. B. 136 James 73 John 151 John H. 111 Margaret 136 Martha 73 N. J. 110
NEVELS, James 140
NEWMAN, 107 C. D. 91 Charles 84 Olivia C. 84 91 Preston 179 R. M. 198
NEWTON, J. M. 83 Minnie 83
NICHOLS, Capt. 128 G. W. 222
NICHOLSON, T. W. 56
NICOLS, George W. 222
NIGHT, John 222
NIOLIN, J. M. Jr. 36 Mr. & Mrs. 36
NIXON, G. D. 91 Geo. D. 91 Laura 91 Thomas Quinn 91
NOLAND, Joseph 209
NOONAN, Fannie 53 James T. 53 Marie 53
NORMAN, J. M. 85 Jno. 180 Lucy Roseland 85
NORRIS, Adeline 75 Bill 164 Marshall 75 Oscar 75
NORSWORTHY, Jennie 41 Josephine Barksdale 41 R. D. 41

NORTH, H. F. 229 R. H. 229 Susan M. 229
NORWOOD, A. J. Jr. 78 90 Ella Smith 78 90 Mahala 91
NUGENT, W. L. 152
NUTALL, James 142 Mrs. James 142
NYSTRAND, Charles 215

O'BRIEN, Grace T. 173 Jerry 211 Julia 211 Louisa 211 Marie 167 Mary 167
O'CONNOR, Josephine 122 Kinnie 122 Tim. 122
O'GRAY, Kate 143
O'HERRIN, Mike 214
O'NEAL, Caroline 125 R. T. 125
O'REILLY, Joseph B. 9 Robert E. 22
O'SULLIVAN, Sallie 166
OAKLEY, Alice 7 Bent. 7 Oscar 7
OATIS, C. R. 133 Myra 133
OBERTI, Father 142
ODEM, Jane Wesley 178
ODEN, Dr. 113
ODOM, John 37
OGDEN, Edmund S. 178 Julia Wickliffe 178
OLDHAM, Mahala 70
OLINGER, David 74 J. D. 74
OLIVER, B. P. 142 Dan 144 Mrs. Capt. 133 Nick 213
ORD, E. O. C. 18
OSBURN, Robert D. 89
OSTERHAUT, Myra Willing 88
OTTERBEIN, Albert 116
OTTO, Jas. B. 41 Mrs. D. H. 163 S. A. 41 Wiley L. 41
OURY, Mrs. E. B. 61
OUSLEY, Harriet Byrne 124
OWEN, Effie Bird 51 J. W. 51 Jno. G. 92 McKie 51
OWENS, Charles 223 Dock 115 182 Muke 85

PACE, Alfred Downs 121 Fannie Percy 121
PACKER, D. B. 82 Helen Lear 82 Mattie B. 82
PADEN, Jno. 156 John 68
PAGE, Elinor Martin 133 Harley 133 Maggie 133 T. 112

PAINE, James 15 Mamie L. 184 Robert 15
PALMER, J. H. 15 Thomas 14
PARISH, David 155 Houston 187 L. P. 144 Mrs. 9 144
PARKER, A. N. 45 D. G. 180 Dave 216 Florence E. 45 J. W. 106 Lewis 51 136 Louis 135 Orville 65 S. S. 33 William 135 Wm. 51 136
PARKS, Geo. 144
PARMORE, Charles 96
PARR, Albert 32
PARSLEY, Cynthia 23 Robert 23
PARSONS, Chas. 36
PATE, George 186 Larken 158 Sue 158 Zachariah David 158
PATTERSON, 101 153 Mrs. A. W. 203 Turner 199 William R. 157
PATTON, G. Farrar 33 John W. 55 Kate H. 72 W. H. 72
PAUL, Otho S. 159
PAXTON, A. J. 128 132 A. M. 227 Annie E. 227 228 H. M. 132 Mary L. 227 Mrs. A. M. 217 William Franklin 132
PAYNE, Jane 213 John 191 Susan 172 W. L. 159
PAYTON, Ephraim G. 101
PEACOCK, Mamie 142 Thos. 142
PEALE, John A. 210
PEARSON, B. T. 86 Fannie A. 86 Jno. 144 Jno. W. 19 Mr. 125 Mrs. L. J. 9
PECK, A. H. 207
PEEBLES, Mary E. 168 Mollie E. 168
PEETS, Dr. 71 Mrs. G. H. 71
PEGRAM, W. G. 6
PENELTON, Willie 218
PENN, H. B. 139 R. G. 139
PENNY, A. C. 121 B. F. 121 Carrie 121
PENRICE, John S. 116
PENSON, Nellie D. 202
PERCY, Fannie 121 LeRoy Pope 121 W. A. 121
PERMENTER, R. D. 180 Rachel 181 Rachel Parker 180
PERNEL, Emma 111

PERRY, 106 111 Fred 107 James 107 Mrs. James 107 Mrs. T. P. 108 T. P. 110
PETERS, Dr. 100
PETERSON, Bryant 202 E. N. 214 Ellen 222 Herman 38 John 213
PETTUS, W. A. 34
PEUGH, Charlie J. 5
PEYTON, Jim 148 Mary 146
PHILLIPS, Antony 225 B. W. 13 Dan 143 Emily Lee 38 F. M. 205 Henry 217 J. S. 158 Leonard 110 T. A. 38
PIACE, Jesse V. 28
PIAZZA, August 82 Joseph 82
PICKINS, Israel W. 74
PIGFORD, J. T. 212
PINKSTON, Eliza 17
PINNIX, Julia 200
PIPES, Chas. A. 199
PITTIFORD, Jack 198
PITTMAN, Susan 160
PLATT, Anna 109 Mahala 220 Mrs. S. A. 108
POE, H. E. 71 Mary 71
POGLE, Julia 108
POINDEXTER, H. L. 207
POITEVANT, Mollie 142
POLK, Susie 215
POLLE, Mrs. L. 109
POLLOCK, Mr. 128
POMATE, Agnes 181
POMET, Louis 177 178
POOL, Wm. P. 203
POPE, Ann 151
PORADY, Ed. 30
PORTER, Alfred 224 Antony 222 E. H. 225 Edward H. 225 W. L. 110
PORTERFIELD, Jesse B. 224 John 213 Julia 222
POSEY, Carnot 54 129 Jasper 54 John 54 128 John T. 54 Mr. 14 N. W. 13
POTTER, George L. 103 194 J. C. 142 Mrs. John 143 Thad. 56
POTTS, J. F. 207
POUND, Mrs. J. A. 198

POWELL, Albert Cage 57 David S. 56 Ella Wright 214 Fannie 56 J. R. 21 56 164 Judge 214 R. B. 211 Thos. 142 W. H. 57 Willie 214
POWER & BARKSDALE, 154
POWER, J. L. 12 87 120 186 John 143 William S. 87 120 Willie 186 Willie S. 12
PRESSELL, D. W. 94
PRESSLY, Frank 169
PRESTON, Ward 218
PREWITT, Harriet N. 20 J. C. 20
PRICE, D. T. 18 Emily 173 Joseph 202 Lewellyn 217 Willie 144
PRIESTER, Jno. 180
PRIESTLEY, E. A. 83 Harry 49 Jessie 163 Lizzie 163 Mrs. Harry 49 Theodore 83 Wm. 163 Wm. M. 83
PRITCHARD, Col. 43 Florence 43 Henry 183
PRITCHETT, J. C. 213
PROCTOR, Jacob 217
PROFILET, L. E. 178 Melanie Thirese 178 Milanie T. 179
PROUDFIT, Alexander 189 E. S. 189 Eliza 189 James 189 John H. 189 W. P. 189
PROVENE, Mrs. 25
PRYOR, 107 111 Fred 108 Mrs. F. 109 Mrs. S. H. 142
PULMAN, Hiram 107
PUNEKY, Phillip 229
PURCELL, Annie 209 H. H. 192 Jake 61 Lella Davis 204 Mark 61
PURSER, D. I. 76 D. J. 76 Willie E. 76
PUTMAN, H. B. 108

QUCK, Walter 108
QUEGLES, Jno. B. 173 Joseph D. 173 Margaret 173
QUIGGINS, O. J. 143
QUIN, Elizabeth 193 I. M. 193
QUINLAN, J. L. 101

RADJESKY, Louis 108 Rachel 111 J. 109
RAFTER, A. M. 56
RAGAN, John M. 102
RAINER, G. C. 196
RAINEY, Mrs. W. V. 203
RAINS, Elizabeth 83
RALPH, John 110
RALSTON, Geo. 175 Robt. 161
RAMBERT, Tyra 67
RANDALL, Capt. 55 James 55 Lot 180
RANDOLPH, Mary Thurston 115 Nannie B. 115 T. E. 228 W. F. 115 Wm. 221
RANKIN, Emaline 181
RANSOM, Alice E. 1 Allice 1 W. M. 1
RATCHLITZ, Julius 107
RATCLIFF, Eletha L. 174 Rufus R. 33 Sarah J. Evans 33 W. Horton 174 Walter S. 33
RATLIFF, Carlos 62 Lucy 62 R. L. 62
RAWLSTON, J. R. 29
RAY, H. J. 45 Lula 58 Robt. 58
RAYFORD, Robert 149
RAYMOND, Doctor 144
REA, Dan 138
READ, Clem 142 Julia 136 Miss 143 Wash 184 Willie 136
RECORD, Corilla 142 G. L. 221 George H. 221
REDDING, Levi 137 Mr. 63
REDFIELD, _. M. 222
REDUS, J. C. 137 James C. 134 Jas. A. 137
REED, Fanny 80 Frank 187 Jno. 180 Louis A. 229 Mr. 136
REES, Daniel 6
REEVES, E. Y. 192 J. R. 192 Mr. 132 Mrs. 45 W. B. 131
REID, John M. T. 169 William M. 50 Wm. 50
REIMER, Henry 216
REINACH, L. 227
REMBERT, Zack 139
RESOR, John R. 158
REYNOLDS, Addie 209 Bruce 192 Elijah 8 Elizabeth 8 Jas. N. 209 Laura 4 Maggie V. 209 Otis 35
RHODES, John 93
RHORBACHER, John J. 153
RHYMES, C. D. 90 Emma 90 Rubie Lucille 90
RIALS, R. B. 139
RICE, John 113

RICHARDS, Mollie E. 49 Mrs. M. V. 161 Thos. 49
RICHARDSON, A. W. 204 Col. 132 E. 24 Ed. 131 J. L. 123 Mathias 16 Silas A. 175 Tabitha 16
RICHMOND, Lucinda 195
RICKETTS, James 26
RICKS, J. W. 17
RIGGAN, J. B. 2 Phelan 2 Mattie J. 2 Robert L. 77
RIGGS, Eliza 77 R. R. 77
RIGLEY, John J. 219
RILEY, Sarah A. 126
RITTMAN, Henry 29
RIVERS, Jeff 222
RIVES, Mrs. 24 O. C. 114
ROACH, Milly 169
ROBB, Carrie B. 123 Eugene A. 123 Fannie Gwyn 123 J. H. 115 121 Mattie Thompson 121
ROBBINS, Laura N. 77 S. L. 77
ROBERSON, Jerry 148
ROBERTS, 202 Julia 144 U. S. 63
ROBERTSHAW, Adele 123 Jas. 123
ROBERTSON, Elam T. 135 Elmira S. 81 Etna 81 Marcus H. 81 Nancy 14 S. M. 200
ROBINSON, 164 C. B. 131 C. F. 7 Cam. M. 101 Charles T. 21 Gabe 190 Gordon 164 J. P. 21 John 35 208 John S. 50 Lillie 7 Mary 152 Mattie 50 S. D. 88 W. H. 150
ROCKETT, H. W. 78
ROES, Barry 142
ROGAN, Ellen 187 L. 187
ROGERS, Alf 145 G. W. 133 Henrietta 109 J. W. 105 106 Mattie E. 133 Moses B. 201
ROGGERS, Patrick 181
ROHRBACHER, John 152 M. Sr. 152
ROLLINS, Albert 143 Dewitt 27
ROSE, Charlotte 50 Cornie 68 Lorell 68 Mamie 68
ROSENBERG, L. Jr. 42 Louis 36
ROSS, Anna E. 43 Billie 26 J. W. 135 James 169 Jas. 172 Joe 128 Louisa 209 May 12 W. B. 158 W. H. 142
ROUSE, W. H. 118

ROUTH, Helen S. 220 Octo 220
ROWAN, T. J. 158 Wm. W. 229
ROWE, A. V. 66 James Hays 66 R. D. 210 Roberta 210 S. E. 210
ROWLAND, Mrs. M. M. 203
ROXY, Corvan 143
ROYAL, A. A. 214 Mary Ella 214 Priscilla 214
ROYALL, Joseph P. 212 Joseph Jr. 212 Mary E. 214 Sallie M. 212
ROYCE, Laura 225 Laura A. 224 225 Owen 224 225
ROZET, George H. 177 Josephine Mandeville 177 Mandeville 177
RUBE, Mr. 153
RUCKER, Charley 10 John W. 53 Mariah M. 53 W. W. 53
RUCKS, J. T. 95 117 L. T. 117 Maggie 95 Mrs. S. J. 102 Sallie B. 95
RUFUS, James 208
RUMPH, J. T. 89
RUPLE, E. 76 J. H. 76 Lizzie 76
RUSHING, James M. 73 L. B. 73
RUSSEL, Mrs. M. A. 173
RUSSELL, Daniel R. 13 James 140 Maud Mayes 47 Mike 47 Miss 140 Mrs. S. U. H. 48 Nannie 47 Silas 141 W. B. 13 W. McN. 202 W. S. 94
RYAN, John 219 John Jr. 219 Mrs. 135
RYLAND, R. H. 27

SADDLER, Rosa 142
SADLER, Dr. 12 187 J. L. 186
SALE, A. P. 79 Emma 68
SALLIS, J. W. 66 Lou 66
SALTZIGER, Henry T. 126
SALZINGER, Henry G. 127
SAMPLE, Mrs. F. E. 194
SANDERFORD, Jno. T. 156
SANDERS, H. S. 60 Henrietta B. 53 J. E. 16 J. H. 112 J. M. 111 Jennie G. 60 Lizzie 217 Matilda 206 Summerfield 60
SANDERSON, Jenny R. 175 Jenny Ralston 175 S. W. W. 175
SANDIFER, John N. 96
SANDS, Ben 110

SANFORD, Mrs. Geo. 108 William 51 135 Wm. 136
SARGENT, Virginia 199
SARTAIN, Dick 34
SASSER, Stephen 70
SAUL, Fannie 68 156 Wm. 68
SAUNDERS, Agatha 143 Ed. 123 Flora 173 Hubbard 206 Mrs. 51 Robert 206
SAVAGE, Emmett 58 Priscilla 58 W. R. 58
SAVERY, J. M. 25
SAWRIE, B. A. 188
SAXTON, Ellen E. 216 Harrison 6
SCANLON, Patrick 213
SCARBER, Henry 156
SCHAFFER, Phil 216
SCHEPHNER, Charles 116
SCHILLING, Michael 69 W. H. 69
SCHLESINGER, H. 102 Huldah 102 Isadore 102 L. 102 Louis 102 Rachel 102
SCHMALHOLZ, F. X. 105
SCHMIDT, H. A. 226 Lizzie 226
SCHNEIDER, Charles 142
SCHNURR, Mrs. Kasemer 225
SCHRETT, Julia 135
SCHWARTZ, Catherine 178 I. 166 J. C. 178 Mrs. J. C. 179 Nora 166
SCONYERS, Jas. 181
SCOTT, 107 Charles 152 D. A. 117 E. M. 152 Eva May 151 Garrett 111 George Y. 152 Georgia Yerger 151 J. W. 124 Jefferson 124 John T. 56 Lottie 173 Margaret 168 181 W. A. 152 W. P. 151 Willie 107
SEALEY, Sarah 225
SEATER, Fannie 46 R. Y. 46
SEELEY, L. W. 224 Sarah 224
SEFFERIED, Eliza S. 162 William T. 162
SEGRIEST, Bardee 87
SELMAN, B. A. P. 17 Lucille 17
SELMON, B. A. P. 18
SEMMES, A. T. 58 B. J. 40 Bena 46 D. A. T. 46 Joseph M. 58
SENTER, R. T. 118
SEPPARD, Lewis 222
SESSIONS, Jessie 37 R. A. J. 206
SETTERIED, Geo. Xavier 162

SEVERT, Mollie 48 Thomas 48
SEVIER, Mollie 48 Thomas 48
SEXTON, J. F. 161 Mrs. 219
SEYPLE, Alex 142
SHACKELFORD, W. A. H. 14 W. H. 13 J. R. 62 Mrs. E. A. 167
SHANKLE, Jas. 142 Robt. 142 W. A. 142
SHANKS, Ella 69 J. J. 69 M. J. 69
SHANNAHAN, Don 110 Mrs. Dan 112
SHANNON, H. E. 210 Wm. B. 150
SHARKEY, S. E. 9
SHARP, Fidello C. 211 Lillie 211
SHARPE, Hunter 11 J. H. 11
SHAW, D. D. 205 Dick 19 187 Helen 111 Mrs. T. B. 110 Smith 19 187
SHAWS, Chas. 108
SHEEHAN, Michael 225
SHEELY, A. C. 157
SHELBY, Evan 126 G. B. 126 Ike 126 Janie P. 126 Janora 126 Thomas 210 Thos. J. 159
SHELLEY, Wm. B. 68
SHELTON, J. H. 122 James 160 S. F. 58 59 140 166 S. M. 9 Susie 122 Susie H. 160 Wm. 59
SHEPPARD, Fannie 128
SHERMAN, Joseph 142
SHIELDS, George 139 Jno. W. 120 John W. 122 Mr. 120 Willie 122
SHIPP, J. W. 93
SHODDY, Mr. 121
SHOREY, Mrs. 108
SHORT, Prince V. 160 Victoria 160 W. H. 160
SHOTWELL, Millie 144
SHOWSE, W. H. 127
SHRETT, Mrs. 136
SHROCK, Caroline 163 Jos. K. 163
SHULTZ, Frank 214
SHURLEY, Emma 70 163 J. R. 70 163
SIEBE, Alice 90
SIGNAIGO, J. A. 84
SIKES, Henry 207
SIMMERMAN, John B. 201
SIMMONS, Clara M. 33 H. A. 71 J. B. 4 J. M. 4 James 25 Jane 199 Jessie 71 Julia 33 Julia M. 197

Mat 187 N. P. 4 S. B. 71 T. M. 197 Thomas Mosby 197 Viney 25

SIMPSON, A. B. 10 Bros. 10 Brothers 185 James 46 John 107 Mattie 199 Sam 10

SIMS, Charles 125 Charlie Estelle 157 Chas. B. 125 John Hampton 113 Lucinda 144 Mrs. 114 R. L. 114 Robbie 125 W. H. 157

SINGLETON, Eliza Yandell 48 Kansas 40 O. R. 48

SIPPEL, Barbara 198 Margaretha 198 Phillip 198

SKILLMAN, Hardy 21

SKINNER, Jno. W. 184

SKOESBURG, son 144

SLATER, Hiram 72 Laura M. 132 Vastine C. 132 W. S. 72

SLAUGHTER, Bettie 52 James M. 50 L. G. 52 Louis 52

SLEVERS, Mrs. M. 109

SLINPENDORTER, John 110

SMALL, Elizabeth 65 Mrs. John 110 Olivia H. 84 Wm. H. 101

SMILEY, James M. 182

SMITH, A. G. 24 Abe 108 Alfannce 128 C. H. 113 Carroll 41 Charles B. 52 Chas. 178 D. L. 61 Dora 16 Edward Nall 150 Elizabeth 37 162 Ellen 136 Eugene 122 Eustis 170 Eva Aubrey 89 Frank 175 Frank P. 109 Frederick 208 Geo. 97 171 Geo. W. 150 Gus 142 Isaac 32 J. C. 78 J. D. 130 J. F. 162 Jack 131 James 39 40 James C. 90 Jas. Mosely 130 Jerry 51 136 John 127 John E. 205 Lake 55 Leodora 223 Leroy 137 Lewis O'amblis 136 Lott 37 Louisa 156 Lula 150 M. E. 156 Maggie B. 133 Mary Clave 41 Matilda 78 90 Mrs. F. P. 108 Mrs. J. E. 126 Nancy 126 Nancy J. 111 Narcissa Jane 17 Oscar 113 Pearle 89 Preston 176 Sallie 55 Sarah E. 68 Susan 169 Thomas B. 17 Victor 142 W. F. 104 W. H. 52 W. I. 156 W. J. 136 W. R. 89 Willie 162 Winnie 107 Wm. 209

SNIDER, Herman 142 206 Katie S. 53 Leonard 53 Sallie 53

SNODGRASS, J. R. 7 M. T. 7

SNOWBERGER, H. M. 126

SOENS, Chas. 119

SOLOMON, Moses 218

SOLUTER, Maria 195 Mr. & Mrs. 195

SOUTHWORTH, Mayor 61

SOW LEE, 107

SOWENS, Charles M. 125

SPAIN, Henry 16

SPAULDING, Mrs. 44

SPEAKS, T. B. 111

SPEARS, Wm. R. 95 190

SPEIRS, Robert B. 24

SPENCER, Matthew 185

SPIGHT, Buren 189

SPIRES, Ross 169

SPIVEY, 8

SPRATT, Henry D. 5

SPRINGER, Benjamin 216

SPRINGS, Phillip 179

SPROLES, S. R. 207

SPURGEON, R. M. 173

ST. CLAIR, Mary 171

STACEY, George Edward 199

STACKHOUSE, Beatrice O. 84 H. C. 84

STAFFORD, Dr. 108 Frank 187 Mrs. 112

STAMPS, Volney 201

STANILAS, Sister 143

STANSBURY, W. M. 199

STANSELL, Georgia Etta 184 S. E. 184 W. N. 188 W. R. 184

STARK, Frank E. 128

STARKE, Wm. E. 220

STATHAM, Edna Earle 67 John B. 67 Mattie A. 67

STEINBERG, 108

STELLA, Sister 143

STENNETT, B. M. 17

STEPHENSON, E. C. 96 F. C. 96 Jack 135 R. 142

STEVENS, Lizzie 43 Oscar 12

STEWARD, Frank 132

STEWART, Annie 143 Fulton A. 204 J. D. 155 204 Jas. D. 120 Leon 16 Mary 143 Steve 111

STINEMAN, Peter 144
STITH, Edna O. 228 Harry 22 Oscar N. 224
STOCKS, A. T. 25
STODDER, Mary 37
STOJOWSKI, Julia 143
STONE, Alfred Holt 132 Carlile 115 Corrine 132 D. L. 112 Ella 132 Ex-Gov. 10 Governor 171 J. H. 143 Mary H. 132 Mrs. 143 Mrs. Jas. 118 O. W. 132 W. R. 103 W. W. 132 Will 97
STONEWALL, Fanny 218
STOREY, Mrs. 107
STORY, M. 51 Milton 136
STOVALL, Josephine 94 R. G. 94 W. G. 205
STOWELL, Lyman 107
STRAIN, Jo. 181
STRANGE, John P. 98
STRATHER, G. 144 Jerry 107
STRATTON, Mr. & Mrs. 163 Ruth 163
STRAUS, Julius 173
STRAUSS, infant 144
STRAWS, Mrs. Archie 143
STREAM, Geo. 108
STREET, C. E. K. 159 Donald Augustus 159 H. G. 205 H. M. 159
STRICKLAND, Elizabeth 196 Mrs. 207 Sandy 151
STRIPPELMAN, F. E. 195
STROTHER, Ann E. 224 225
STUART, W. B. 31
STUBBS, Charley Jr. 10 Jesse Embry 185 Jessie 10
STURGES, Alice 78 Nellie 78 Theodore 78
SUBLETT, J. M. 88
SUDDUTH, R. B. 197
SUGG, Matt 15
SUGGS, Walter 19
SULLIVAN, Capt. 96 John F. 222 Johnnie T. 164 Sarah E. 164 Thos. 36 Thos. L. 164
SUMELL, A. 128
SUMLIN, Andrew 7
SUMLING, 146
SUMMERFIELD, Johonie Jones 39 May 39 William W. 39

SUMMERS, Mrs. E. J. 82
SUMRALL, Elisha 82
SURRATT, M. 12
SUTHERLAND, 53
SUTTEL, Mike 138
SUTTON, Amanda 144 J. M. 100 James M. 125 126 Laura 100 Mrs. Lycian 71 Steve 108
SWAFFORD, Mary E. 208
SWAN, Henry 137
SWANN, Geo. T. 104
SWETT, Mrs. 51
SWINNEY, C. K. 141
SWINTON, John 222
SWITZER, Nannette 127
SYKES, James 60
SYLVESTER, Tom 110
SYMS, George 214

TABB, Ross 204 Wm. 162
TAFFE, Charles F. 212 Mrs. K. J. 212
TALIBERT, Loyd 113
TANDLER, Isaac 142
TANKERSLEY, Warren 47
TANNER, W. H. 61
TAPLEY, James 162
TAPPAN, Mrs. M. B. 225
TARRY, Edmund 53 Eugenia H. 53
TATE, Caswell 155 186 J. M. 205 Jimmie 205 Mrs. M. A. 205 Sarah A. 155 186
TAYLOR, Ben. 41 Benjamin S. 183 H. 226 H. L. 200 J. M. 32 Louis 200 M. L. 32 Mary E. 32 Mary Grace 200 Nathaniel 163 Richard 40 Tillman 199 W. A. 161 W. H. 88 Willie 89 Wm. 109
TEAL, C. J. 131
TELFAR, Wm. 107
TERREL, Ermira 136 Judge 36
TERRELL, J. 51 John S. 134 136
TERRY, W. D. 157
THAMES, Archie 75
THERRELL, Benjamin E. 76 Sarah J. 76 Thomas Adde 76
THIGPEN, J. Gray 47
THOMAS, Ella 216 G. 144 Jacob Tristem 198 Jo. 210 M. L. J. 198 Martin 144 Mary 27 223

Mrs. E. A. 142 T. A. 211 T. S. 198 Wade R. 157
THOMPSON, Bryant B. 183 Charles 218 Ellen 173 Harriet B. 183 Herbert 54 129 J. H. 91 J. P. Stree 196 Jacob 96 165 Jesse 91 Jestana 211 Jimmie 88 Julius 129 L. W. 53 Lewis 54 143 Mrs. Louis 143 Rachel 147 S. M. 17 29 30 155 183 Sam 183 Samuel Moore 183 Victor 183 Victor W. 155
THORN, Neville H. 228
THORNTON, Henry 111
THRELKELD, S. 147
THROCKMORTON, Eliza 217
TIDWELL, A. J. 204
TIERNAN, John 145 Mike 144
TIERNEY, John J. 210
TIGERT, Elisabeth 155 Elizabeth 186 Mrs. Wm. 192 Sallie 155 186 Thomas 186 Thos. 155
TILLEY, W. Jr. 111
TILLMAN, A. J. 89
TIMBES, W. C. 26
TIPP, Reuben 25
TISON, Col. 16 W. H. H. 123 William H. H. 12
TOBIN, J. E. 145
TODD, W. R. 142
TOWLER, W. P. 23 45
TOWNS, Governor 45 John G. 45
TOWNSEND, Charles 20
TRAMMELL, Mrs. 108
TRAUBE, L. L. 32 33
TREMBLE, 110
TRIGG, A. B. 110 Davis B. 101 W. R. 101
TRIMBLE, B. F. 146
TRIPLETT, Wm. 60
TRYFORD, John R. 224
TUCKER, A. Fenton 141 Gen. 19 W. F. 187 Wm. F. 87
TURK, Capt. 49
TURNBULL, Fredeerick G. 115 Mary B. 115
TURNER, Ada 204 Agnes 175 176 Arch 62 Irvin 127 Robert S. 160 Sarinthia F. 69
TUTT, W. G. 116

TYLER, H. C. 83 H. N. 83 James 203 Otto 83 Virginia A. 199

ULMAR, Harriet C. 217
ULRICH, Rachie 176
UNDERWOOD, Toll 109
UPSHAW, E. W. 143

VAIDEN, C. M. 42 Coles Meade 150 Cowles Meade 116
VALIANT, Mrs. F. 117
VAN COURT, Annie G. 180 181 E. J. 180
VAN NORMAN, P. V. 207
VANCE, J. F. 141 John F. 62 167
VANDENBURG, Laura Annie 222 Mrs. S. A. 222
VANDERFORD, Elder Paralee 206 Mr. & Mrs. 206
VANDIVE, Henry 144
VANZANT, Eugene Stanley 35 Sallie 35 W. J. 35
VARNADO, I. E. 73
VAUGHN, Henry 111 W. R. 171
VEAL, Jennie 67
VERNON, Columbus 100
VICKARS, Lena Kelly 158 Wm. 158
VICKERS, F. F. 204
VICTORIA, Sister 144
VIERS, W. H. 96
VIRGINIA, Mollie 144
VOELLINGER, Chas. Eddie 209 Rozina 209 Wm. 207

WACTOR, J. R. 207
WADDELL, A. M. 160
WADE, Benj. 174 Bennie 174 Matilda 167 Mittie 174 Thos. 143
WAGNER, Frank 109
WAH_ER, John 51
WAINE, George P. 105
WAITE, Julia 142
WALCOTT, T. G. 122 160
WALKER, boys 121 Brothers 11 34 155 Belle Orville 118 C. H. 144 Daisy Euphemia 161 Eli 144 Emily T. 38 G. B. 18 G. W. 71 J. P. 121 J. S. 115 118 131 James 142 Jas. W. 161 John M. 202 Martha 144 213 Mary 137 Mattie 161 Miss 135 Ned 35

Orville Blanton 131 Ruth V. 194
Wash 108 Will 47 William
Jason 118 Wm. 194 Wm. F.
38
WALL, Abe 110 Francis 217
WALLACE, Ephraim 50 F. 223
Freddie 227 John G. 163
Joseph S. 122
WAINE, G. P. 215
WALTER, Avant 143 Frank 143 H.
W. 143 Jimmie 143
WALTERS, John Henry 158
WALTON, A. J. 180 Dillania 157
Eliza J. 23 Helen C. 180 Thos.
157 William H. 23
WAMBLE, Sarah E. 2 T. J. 2
WARD, B. F. 61 Jane V. 53 John F.
127 Mrs. A. 111 Robert 61 W.
T. 92
WARDEN, Nellie 110
WARE, Luis 108
WARFIELD, Kittie 177
WARNACK, Thomas C. 193
WARREN, Jesse 30
WASHINGTON, Caroline 143 H. 73
Henry 151 Margaret 181 Miles
168 Wm. 144
WATERS, Henry 181 Joseph 199
WATRONS, H. T. 4
WATSON & WEST, 20
WATSON, Joshua 144 Judge 115
Louis D. 229 Melinda 176 Mrs.
R. L. 143 Olivia D. 203 229 R.
L. 142 W. F. 115
WATTS, A. S. 161 Jacob 110 John
98
WAYS, Ah 113
WAZEE, Aaron 61
WEATHERBEE & BROWN, 97
WEATHERBEE, Eva 108 L. P. 110
Wes. 111
WEATHERBY, Hezekiah 156
WEATHERSBY, Eugene 27 T. H. 21
54 William 27
WEAVER, Frederick 5
WEBB, Ann Eliza 78 Jacob M. 192
Wm. 213
WEBBER, A. W. 101 child 144 J. W.
143 Peter 143
WEBER, Adam 58 William 213
WEEKS, Eugene L. 159

WEIGHTMAN, Lou 203
WEIR, Walter 173
WEISENFELDT, Mrs. L. 111
WELBORN, 122
WELBOURN, Sallie Fitzhugh 46
WELCH, Cydny 142 Henry 173 Joe
24 John 24 Mr. 142
WELDON, W. T. 171
WELIZENFELDT, L. 110
WELLS, Alice 70 Elizabeth 175
Fayette 193 J. M. 10 185 Jim
143 144 Lee 70 Mary 127 Mrs.
Jim 143 Sallie L. 10 185 W.
Lum 70 Willie B. 127 Wm. E.
171
WELSH, Jos. 199
WENTWORTH, 35 Rowan 206
WERLES, J. D. 100
WERLOIN, Philip P. 33
WEST, A. M. 165 F. H. 96 G. J. 212
John M. 20 Julia A. 212 Sidney
165
WESTBROOK, J. E. 198 Sarah Jane
195 W. H. 195
WESTERFIELD, Anna 207 Mrs. 136
WETHERBEE, Mable 112 Mrs. L. P.
108
WETHERS, Ellen 211
WHARTON, Jack 87 T. J. Jr. 44
Thomas 87
WHEATLY, David Milton 17 M. H. 17
T. J. 17
WHEELER, Albert 110 E. B. 28 89
127 179 R. B. 20
WHITE, Beontine 107 Capt. 136 E.
50 George 51 136 George
Adolphus 30 J. F. 30 J. J. 208
James 217 Margaret 173 Mary
30 111 Mary Ann 215 Nora 215
Sarah Emily 30 Susan F. 50
Vernon 18 Willie B. 110
WHITEHEAD, Mr. & Mrs. 123 P. F.
222 224 Peter F. 226 Rennah
123 Sid 81
WHITER, Sherisy 112
WHITEWAY, Robert Thomas 126
WHITFIELD, Edith 76 Emma 76
Lucy 4 Mr. 149 Needham J. 4
O. H. 22 R. H. 76 Raynor 148
Robert M. 76
WHITLOCK, Ellen 180

WHITLOW, Sarah A. 191
WHITTINGTON, A. J. 178
WHITWORTH, S. H. 33
WICKER, E. J. 198
WIER, Issabella Catharine 186
WIES, Capt. 136
WIGGINS, Ella 39
WILES, J. M. 200 Jennie 64 Jennie E. 64 William W. 64 James C. 64
WILEZINSKI, Joe 128
WILKERSON, Mrs. 135
WILKES, Burwell B. 78
WILKINS, Miss R. R. 171
WILKINSON, Martha 207 Miss 207 Mrs. 51 Sue 166
WILKOWSKI & CO., 106
WILLIAMS & POSEY, 54
WILLIAMS, A. G. 23 Anna 124 Anna J. 64 Annie Boyd 6 Benjamin 127 Bessie Davis 6 Bryant 175 C. C. 6 C. P. 124 Carbelle 64 Caroline 201 Charles P. 124 Charley J. 72 Chas. 110 Cinderella 145 Dr. 42 Edward 215 Felix 60 Frank 229 Gambrell 67 Grant 99 Henrietta 179 J. A. 51 135 J. L. 12 James 63 James A. 136 Joe 135 John 194 Letty 178 Lucy 210 Malissa 12 Margaret 110 Merritt 124 Mrs. 21 Nicey 213 P. C. 64 67 Percy C. 72 Rebecca 179 Susan 181 219 W. B. 21 W. T. 42 William 167
WILLIAMSON, Christian Kerner 90 John 90 114
WILLIS, E. B. 218 Ed. 144 William 182
WILLS, J. Q. 103
WILSON, 138 Alex 80 Berry 134 Bill 80 Dan 113 Ed 28 29 138 219 Henry 179 180 John 123 Lina 23 Mrs. 39 142 Samuel T. 24 131 T. 23
WILTSHIRE, A. T. 142
WINBORN, Doss 7 Hugh 143 Sheriff 7
WING, George 142
WINKER, J. 107
WINKLER, Dr. 190 E. T. 189

WINTER, John 112 Katie W. 217 R. H. 217
WINTERS, Eddie 113
WIRA, Herman 216
WITHERS, Alice 167 C. A. 162 Mary 146 Sallie N. 162
WITHERSPOON, Jno. G. 91 Sarah 91 V. V. 91
WITKOWSKI, Gustav 123
WOFFORD, James 222
WOLCOTT, Chas. 168
WOLFF, Eugene T. 185 Francis A. 185
WOLVERTON, W. H. 154
WOMACK, J. H. 7 Mary 7
WOMMOCK, Mrs. 7
WOOD, Anna 169 C. W. 62 E. G. 202 Eliza A. 183 J. W. 68 Joseph 2 Licurgus S. 2 Mrs. B. U. 206 Nancy 2 Samuel J. 134
WOODRUFF, Dave 106
WOODSON, Marshall 111
WOODWARD, Dr. 157
WOOTEN, Jeff 153 Willie 142
WORD, Laura 1 Lavina 184 Leatha 1 Mrs. 46 Thomas 1 184
WORSHAM, Ella 202 Martha 145
WORTHINGTON, Amanda 118 120 Hal 199 Mrs. B. T. 106 S. 113 W. M. 101 115 118
WRIGHT, Buck 62 Charles W. 23 G. M. 118 G. W. 187 John 20 Mrs. 118
WYATT, Eddie Thomas 208 Fannie B. 208 G. W. 208
WYNN, Robt. 163
WYNNE, Effie 48

YAGER, Andrew 101 Lula C. 101 Margaret 101
YANCY, Mrs. 143 Wm. 143
YARBOROUGH, 80 Mary E. 80
YARBROUGH, John S. 55 Martha Y. 55
YATES, L. D. 139 Mrs. M. E. 23
YEISER, Emma B. 225 Emma Ballou 225 John G. 225 Thomas C. 225
YERGER, Alex 117 Arthur R. 110 Geo. S. 199 Mrs. E. B. 117 Mrs. Shall 129 Shall 32 William 32

259

YEWELL, Squire 144
YOCUM, Sophia 111
YOUNG, D. E. 109 Frank A. 29 Geo. F. 15 Jas. 107 Mr. & Mrs. 142 Mrs. 108 Mrs. J. H. 101 Ruth 181 Sarah J. 15 Terry 203 Thomas 209 210 Victoria A. 209 210 Virginia 209 210
YOWELL, W. B. 147

ZEIGLER, Caroline 107
ZIMMER, Spencer 173